Gen Men

Gen Men

What the Men of Genesis Can Teach Us Today

D. ERIC SCHANSBERG

RESOURCE *Publications* · Eugene, Oregon

GEN MEN
What the Men of Genesis Can Teach Us Today

Copyright © 2025 D. Eric Schansberg. All rights reserved. Except for brief quotations in critical publications or reviews, no part of this book may be reproduced in any manner without prior written permission from the publisher. Write: Permissions, Wipf and Stock Publishers, 199 W. 8th Ave., Suite 3, Eugene, OR 97401.

Resource Publications
An Imprint of Wipf and Stock Publishers
199 W. 8th Ave., Suite 3
Eugene, OR 97401

www.wipfandstock.com

PAPERBACK ISBN: 979-8-3852-3531-5
HARDCOVER ISBN: 979-8-3852-3532-2
EBOOK ISBN: 979-8-3852-3533-9

10/09/25

Scripture quotations taken from The Holy Bible, New International Version®, NIV®. Copyright © 1973, 1978, 1984, 2011 by Biblica, Inc. Used with permission of Zondervan. All rights reserved worldwide. www.zondervan.com

To Tonia and "the boys"
who are in the process of becoming fine young men

Contents

Acknowledgments		ix
Introduction		1
1	Silence and Violence	11
2	Treading Water vs. Moving the World	23
3	Leave and Go	35
4	Lies vs. Truth in Love	46
5	Magnanimous and Mighty	56
6	In vs. Of the World	66
7	Patience vs. Pushing	76
8	Faith and Reason	87
9	Passion vs. Apathy	97
10	Cleverness and Perseverance	109
11	Placate and Wrestle	121
12	Vengeance and Jealousy	131
13	Purity and Productivity	143
14	Repentance and Leadership	153
15	Guilt vs. Grace	165
Epilogue		175
Select Bibliography		181

Acknowledgments

THANKS TO MAXIE BURCH and Dwight Edwards for inspiring my love for the Bible. Thanks to Bob Russell, Dave Stone, and Kyle Idleman for their faithfulness in ministry at Southeast Christian Church.

Thanks to Joe Donaldson for giving me the opportunity to lead a young adult Bible study in January 1993. Thanks to Kurt Sauder for our partnership in ministry through Southeast and Further Still Ministries.

Thanks to Dallas Willard and C.S. Lewis for their writings. Thanks to the Jewish scholars I've read and all of the Sunday night Bible study groups who have had a hand in helping me explore the great book of Genesis.

Thanks to Bob Reed for helping me become an econ prof and shaping the way my family would look. Thanks to Dad and Mom for helping me where I am and who I am. Thanks to my wife Tonia for putting up with me and giving me space to complete this project.

Thanks to Jesus who saved a bozo like me, changed my life, and empowers me through the Holy Spirit and the Scriptures to lead a life of depth and influence.

Introduction

A FEW WEEKS BEFORE Covid closed down the world, I gave stand-up comedy a whirl. On a weekday evening, I went to a bar that served as a "minor league" opportunity to practice, before I'd have a few minutes at a comedy club on a weekend. There were a few rookies and a bunch of veterans. All of us were "trying" our material—the lines, the stories, and the delivery.

My big joke was about the director of TARC, the local government bus system. He had recently been fired after repeated episodes of sexual harassment. My punchline: He was an example of "TARC-sick masculinity." Somewhere between funny, amusing, and a dad joke. Not exactly Nate Bargatze, Brian Regan, or Jim Gaffigan. Covid ultimately cancelled my chance at the big leagues. But it was already obvious that I shouldn't quit my day job. Still, I'm glad I gave it the old college try.

Part of humor is taking the audience to unexpected places. I was talking about mundane topics: city buses and a jerk taking advantage of his authority. But suddenly, I had a pun about a social ill that gets a lot of attention. The term "toxic masculinity" is used to describe all sorts of behaviors—from clear problems to debatable issues. What's *not* debatable: Too many men and boys are having trouble and making trouble. And when they aren't doing well, it's not good for them, families, or society.

There's so much at stake here. Men have the capacity to be so productive or to cause so much harm. Unfortunately, males are on the struggle bus far too often. Men are much more likely to experience suicide and homelessness, to use and become addicted to drugs, to murder and to be murdered, to be in prison and on parole. They are more likely to be disruptive in K-12 education and less likely to do well at any level of schooling. Of men ages 25–54 with only a high school education, one-third are not in the labor force.[1] And the cycle can easily perpetuate. When men fail as fathers, then mothers, daughters, and especially sons are harmed.[2]

We'll see this in spades throughout Genesis. As one of its primary themes, God seems especially concerned with men in terms of both what they can accomplish and the damage they can cause. And this, not just for themselves, but for their immediate family, the world around them, and the generations to come. The stories in Genesis range from the passivity of Adam to the terrible choices of Joseph's brothers; from the growth of Jacob and Judah to the regression of Lot and the limitations of Noah; from the faux masculinity of Lamech and Reuben to the true manhood of Abraham and Joseph.

WHAT DOES THE WORLD OFFER?

The world has many strategies to deal with the problems of men and the social ills that result. One is the force of government. Men keep our police and parole officers busy. Men fill our judicial system—our courtrooms, detention centers, jails, and prisons. A century ago, the "temperance movement" successfully lobbied the government to prohibit alcohol, concerned especially about its use by men.

Unfortunately, the government's 60-year-old "War on Poverty" has been an indirect war *on* men, as the State has increasingly substituted itself *for* men, especially in the lower-income classes. Women with children only receive financial support (or receive much more support) from the government if they are unmarried, strongly encouraging single-parent households. This also encourages men to mooch on women in relationships, further reducing men's incentives to work and eroding their character.

When government and society try to address more modest problems, its efforts are centered on female-dominated professionals in social work, counseling, and education. Perhaps women generally have a comparative advantage in providing this sort of assistance. But to borrow from the title of a famous book decades ago: If "Men are from Mars" and "Women are from Venus," maybe it'd be better to have a lot more older Martians working with younger Martians.

1. Reeves, *Of Boys and Men*, 19.
2. As examples in the literature, see: Melissa Kearney's book, *The Two-Parent Privilege* and Brad Wilcox et al., *Good Fathers, Flourishing Kids* (cosm.aei.org/wp-content/uploads/2025/06/UVA-Good-Fathers-Flourishing-Kids-Report.pdf).

Introduction

In his book *Of Boys and Men*, Richard Reeves brings welcome attention to male struggles in contemporary society, focusing especially on education, labor markets, and family. Traditionally, the world has defined manhood around three categories: to protect, procreate, and provide. But we mostly rely on the government to *protect* us today. As for *procreation*: marriage, children, and family are not valued as highly these days. And men are increasingly seen as supplemental and secondary in this arena. So, these deeply formative roles for men as husbands and fathers have also diminished.

The ability to *provide* has become more difficult with the failure of increasingly unstable families and expensive but ineffective government K-12 schools to prepare men for modern economic realities. The emergence of a more-competitive global marketplace has been a boon for consumers and skilled workers, but tough on many businesses and people with fewer labor market skills. The growth of Social Security Disability Insurance (SSDI) payments has made it tempting for many less-skilled but able-bodied men to stay on welfare and remain indigent—instead of choosing the work force, a career pathway, and the dignity of self-actualization.

Women are generally more successful than men with the process of education and have emerged as more productive members in the modern economy. As women have increased their status and improved their options, men have become more disposable. With diminished opportunities to protect, procreate, and provide, what does the world offer to men and what can men offer the world? With these new social norms—often lacking value, identity, and purpose—how can men avoid seeing themselves as worth less, or even worthless?[3]

Even when discussing the most regrettable behaviors of males, Reeves argues that "toxic masculinity" is an unethical, impractical, and inconsistent term.[4] The label is used far too broadly and it's *unethical* to crush immaturity and to slander neutral traits which occur naturally in men. The language is *impractical* when it pushes boys and men to the "online manosphere" instead of engaging them in dialogue and providing them with better role models. And the phrase is *inconsistent*, since the same terminology

---

3. Reeves (*Of Boys and Men*, 127) quotes George Gilder on the temptation for men to become "outlaws or exiles."

4. Nancy Pearcey connects beliefs about "toxic masculinity" to Darwinism, natural selection, and Social Darwinism ("Degraded Conceptions," *Salvo*, Summer 2025, 13). Her book, *The Toxic War on Masculinity*, provides an excellent historical and contemporary discussion of the topic from a biblical worldview.

is not applied to females who behave badly. (Imagine describing female stereotypes as "toxic femininity.")

Reeves' worldview is moderate to Left, but he's critical of his own tribe. He notes that the Right may make too much of gender differences, but it's clear in this realm that the Left downplays science in general and biology in particular. Here, the Left also inverts its usual penchant for blaming external factors rather than emphasizing personal responsibility. And the Left is only willing to talk about gender when it comes to men's advantages and women's disadvantages. This approach is intellectually dishonest and not helpful. Reeves is careful to say that one can be in support of both men and women—that we can hold two thoughts in our heads at the same time. From a worldly (and a biblical) perspective, the answer cannot be helping one gender by denigrating the other.

But Reeves' proposed solutions are less impressive, suffering from the inherent limits of public policy, unwarranted optimism about some well-intentioned ideas, and his reluctance to discuss certain solutions. (Most notably, he makes no mention of religion or the Church!) Unfortunately, there isn't much that government can do. Potentially helpful policies are not politically palatable. It's exceedingly common to overestimate the effectiveness of government activism. And in large part, these are cultural problems and a matter of personal responsibility—better handled by civil society, family, and individuals. At the end of the day, Reeves' book is really good at pointing fingers, but not so useful for finding answers.

WHAT'S THE CHURCH DOING?

The common (and easily accessible) metrics on organized religion have declined in recent years. It's not clear whether this is mostly a decline in "Christendom" (the cultural influence of Christianity) or something more important. When Christianity fades as an institution, people are less likely to loosely align with it. Church attendance is down, but are there fewer disciples of Jesus? Good news: The lines are more clearly drawn between those inside and outside the faith—and fewer people are likely to imagine that they're in the Kingdom when they're not.

In any case, for the first time in recorded history, young men are more attracted to the Church than young women.[5] Why? Perhaps because the

---

5. See Graham, "With Gen Z, Men Are Now More Religious" (based on research by the Barna Group: barna.com/gen-z-volume-3/). For the same in England, see Evans, "No

Introduction

Church is the only contemporary institution which communicates that men have meaning, purpose, and value. Every other prominent social structure treats masculinity as neutral or negative. Hollywood often makes fun of men. Schools and the culture try hard to tame boys. Some well-intentioned efforts to elevate women end up dissing men. In stark contrast, the Church generally places a high value on men—as humans and as men.

Within a close walk with Jesus, being a good husband and father is certainly a top-tier priority inside the Church. The word "patriarchy" is related to the Latin for "father" (*pater*) and the Greek for "family" (*patria*). Although the English term has baggage, it points to the importance of marriage and family—and encourages us to aim for excellence in both. Likewise, the title "husband" comes from words meaning "house" and "bound"—again, that men are built to be husbands and fathers, bound to a house and a home. These are things to applaud and pursue, not to criticize and avoid.

More broadly, we're talking about discipleship. But it is quite common for churches to rely far too heavily on preaching. This approach obviously falls far short of the ministry model of Jesus. He spent time with individuals and preached to the crowds on occasion, but the vast bulk of his time was apprenticing the 12 disciples. Arguably, the top mission of the local church is to fulfill Ephesians 4:11–16, training up men and women to spiritual maturity and continual growth. In this, sermons are useful, but ultimately quite limited in their ability to disciple. From there, church leaders usually lack a robust vision for making disciple-makers and developing layleaders. And if they give this more than lip service, they rarely have a coherent plan to make it happen.[6]

That said, churches generally do better with discipling women than men. Men's ministries are relatively rare. And when they exist, they're usually some combination of a monthly breakfast, periodic service opportunities, and some light Bible study.[7] What's generally asked of men? Stay out of trouble; be a good husband and father; engage in modest service; contribute money to the church; and perhaps provide leadership in the church based on business acumen, worldly skills, and (hopefully) a biblical worldview.

Sex, No Booze, We're Off to Church."

6. I have a 2018 article in *Touchstone* ("The Great Omission") that compares a key phrase in the Great Commission to "teaching them to obey all there is to know about economics."

7. Check out The Babylon Bee's funny/sad post on quarterly pancake breakfasts for men: Babylon Bee, "Church Unsure Why Men Are Struggling."

All of these are fine, but not exactly a robust fulfillment of Jesus' call to be a Kingdom worker or a disciple-maker.[8]

Even if we ignore the biblical mandates to train laypeople, much more attention is obviously required to deal with the problems and opportunities connected to contemporary manhood. Women seem to arrive at "womanhood" more naturally. After all, how often do you hear women exhorted to "woman up" or to "be a woman"? How often is it said that we need to "make a woman out of her"? Becoming a man seems to require more effort and intentionality—which we'll see in the book of Genesis, as God purposefully works with a variety of men.

DOMINANT, DOMESTICATED, DOORMAT, OR DIVINE?

When we think of *manly men*, it's easy to caricature them as domineering jerks. But that's certainly not God's vision of "manhood" in Genesis or the rest of the Bible. A godly man loves his wife as Christ loved the church, giving himself up for her. He loves his children and is heavily involved in parenting. He's a productive worker, a good neighbor, and an effective citizen. He's an excellent example to emulate; he's a wise mentor pouring his life into others; he's a flesh-and-blood inspiration to follow.

When we think of *domesticated men*, it's tempting to imagine them as doormats. But we won't see this from the godly men in Genesis. Joseph will persevere through remarkably difficult circumstances; Judah will offer to sell himself into slavery to save one of his brothers; and Abraham is amazing in so many different ways.

Likewise, Jesus was much more than "a nice guy." Read a few verses of Matthew 23; consider when he cleared the Temple; remember how he provoked the Pharisees; recall how he challenged the disciples and messed with the Canaanite woman (Matt 15:21–28). He was the first person you'd

---

8. This is at the heart of my work with Kurt Sauder at Southeast Christian Church (Louisville, KY) and through Further Still Ministries. We've been tilling this ground for 25+ years, including two curricula for training layleaders (*Thoroughly Equipped* and *Getting Equipped*) and two books which lay out a vision and coherent plans for making disciple-makers (*Enough Horses in the Barn* and *Roll Up Your Sleeves*). In trying to get people into the Bible, I've written a Bible literacy project called *The Word Diet*. And I have a radio show and podcast called The Word Diet for those who want in-depth Bible study. More information about all of these is available at ThoroughlyEquipped.org and GettingEquipped.life.

INTRODUCTION

want at your party and the last man that the religious leaders wanted alive. As Dorothy Sayers expressed it:

> The people who hanged Christ never, to do them justice, accused him of being a bore; on the contrary, they thought him too dynamic to be safe. It has been left for later generations to muffle up that shattering personality and surround him with an atmosphere of tedium. We have efficiently pared the claws of the Lion of Judah, certified him 'meek and mild' and recommended him as a fitting household pet for pale curates and pious old ladies . . . Somehow or other, and with the best intentions, we have shown the world the typical Christian in the likeness of a crashing and rather ill-natured bore—and this in the name of one who assuredly never bored a soul in those 33 years during which he passed through the world like a flame.[9]

Putting it another way: Being a nice guy falls far short of what God intends. Being a good husband, father, and worker is laudable—and part of God's plan for most men. It is good to protect, procreate, and provide effectively. But these are not the ultimates. The Bible, starting with the narratives of Genesis and running through the cross of Christ, enunciates a vision of men that is built on faith in God, loving like Christ, walking in the Spirit, a vibrant hope, an eternal perspective, and making a difference in the world.

In particular, the Cross of Christ points to sacrifice and selflessness—as Christ loved the Church and gave Himself up for it, putting it above Himself (Eph 5:25, Phil 2:3–4). It's the Cross that leads to our crucifixion to the World and the Flesh (Gal 5:24, 6:14). It's at the Cross where we see our own sinfulness; where we embrace the unconditional love of Christ and the extravagant grace of God; where we begin to experience the transforming power of the Spirit through repentance, restoration, and growth.

How do we raise up men who follow Christ and love people like this? Ideally, it starts with being raised in a good family—a glorious marriage with effective parents who love their children and work sacrificially for their good. Supplementing this—or substituting for it when it's not available—should be distant family, neighbors, members of the local church, and non-profits in the community. Long-term small group discipleship is another key ingredient, simulating the ministry model of Jesus with his disciples.

---

9. Sayers, *Letters to a Diminished Church*.

We need more mentor/mentee relationships and men who can humbly but confidently follow Paul's example by being a model for others to emulate. We need to exhort men to pursue Paul/Timothy relationships—as Timothy to a Paul with more wisdom; and as Paul to a Timothy who is younger in the faith. In this, it's vital to encourage inter-generational ministry—as older men come off the bench to pour into the boys and young men who need them. And we need to encourage men to have Paul/Barnabus relationships with peers. Men should find a small band of brothers with whom they walk with the Lord, live life, and do battle.

Have you seen video of Mamoudou Gassama, the immigrant from Mali who became a real-life version of Spiderman? In 2018, Gassama scaled four stories of a building in Paris to save a four-year-old boy who was holding onto a balcony rail when his father left him unattended. What a metaphor for what's at stake in the face of the world's frequent apathy and selfishness: an inattentive father, a crowd of people who stood watching, a man who took amazing action, and a boy's life hanging in the balance. Indeed, with great power comes great responsibility.

BIBLICAL MEN, BIBLICAL WOMEN, DISCIPLES OF JESUS

In the world of men's ministry, there are efforts to define an ideal man in biblical terms. The "four pillars of manhood" from Robert Lewis are as good as any: "reject passivity; accept responsibility; lead courageously; and expect God's greater reward."[10] For a "biblical woman," Proverbs 31 is a popular and convenient shortcut to define the concept. But such efforts largely conflate gender with discipleship, since most of these attributes should be pursued by all of us in our apprenticeship with Jesus, whether male or female.

For men, one can make a decent case for "protect, procreate, and provide." But procreate requires male and female. Provide and produce are for both men and women—from Genesis 2's calling to Paul's injunction to work (I Thess 4:11–12, II Thess 3:10). Sure, men are supposed to be productive, but don't forget about the industrious Proverbs 31 woman. The strongest case for a particularly male attribute would be "protect," given Adam preceding Eve, I Peter 3:7's command, and the usual prowess and size

---

10. Lewis, *Quest for Authentic Manhood*. In more recent work that builds on Lewis' legacy, BetterMan defines "a real man" as one who "courageously follows God's Word, loves and protects God's Woman, excels at God's Work, and improves God's World."

INTRODUCTION

advantage of men. "God is Father to the fatherless and defends the widow." (Ps 68:5) Even so, such protection is still grounded in the universal biblical calls to servant-leadership, caring for the vulnerable, and self-sacrifice.

Even a famous passage like Ephesians 5:33 is doubly aimed at both men and women. Paul writes, "Husbands, love your wives. And wives, respect your husbands." Beyond providing a gender-specific command to both marriage partners, note that both phrases implicitly address the other party. When Paul instructs me to love my wife Tonia, he's implicitly telling Tonia to be as lovable as possible. When he exhorts Tonia to respect me, the flip side is that I should strive to be as respectable as possible.

In any case, this book is motivated in large part by my concern about the state of men in America and my callings from the Lord to men's ministry, making disciple-makers, and training layleaders. Further, the book is about the men of Genesis—and I am particularly interested in talking about its men for today's men. As such, the book is angled toward men and I fervently hope that the book is read widely by men. All that said, as with everything else in the Bible, there is a ton in the book of Genesis for women as well. So, I am confident that everyone who reads this book will find plenty of commentary and applications to challenge them in their apprenticeship with Jesus.

BEFORE WE GET STARTED . . .

A few final words before we dig in. I love the Bible. I've been reading and studying it diligently for 40+ years, since I was awakened to its power in college. And I believe the Old Testament is greatly under-rated. I fell in love with it when Dwight Edwards spent eight months preaching through Joshua 35 years ago in Texas. Its narratives are powerful, especially in a post-modern era which emphasizes the importance of story. And of all the books in the Old Testament, none is more powerful than Genesis—its opening themes of Creation, Fall, and Redemption; God's efforts to redeem the world through Adam, Noah, and then Abraham with his descendants; its powerful stories that communicate universal principles about the character of God and the human condition. There is so much to say about Genesis! (As such, the book is loaded with commentary. Some of it is too much of a tangent and is relegated to footnotes.)

We tend to forget that Jesus, Paul, the apostles, and the New Testament church relied on the Old Testament as their "bible." Not surprising, it still has tremendous use and applicability to us today—in describing God, depicting His work in history, and pointing forward to the ministry of Jesus. Beyond this, the Old Testament is immensely helpful as a divine source of moral doctrine and practical ethics—not merely laws and commands, but by providing so many examples of what to do and what *not* to do. This is where Genesis shines. In the first half of I Corinthians 10, Paul writes at length about how "these stories" were written down as examples and types for us. Jesus encouraged his listeners to "remember Lot's wife" (Luke 17:32), but there are many more stories to remember and apply from Genesis. Why would we forsake or downplay this rich resource?

It's not necessary, but I encourage you to read the relevant Bible passages before my comments. At the front of each chapter, I offer a comprehensive plan to read through Genesis and a slimmer "greatest hits" approach. In particular, I want to exhort you to read the Bible if this is not a comfortable discipline for you. It's important for you to engage the text on your own—not merely to read what someone is writing about something. Please let this book be a supplement rather than a substitute for reading the Bible. For what it's worth, when I quote Scripture, I'm usually relying on the NIV. But you should feel free to read whatever version you want. If you're a long-time reader of the Bible, I would recommend trying a different translation, so that your eyes can more easily see the text afresh.

I also offer some memory verse options for those who already practice this spiritual discipline and for those who might give it a try now. In our discipleship curricula, we offer techniques to help with Bible memory. My favorite is to use the first initial of every word as a crutch while I'm memorizing the words. But we also suggest organizing it phrase-by-phrase, writing it backwards, and writing every other word. The brain is a funny thing—as is the process of learning. So, please try something new, especially if you have not had success with this previously.

As you'll see soon, the chapters are titled and built around pairs of words or phrases which either complement or contrast with each other. I've done this in an attempt to make the lessons more memorable. This inevitably resulted in some stretching to fit the primary points of each chapter into the framework. So, in advance, I appreciate whatever forgiveness you can offer for my liberalities there—or any errors that remain, despite the efforts of my editor Kaylee Anderson and the folks at Wipf & Stock. I hope you enjoy the book; learn a ton about the great book of Genesis; and are inspired and empowered to make a greater difference in God's Kingdom!

1

Silence and Violence

COMPLETE TEXT: GENESIS 1:1–2:3, 3:1–6:5
RECOMMENDED READING: 1:26–2:3, 3:1–4:16
POTENTIAL MEMORY VERSES: 1:26, 1:28, 3:6, 4:7

"First they came for the Communists, and I did not speak out, because I was not a Communist. Then they came for the Trade Unionists, and I did not speak out, because I was not a Trade Unionist. Then they came for the Jews, and I did not speak out, because I was not a Jew. Then they came for me, and there was no one left to speak for me."

This is a poetic version of Martin Niemoller's famous critique of German Christian leaders—for their failure to aggressively oppose the emerging Nazi regime. Niemoller did not compare their silence with Nazi violence. But he observed that the two acted in tandem. When some men badly misunderstood the world around them, other men took advantage of their ignorance and naivete to seize power. When some men failed to speak and to act, other men used their power to crush individuals and stagger the world.

The same pair of problems are a plague on society today: the silence and the violence of men. From absent fathers drawn away by cultural influences and pushed away by welfare policies to gang-bangers who wreak havoc on inner-city streets with drugs and guns. From guys who spend themselves on video games and porn to men who yell at their kids and engage in domestic violence against women. It turns out that "toxic masculinity" comes in two flavors: acting like thugs and mostly just taking up oxygen.

These are not new problems; it's been this way throughout recorded history. Adam refuses to speak and act; Cain kills his brother. As the Bible unfolds, the same pattern continues. King Darius is clueless while his advisors work to corrupt or eliminate Daniel. King Xerxes parties while his top lieutenant Haman plots the destruction of the Jews. Pilate refuses to act decisively at the trial of Jesus and Peter slices off an ear in the Garden. In fact, one can compose a history of the world through this lens—in particular, the use of government power against individuals and peoples. But behind the scenes, oh so quietly, there is the complicit acquiescence of those who failed to say or do anything.

Maybe you're thinking your choices are not so grand; your impact is not that great. Let's turn our eyes closer to home, where we can see the temptations to silence and violence in our everyday lives. Won't our failures and successes here make a profound difference in our marriages, with our kids, and within our workplaces? Won't our decisions have a significant impact on our communities, within the local church, and for the Kingdom?

Apparently, God thinks so. In Ephesians 2:8-9, Paul makes clear that we cannot be saved by good works. But in the next verse, he writes: "For we are God's workmanship, created in Christ Jesus to do good works, which God prepared in advance for us to do." We are God's works of art—and a good God would not create us for silence or violence. We were created to do good works—not just to avoid bad works. And these works were "prepared in advance" to be done with other masterpieces. So, God has been waiting for you to enter his Kingdom; to be comfortable in the goodness of the Kingdom; and to do certain things *for* Him and others—*with* Him and others—through His Kingdom.

Niemoller was part of a large group that supported Hitler's rise to power in 1933. But soon, Niemoller criticized the new regime and eventually led an opposition movement of clergy. Unfortunately, many others lacked the courage to join. He regretted his own late conversion to opposition, but at least he converted. He was arrested in 1937 and imprisoned in concentration camps until the end of the war. Many others continued in their silence—in safety and cowardice—complicit in allowing the horrific violence to continue without even a contrary word.

Dietrich Bonhoeffer was part of the same movement. Ironically, Bonhoeffer had written a chapter arguing for pacifism in his classic 1937 book,

Silence and Violence

The Cost of Discipleship. He was willing to speak out but not act out against the Nazi regime. Later, he changed his mind—even to the point of joining an assassination attempt on Hitler. Bonhoeffer was imprisoned in 1943 and executed just days before the end of the war. Sometimes, speaking out is sufficient; other times, more is required; in any case, silence is not enough.

ADAM AND CAIN

The silence and violence of men are two of the opening concepts in Genesis—and arguably, the two primary concepts just after the Fall. First themes are often crucial, so it's important for us to pay attention here. In Genesis 1–2, the Bible opens with the goodness of God's creation; the material and spiritual aspects of humanity; the nature of our work and calling from God; and both the equality and complementarity of husbands and wives.

But in Genesis 3, things go sideways: Eve is tempted by the Devil while Adam is silent (3:6). In Genesis 4, the narrative of the next generation is dominated by violence, as Cain murders Abel. Adam is quiet; Cain talks junk to God. Adam stands there like a dope while his wife is being tempted; Cain gets angry and takes action, premeditating Abel's murder. Adam's problem is passivity; Cain's problem is activity. Adam's failure is a "sin of omission"—a failure to do the right thing; Cain's failure is a "sin of commission"—doing the wrong thing.

Both types of sin can cause tremendous damage. Sins of commission are usually more obvious—by their nature. We see the sins take place and can often see the harms caused; they are more concrete. Murder, rape, and theft; sexual immorality, slander, and drunkenness; anger, greed, and gluttony. We often do things that we should not do. Sins of omission are usually more subtle—by their nature. They're *not* done, so they are more difficult to "see" or even to imagine; they are more abstract. Yet, they can be just as damaging. Failing to encourage our children; refusing to help someone in need; unwilling to practice robust hospitality. We often fail to do things that we should. (Thankfully, God's grace covers both categories!)

My wife and I run a small group for young adults and we've seen both sins bear fruit within the parenting they've had. Overbearing, legalistic, and abusive on the one hand. Neglecting basic needs, refusing to provide discipline, and failing to encourage on the other hand. Which is worse: raised by wolves or by hard-core helicopter parents? I don't know, but they're both damaging.

THE SILENCE OF ADAM

Although Eve is famous for biting into the fruit, Adam gets the lion's share of the biblical blame.[1] After all, who does the Lord approach in Genesis 3:9? But what was Adam's first sin? Maybe it was bad teaching, as he passed along God's instructions to Eve. Maybe it was his participation in the debacle at all, given his greater knowledge, accountability, and call to leadership (2:16–17). Eve yielded to a supernatural being; Adam merely succumbed to peer pressure. And pride must be considered a root cause, putting his own agenda above God's.

In any case, we know that a key sin in Genesis 3 was Adam's silence—his sin of omission. As Larry Crabb notes: "Silence is not golden, it is deadly. Adam's silence was lethal."[2] Ironically, Adam had spoken in Genesis 2, naming the animals on his own and breaking into poetry when he sees Eve. And Adam was made in the image of God who had spoken Creation into existence. God spoke and turned darkness and chaos into light, order, and beauty. Through Adam's silence, all of this was reversed.

For us, it is clear—from the Biblical record in general and the ministry of Jesus in particular—that God is not at all interested in this approach to manhood. We're not on Earth to kill time. We're called to steward the time, talent, and treasure we've been given—to be blessed by God, in order to be a blessing to God and others. We're not simply supposed to stay out of trouble until we're whisked into Paradise on the occasion of our bodily deaths. We are to be "thoroughly equipped for every good work" (II Tim 3:17) through the Word and the Spirit.

MIGHT MAKES RIGHT IN A MAN'S WORLD

The climactic sin of the second generation of mankind is heinous. Deliberate murder followed by callous indifference—and all of this, after a warning and encouragement from the Lord. Instead of Adam and Eve's shame, Cain substitutes flippancy and hardness of heart—with little fear or desire for relationship with the Lord. What an ominous start to human history and the divine project: The first wholly human being—the first person with an umbilical cord (and a belly button)—is a murderer.

---

1. See: Rom 5:12–19, I Cor 15:22,45. I Tim 2:14 notes that Eve was deceived, but that doesn't pin her with the blame for "original sin."
2. Crabb, *The Silence of Adam*, 98.

Silence and Violence

Cain's decision to kill Abel is the initial biblical example of "might makes right" and what it looks like to be in "a man's world." The pattern proceeds as Genesis 4 continues. In the 7th generation from Adam through Cain, Lamech is a mess, starting polygamy and altering God's ideal plan for marriage and family. He wants more women, more kids, and more power. Then, Lamech loudly and proudly kills someone who had wronged him. In fact, Lamech implies that he is greater than God, given that his promised vengeance is seven times greater than God's with Cain. The narrative serves to compare Cain with Lamech: The city and civilization established by Cain begin with self-sufficiency and fratricide, before extending to a god-like desire to rule over others.

By the time of Noah, both concepts have grown to horrific levels. In Genesis 6:5,11–12, evil is portrayed as extreme and universal: "how great the wickedness had become"—with "corrupt people" engaged in "corrupt ways," "corrupt in God's sight" and "full of violence." The actions are bad enough, but beyond this, "every inclination of the thoughts of the human heart was only evil all the time." Apparently, they wanted to do even more evil, but were limited by natural consequences. Unconcerned with what was *right*, they were willing to do whatever their *might* would allow—and only worried about others using their might on them in return.

However one interprets the strange description of the Nephilim in Genesis 6:1–4, it's clear that the narrator is describing *a man's world*—with worldly "heroes" who were "men of renown," objectifying and using women as they saw fit. Heroic from the world's standpoint, but not at all within God's vision for humans and the world they inhabit. (In the next chapter, we'll see God's response to all of this through the Flood narrative with Noah and the Ark—and ultimately, Noah's inability to move beyond that world.)

If you do the math with the ages in Genesis, you learn that Noah was the first (recorded) man to be born into a world that had become fully conscious of mortality—after Adam had finally died.[3] Physical death had been promised by God but not delivered for hundreds of years. (This is similar to us: We know about death intellectually, but then it becomes experiential for us when a close relative or friend dies—or we have a serious car accident or health scare.) How did men respond? Not well.

Again, it is clear from the Biblical record that God is opposed to this approach to manhood. It's to be peacemaking instead of inciting violence.

---

3. At least in terms of what's recorded, the only other deaths were *not* natural: the murders by Cain and Lamech.

Humility instead of pride. Building up rather than tearing down. Love instead of hatred. Overcoming evil with good rather than evil. Loving our wives as Christ sacrificially loved the church. Service and sacrifice instead of selfishness.

Throughout the Bible, there are repeated warnings about improper human dominion, the oppressive exercise of authority over others, and the potential for idolatry toward the power of government. It's supposed to be the opposite—a call to care for the vulnerable, rather than taking advantage of my power and your weakness. The Torah lays out the responsibility of Israel to be kind to the orphan, the widow, the stranger. (James 1:25 will later describe this as "pure and faultless religion.") God communicated with Hagar (an Egyptian slave woman) more than Sarah (the mother of the promised child Isaac). The Lord of History arranged for Tamar, Rahab, Ruth, and Bathsheba to be in the lineage of Christ. Jesus constantly worked with the vulnerable and the social outcast—from the Samaritan Woman and "the woman caught in adultery" to lepers and profligate sinners.

BAD THEOLOGY AND ANTHROPOLOGY

We see some of the steps of Adam and Eve's sin quite clearly: Eve looked, took, ate, and gave some to Adam—and he failed to intervene. At any point, they could have turned back, but instead, they continued their slide down the slippery slope of sin. Temptation is not a sin, but how we respond to it can be. They couldn't think clearly; they believed the doubts about God's goodness; they failed to flee; and they didn't "just say no."

Adam and Eve didn't handle the Devil's arguments well. He injected doubt about God's word ("Did God really say . . . ?"). He challenged God's love and benevolence by ripping "you must not eat . . . " from its bountiful context (2:16–17). He twisted truths into half-truths. He denied God's judgment, questioned His authority and power, and impugned His character and motives.

This is par for an unfortunate course. Satan presents the bait but hides the hook. He appeals to the body and the soul, promoting pleasure and pride. He promotes the short-run benefits of sin and downplays its long-run costs. He tempts us to love the gifts rather than the Giver. He tries to get us to forget our innumerable blessings and to focus on forbidden fruit or what we don't have. He implies that God is strict, stingy, selfish, and finite.

Silence and Violence

Satan wants us to choose his kind of life (independence, pride, and rebellion) over God's kind of life (love, faith, and obedience). This gets to the crux of basic theology: Does God *know* what's best for us and *want* what's best for us 100% or 94% of the time? If it's 100%, then the obvious choice is to always follow a good and great God. If it's 94%, we should look for the 6% where God is a Moron or a Cosmic Killjoy—and then, go the other direction.

Cain brings a mediocre offering ("some" vs. firstborn) when it was convenient ("in the course of time"). God rejects it—although not Cain himself—and offers encouragement and a blessing if it's done well. But Cain is livid at God's response—at least relative to God's satisfaction with Abel's offering. In his wounded pride, Cain ignores God's kind warning ("sin is crouching at your door"); blows off His exhortation to "master" his desires; and kills his little brother—a human being made in God's image, a good man who had (apparently) done nothing wrong. Cain kills Abel under false pretenses, with pre-meditation, out of jealous and perverse competition (when Cain was likely favored as the older son). And then instead of confession and repentance, Cain gets sarcastic with God through his infamous question: "Am I my brother's keeper?"[4]

How did Adam and Cain arrive at their sins? In large part, it happened because of flaws in their understanding of God and their relationship with God. More broadly, one can be disinterested in starting or fostering that relationship. Or one can relate to God and others eagerly but improperly—for example, through bad theology (misunderstanding God) or bad anthropology (misunderstanding God's vision for humans).

Legalism is a common mistake which combines both categories, imagining that God is looking for certain behaviors to enter into relationship with Him or to earn continuing relationship with Him—a check-the-box, black-and-white, canned approach to satisfying God. Not surprisingly, it results in a wooden and judgmental approach to non-Christians and Christians. Eve added a legalism to what God had said, going beyond the command not to *eat* from the one tree to a prohibition on *touching* it. Whether taught by Adam or invented by Eve, it was a well-intentioned self-control mechanism, but not God's word.

---

4. Cain and Abel are key to the framework of John Steinbeck's classic novel, *East of Eden*. All of the A characters are like Abel; all of the C characters are like Cain. The book also wrestles with free will and determinism, especially through the servant, Lee.

For Cain, God is to be ignored as possible, appeased when necessary, and manipulated as useful—approaching God on one's own terms, if at all. (We'll see some of the same principles with the Tower of Babel narrative in Genesis 11.) For many people, relationship with God is largely a matter of indifference. But when interaction with God emerges, they experience it through frustration, sarcasm, flippancy, and anger.

RECOVERING FROM SIN

Adam struggles throughout most of Genesis 3. He fails to intervene with the Serpent on behalf of Eve. He tries to cover their shame with mask-like fig leaves, instead of going to God in repentance. Their makeshift underwear is inadequate as they hide from God—now afraid of fellowship and even His voice. Then with fig-leaf language, Adam points to his nakedness not his disobedience; he makes excuses instead of apologizing; he blames God and Eve instead of taking responsibility.

But after the punishments are meted out (to Adam and Eve) and the curses are pronounced (to the ground and the Serpent), our Savior is prophesied (the bitten heel and crushed head), and Adam recovers nicely at the end of the narrative. He names the woman "Eve" at this point, meaning "mother of the living."[5] And he busts into poetry and looks hopefully to a glorious future—re-established relationship with the Lord, revitalized relationship with Eve, and renewed commitment to the mission of being fruitful, multiplying, and extending (healthy) dominion over the earth.

In contrast, Cain never seems to get it. We don't even know why he made the offering—perhaps to placate God and hope for better growing conditions. In any case, Cain does it halfway—while Abel, following his example, ironically takes it in the right spirit. Cain receives a kind warning from God but spurns it, even to the point of dropping sarcasm when he rejects the counsel and murders his brother. And then, when the punishment comes, Cain's response is whining and complaining: It's "more than I can bear"! All he offers is fear, despair, and self-pity—along with a bunch of first-person pronouns when he's not shifting blame. As with his parents, we see Cain evading responsibility rather than embracing introspection, remorse, and repentance. Finally, notice that Cain "went out" (4:16) while

---

5. I would have considered names such as "thanks for the fruit" or "Snapple" (short for snake and apple)!

Adam is "driven out." (3:24) Adam wants to rebuild and maintain a relationship with God; Cain is ready to move on.

ACTIVITY AND PASSIVITY

As Genesis 4 opens, Eve gives birth to Cain and names him. (Again, where is Adam? We won't read about him at all in the rest of this account. Ironically, he names the animals, but not his own sons.) The second generation is offered the choice of obedience or rebellion, life or death—and Cain chooses poorly. The root of sin in Genesis 3 leads to more fruit in Genesis 4, as sin continues in the family tree. Where are Adam and Eve in the sibling rivalry? The text simply indicates more silence.

Since Adam's sin in Genesis 3 is first, silence and passivity may be the greater general temptations for men—while the violence and bad activity of Genesis 4 are significant but secondary concerns. This is contrary to the world's view of things, where sins of commission are usually judged much more harshly than sins of omission. Then again, if Adam represents men who want a relationship with God and Cain represents those who are not interested, perhaps the point is that silence, cowardice, and passivity are the temptations most relevant to *Christian* men—while indifference, pride, and violence are generally the greater concern for *non-Christian* men.

Focusing on Christians, it's certainly possible (and in fact, sadly common) for men to struggle with anger, objectify women, pursue their own agendas, etc. But given the overarching emphasis on grace, love, and kindness in a Christian worldview, it seems probable that passivity is the more likely problem. Still, men are not called to be doormats or merely nice guys. (Of course, there is no biblical license for being a jerk or a dictator either!) To combat passivity, it's important that we have better theology and a robust vision for the great things that God wants for us and from us. And as a practical matter, especially if one struggles here, it's better to err on the side of doing and saying too much.

Our commission is to fulfill the Creation Mandate as those "made in the image of God" in Genesis 1:26–28 (as we'll discuss more in the next chapter). But the call to exercise proper dominion in Genesis 1 becomes far more challenging after the Fall in Genesis 3—in particular, raising a family and making a living. From another angle, the charge is to reverse and redeem what Francis Schaeffer describes as deaths or separations that resulted from the Fall:

- Psychological (3:7)—man from himself (self-consciousness, guilt, shame)
- Spiritual (3:8)—man from God (fear, hiding, ignoring grace and repentance)
- Sociological (3:11-13, 16b)—man from man (blaming others, trouble at home)
- Environmental (3:15a, 17a)—man from nature (pollution, degradation, abuse)
- Economic (3:17-19a)—man from work and provision (toil, increased scarcity)
- Physical (3:16a, 19b)—man from life (pain, suffering, aging, disease, death)

In other words, the Fall resulted in a hostile world filled with fragile and broken people. What is prophesied in Genesis 3 comes true, in spades, in Genesis 4. Too often, lives will be dominated by despair, darkness, distance, destruction, deprivation, difficulty, and death. Ironically, the solution to these problems is another death: "death to self" (Rom 6:11), being crucified to the World and our Sinful Nature (Gal 5:24, 6:14), as we follow in the footsteps of Jesus who was crucified for our sins. In Romans 8:18-25, Paul writes about the hope and redemption that are available to us—now in part (as Creation groans) and eventually in full (as we walk and wait in the meantime). The call is to accept the grace of God and to extend it to others; to be blessed by God so we can bless others; to keep in step with the Spirit and to love others robustly.

This can involve difficult moments—for example, repenting as necessary and exhorting others to make changes in their lives. Take responsibility; embrace accountability; and provide restitution when appropriate. Repent, restore, and redeem. Get up after you stumble (Prov 24:16); learn and progress; practice spiritual disciplines and strive for growth. None of these things are easy. Paul prays that we would have the power to grasp God's love (Eph 3:18); apparently, embracing and applying that love often requires strength. Being nice is not enough; being a good guy is not sufficient.

This is modeled briefly but well by Enoch in Genesis 5:21-24. As Lamech, Enoch is also the 7th generation from Adam—through 3rd son Seth this time. His line is not given credit for any innovations—other than Enoch's close relationship with God. Throughout Genesis 5, people "lived,"

Silence and Violence

but Enoch "walked with God," implying his choices and purpose.[6] In fact, Enoch is so impressive that he joins Elijah and Jesus in being whisked into Heaven, instead of going there through death. We don't know much about his life, but we can infer his theology from Hebrews 11:1–6. Enoch believed in (and thus, walked with) the good and great God of Creation. And we can imagine how a man like that would love all sorts of people.

WRAPPING UP . . .

As an economist who focuses on public policy, I love Florence King's semi-spoof of Niemoller's point: "When they came for the smokers, I kept silent because I don't smoke. When they came for the meat eaters, I kept silent because I'm a vegetarian. When they came for the gun owners, I kept silent because I'm a pacifist. When they came for the drivers, I kept silent because I'm a bicyclist. They never did come for me. I'm still here because there's nobody left in the secret police except sissies with rickets."[7]

Her humor underlines the seriousness of the concern. In particular, we should defend the (legitimate) rights of others when they are under attack by powerful others—even when we don't want to exercise the same rights. I may not use a gun, but I'll defend the 2nd Amendment. I don't agree with you, but I'll defend your right to free speech. You worship a different God, but I'll defend your rights to conscience and the free exercise of religion.

The same is true with legalism in the church. Even if I don't want the occasional beer or glass of wine, I'll passionately defend you from the legalists who want to condemn and attack you for this. I may not agree with you on Calvinism, belonging to a certain church, or speaking in tongues, but I'll argue vehemently with those who imagine you're not going to Heaven because of your views on those topics. All of this requires vision, wisdom, and courage that extends far beyond niceness.

Neither silence nor violence is the answer to how God wants us to get around in this world. We should avoid anger, ridicule, and coercion—relying instead on kindness, persuasion, and freedom. We should speak up and be active in our world, especially in the face of oppression, violence, and

---

6. Is it a coincidence that his relationship with God deepens after the birth of his son Methuselah? Think about how often the birth of a first child changes life dramatically—spiritually and otherwise.

7. King, *Florence King Reader*, 330.

hatred—and despite temptations toward apathy and passivity. We should avoid both the silence of Adam and the violence of Cain—and as appropriate, to use our voice to oppose injustice through the violence of others.

2

Treading Water vs. Moving the World

COMPLETE TEXT: GENESIS 2:4–25, 6:6–11:9
RECOMMENDED READING: 2:4–25, 6:7–22, 8:13–9:17
POTENTIAL MEMORY VERSES: 2:7, 2:18, 2:24

When people retire from our School of Business, we throw a party with a lunch, a cake, a parting gift, and colleagues sharing memories. The stories are a collection of fond recollections and poking fun. The tales induce laughter and occasionally tears—as we remember some of what has made the retiree special, productive, and worthy of honor, especially in our work together.

Two of these retirement shindigs haunt me a bit. The first was a colleague who refused the party. We were surprised by this; it hadn't happened before (and hasn't happened since). We're not sure why; the best guess was that he couldn't handle the roast part of the festivities. But I also don't think there would been many great stories to share. He would have been broadly celebrated for his ample service to the School and being a good guy, but that's about as far as it would have gone.

So, maybe he made the right decision to avoid the party—and this takes me to the second example. With this colleague, when we got to the stories, nobody had *anything* to say. The initial silence was awkward; the continuing silence was extremely uncomfortable. Eventually, a few people strained to say pleasant things and then it was over. He had been a good enough colleague and he is a really nice guy. But there were no memories to share and he hadn't moved any of us.

Now that I've thrown two former colleagues under the bus, let me get underneath there with them. After my third semester of college, I was kicked out of school for bad grades. I was really smart, but not a *student*—a combination that didn't work when I was "studying" to become an engineer. (It would be more accurate to say that I was majoring in Video Games.) My parents had divorced and my mom had been the driving force behind my education. When I shared the news about my grades with her, she simply said "You're just trying to be average." Ouch! But she was right. After four months of early-morning full-time work at McDonald's, I was ready to strive for something above-average at school.

Sometimes, average may be the best you can do—and that's fine. And within God's Kingdom, there is purpose and even glory in the middling and the mundane. But only having a vision for mediocrity, settling for average when so much more is possible, succumbing to fear instead of living by faith and taking risks? We learn from the Parable of the Talents that the Lord's response to such stewardship is to label it "wicked and lazy." (Matt 25:26)

There are other occasions where people move the needle big-time, but in the wrong direction. They're memorable; they may even make the history books. But their impact is regrettable. Here, think of dictators, mobs, and cults—with "effective" leaders and "impressive" results but destructive outcomes. In contrast, the call for Christians is to make a *positive and significant* difference in God's Kingdom, extending the grace they have received, emulating Christ and living by the Spirit.

TREADING WATER AT THE TOWER OF BABEL

From a worldly perspective, the Tower of Babel in Genesis 11 was a praiseworthy project—before the work was disrupted by God. The people displayed noteworthy unity around a common goal; they worked hard; and they seemed to accomplish their goals efficiently enough. They built a city and a tower "to the heavens," but largely in service of "making a name" for themselves. Ironically, their name *is* saved for posterity, but not as they intended. The project is now a monument to futility, a symbol of supposed self-sufficiency, the pursuit of fame, temptation to pride, and hard work for naught.

The tower was probably a ziggurat—a mini-temple in the sky, as if reaching toward the gods in the heavens. But given their motives, it was coming near to God—in height rather than holiness. In Genesis 6:4, the Nephilim had accomplished the same, earning "renown"—literally a "name." Both followed in the footsteps of the Serpent's temptation to "be like God." If Babel was an attempt to "get closer to God," it is noteworthy that God "came down" twice in the narrative, indicating their failure. God disrupted their language and injected chaos into their improper order—in contrast to His creation of (good) order from chaos through His speech in Genesis 1-2 and Adam's creation of chaos from order by his silence in Genesis 3.

The Babel'ers were also unified in avoiding God's command for them to exercise dominion of the entire earth. There's nothing wrong with fame *per se*—if grounded in God and His will, if accomplished as a by-product rather than pursued as a goal. Ironically, God will promise the same to Abraham: a great name (12:2), a great/mighty nation (18:18), a multitude of nations (17:4-6,16), and the father of kings (17:6,16). If Babel represents the potential dangers of self-sufficiency, urbanization, and "bad unity," this underlines the very different approach of God to Abraham in the next story: a journey of faith, walking with God, and living in tents.

One of the angles for understanding Genesis 1-11 is to see its opening narratives as polemic against similar pagan myths, with their flawed theology and anthropology.[1] For example, Israel's Creation account assumes the pre-existence of God who merely speaks the universe into existence—whereas the pagan stories underline the limits and vulnerabilities of their gods. Both depict man as created from clay, but God's breath of life sets humans apart in value and purpose—whereas the pagans see the creation of man as an afterthought whose purpose is to be a slave to the gods. God creates light, order, and beauty, desiring to have relationship with humans—whereas the pagan gods are arbitrary and capricious (if not evil), using humans as cogs in the machine. In the *Epic of Gilgamesh*, the ark is a cube that couldn't have floated during the Flood. And so on.

Likewise, the Babel stories are different. The building materials in the Bible's account are part of its subtle critique. The pagans use brick and tar—with all of the impressive human ingenuity implied by this scientific advance. In contrast, the Jews used stone and mortar. Although not as impressive from a technological standpoint, these are natural and stronger building materials. It's also interesting that the Babel bricks were moistened dust from the ground and refined by fire. This was similar to God's creation

---

1. Nahum Sarna's *Understanding Genesis* is exceedingly helpful on this.

of dust moistened by God's breath, cleansed by water, and refined by fire—but a counterfeit for God's creative activity.

We saw the same bent toward earthly "progress" in the line of Cain (4:17-24). He built a city that he named after his son. Seven generations after Adam, Lamech invented polygamy—portrayed as a social innovation. One of Lamech's sons was described as "the father of those who live in tents and raise livestock"—shepherding and animal husbandry. Another son was "the father of all who play stringed instruments and pipes"—music and the arts. Another forged tools from bronze and iron—indicative of science, industry, and military prowess. All impressive, widely varied, and mostly useful as civilization flourishes. But it was all soberly connected to the troubled line of Cain. And there was no mention of God or faith, implicitly pointing to selfish agendas and the prevalence of pride.

Like money, such tools can be used for good or for ill. Coming out of Egyptian bondage, Israel spent the wealth it gained upon its release—some for the Golden Calf and some for the Tabernacle. In I Timothy 6:10, Paul warns about "the love of money" as "a root of all kinds of evil." But a few verses later, he exhorts the wealthy to be "rich in good deeds." Economists focus on markets: an amazing way to foster trade, consumption, and production. But what is being consumed? Social media has many great uses, but has caused so much trouble. What are we doing with what we have? Babel represents the use of worldly means to pursue worldly ends. But from a Kingdom perspective, it reduces to the passionate pursuit of treading water.

In Acts 2, the Holy Spirit comes on all believers at Pentecost. In many ways, this moment is the anti-Babel or more positively, the resolution and redemption of the Babel narrative. Again, amazing unity in the face of diversity. Again, multiple tongues are present. But this time, the unity and diversity will glorify God and drive His Kingdom further. As it was after Babel, now it's the Church that will scatter to the ends of the Earth and spread the Gospel.

GOD'S DESIGN FOR HUMANS

As we saw "in the beginning," we are made in God's image (1:26-28), implying an agenda—with means and ends—in line with God's will in His good and great Kingdom. We are blessed and called to increase in number and to be fruitful, filling the world with children and properly ruling the (social and natural) world through effective human governance. Work was initially a full-fledged blessing—a pre-Fall institution that was corrupted by the Fall. God was the first worker (2:2,15). In the New Jerusalem, we will have work to do. Until then, we work with God to redeem the work we have in front of us. What is our work? Ideally, robust families, productive careers, enjoyable vocations, effective ministries, and creative hobbies.

In all of the above, created in the image of a Creator God, we are to convert chaos into order and to act with purpose within God's will. We are to be people whose word is good—like God—that when it is said, it is as good as done. We are to value and enjoy God's creation as good. We are to be creative and to create things of use and beauty within our work, working to redeem work. We are to exercise proper dominion over nature and the resources over which God has given us stewardship. We are to bless God and others—as we have been blessed by God. We are to respect the inherent value and equality of all people—and their individual differences (1:26-27). We are to pursue relationship, teamwork, and community as we do our work. We are to empower others—as we've been empowered by God. And we are to view ourselves as God's royal ambassadors to the world (II Cor 5:17-20).

Adam was made of dust and God's breath (2:7)—the material and the spiritual; body, soul, and spirit. Dust is formless (as the universe in 1:2), dry (alluding to our need for Jesus and the Holy Spirit as the spring of living waters [John 7:38-39]), and oh so common. As Matthew Henry quipped, "the same infinite power that made the world [out] of nothing, made man [out] of next to nothing."[2] God condescended to make something in His image—out of dirt. This should make it easier for us to stay humble! But we are also formed with God's "breath of life." It's ironic that breath usually scatters; here, it serves to bring us together gloriously. The combination is earthly and divine, natural and supernatural. We need both; we can't drop either. Our bodies tie us to the animals, while our souls direct us toward God. We are tempted to be too worldly—or to be so heavenly-minded that we're no earthly good—when our calling is to live on Earth with eternity in mind.

After creating Adam, God put him in a garden. This underlines our participation within God's provision. God could have had Adam simply picking fruit and nuts for food; instead, he works in the beauty and bounty of a garden—a picture of growth, cultivation, and then fruit. In fact, the first institution given to Adam was his work—his purpose on earth, from

---

2. Henry, *Commentary*, 11.

career and job to vocation and family. So too, we find much of our identity and our satisfaction from God in our work.

Soon after, in Adam's loneliness, it was "not good for man to be alone." The animals were not good enough and God alone was not ideal. Even though Adam had walked with God and had work and purpose, he still needed Eve to complete him. As Henry said: "Perfect solitude would turn a paradise into a desert and a palace into a dungeon."[3] So God gave Adam a "helper" (2:24-25)—a term usually used for God—a partner for his work; a pairing for the crucial work of marriage and parenting; the beginnings of community and society.

In the Garden of Eden, Adam and Eve were spiritually united, emotionally available, and physically connected. God designed marriage for procreation and pleasure; to be partners in Kingdom work (2:18,20); to provide mutual joy, comfort, and companionship. Clearly, from the beginning, biblical marriage is meant to be monogamous, heterosexual, and for a lifetime. This is good for the couple, but also provides security for children and stability for society and the nation.

Why was Eve made from Adam's rib? I love the Henry quote you often hear at weddings: "The woman was made out of a rib out of the side of Adam; not made out of his head to rule over him, nor out of his feet to be trampled upon by him, but out of his side to be equal with him, under his arm to be protected, and near his heart to be beloved."[4] How precious and powerful!

Adam had given names to the animals, but now he busts out with some poetry. From there, they are "united"—what the KJV calls "cleave." In the future, bride and groom will face a call to "leave" their parents to start a new household. This can be a serious problem in marriage: failing to leave or to cleave. But it is unbiblical to not sever the umbilical cord!

In the Garden, Adam and Eve were given tremendous bounty and freedom, but also modest limits (2:16-17). God is portrayed as Creator, Benefactor, and now Lawgiver. Life in the Kingdom is not "anything goes," but is rooted in the goodness of the limits that God has given us. Likewise, freedom should always be grounded in responsibility—in the opportunities and limits of the human person. There was still a choice to be made and for free will to be exercised. Why? We can stand in opposition to God, so that

---

3. Henry, *Commentary*, 15.
4. Henry, *Commentary*, 16.

ESCAPING THE FLOOD

Adam and Eve were set up to be productive in work and family, fulfilling the commission to be fruitful, multiply, and extend dominion over the Earth. In contrast, the people of Babel were figuratively treading water by building a monument to themselves. And Noah ends up floating on the waters of the Flood in the Ark. His context: Given the violence, selfishness, and heroism of Cain and Co., the world was dominated by "might makes right" in "a man's world." So, now what?

In Genesis 6:8–10, we read "But Noah . . . " He is the exception to the rule. His righteousness is surrounded by evil—literally and in the narrative. (Notice how 6:8–10 is bookended by evil in 6:5–7 and 6:11–12.) He was not a perfect man, but he "walked with God" and he was "blameless among the people of his time"—in absolute or at least relative terms, despite the peer pressure of the world around him. Noah is repeatedly commended for his righteousness and then, for building the Ark in obedience. Not only does he save his family and pairs of each animal. More broadly, he saves "mankind" and the animal kingdom—in what turns out to be a fresh start, a new beginning, another opportunity for man to get it right in terms of dominion, multiplying, and fruitfulness.

As a result, Noah is blessed and receives a new covenant from the Lord. In the New Testament, he is in the "Hall of Faith" of Hebrews 11. His work with the Ark and the Flood waters are described as a symbol of baptism (I Pet 3:20–21). And he is described as a "preacher of righteousness," stepping into the "watchman" role described in the Old Testament. The watchman warns the people—and if they don't listen, their blood is on their own hands. If the watchman doesn't deliver the message, then he is responsible.[5] Noah preached righteousness; his life exhibited holiness and righteousness; and he offered them a way to be saved that they refused.

But there are problems with Noah as well. The most obvious is his drunkenness after the Flood. Maybe he had PFSD (Post-Flood Stress Disorder) that drove him to drink. Can you imagine what it would have been like to build the Ark around your neighbors (when they may have never

---

5. Because of this powerful concept (especially in Ezekiel 33) and the writings of Watchman Nee, we blessed our fourth son with Watchman as his middle name.

experienced rain); to experience the Flood in the Ark with all of those animals; to see the staggering carnage afterwards; to bear such responsibility before and after the Flood; and to be alone on the Earth with your family afterwards?!

Was the drunkenness a one-time slip or a recurring problem? Maybe he didn't know the wine's potency or just took his drinking too far. Perhaps he struggled with all of his newfound spare time.[6] In any case, this moment robs him of some dignity and authority. The responses of his sons are noteworthy; Ham is certainly a mess, but the other two respond admirably. Noah's response to Ham seems over-the-top, but perhaps we should imagine a larger context when we see his glee at Noah's stumble. Surely this was in keeping with Ham's (lack of) character. Cain had asked about being his brother's keeper; here, Ham fails to be his father's keeper.

But there is another less-obvious problem. Notice the command to get on the Ark in the old world's style (6:18). As such, Noah gets on the Ark men first and women second (7:7,13). But God commands him to get off the Ark in a different order: Noah, *then his wife*, and then his sons with their wives (8:16). In other words, God wants his wife elevated over his sons—a repudiation of "the man's world" prior to the Flood. But look how Noah gets off the Ark (8:18). He disobeys God, but perhaps more important, he doesn't understand what God is trying to do—a sign that this approach to dealing with humans is not going to work well.[7] Starting fresh with the best man available out of a man's world is not as promising as one might hope.

Noah starts off so strong. He completes an amazing task, but has a rough finish. In the narrative, he seems to follow Adam in passivity and silence—and Cain in his anger. (No words are recorded for Noah, except the post-drunk aftermath with his sons.) And he has a subtle yet crucial act of disobedience, emulating the pre-Flood world in exiting the Ark. Ultimately, as we look forward to the Babel narrative, he fails to move the culture beyond its Cain-like tendencies.[8]

---

6. Solomon is another example of this concern: an active building agenda for the first 20 years of his reign, but then apparently, a lot less work and a lot more trouble in his last 20 years.

7. Similarly, the Bible has few mentions of women's names, until their elevated and vital roles with the patriarchs.

8. In II Pet 2:5, Noah is described as a "preacher of righteousness." But a few verses later, Noah and Lot are compared favorably to each other. Given Lot's problems, this doesn't reflect well on Noah.

Treading Water vs. Moving the World

GREATNESS IN THE KINGDOM AND MOVING THE WORLD

Noah is in the pantheon of Biblical paragons. As Christians, we're used to seeing these heroes as largely interchangeable. But he is not a top-tier hero for Jews. Why? To the Jewish mind (and a careful reading of the Old Testament), Abraham, Moses, and David stand out above the rest. In particular, why is Abraham considered so much greater than Noah?

What did Noah say to those around him? It's unrecorded in the Old Testament and unknown in the New Testament except two vague references. Hebrews 11:7 says "by his faith he condemned the world" and II Peter 2:5's reference to him as a "preacher of righteousness." Here's what we do know: When it's time to build the Ark and save his family—unlike Abraham in Genesis 18—there was no intervention by Noah with the Lord on behalf of those to be destroyed. Abraham argued with the Lord on behalf of strangers, while Noah didn't even advocate for his neighbors. Adam's troubles with silence and sins of omission echo in Noah's story. In a word, Noah stayed dry, but Abraham got his hands dirty.

Jonathan Sacks gives us a preview of what we'll see from Abraham: God "seeks from us something other and greater than obedience, namely responsibility . . . the hero of faith was not Noah but Abraham . . . What might an Abraham have said when confronted with the possibility of a flood? . . . Abraham might have saved the world. Noah saved only himself and his family. Abraham might have failed, but Noah—at least on the evidence of the text—did not even try . . . Noah's end—drunk, disheveled, an embarrassment to his children—eloquently tells us that if you save yourself while doing nothing to save the world," it's far from ideal.[9] In other words, obedience is not enough for greatness in the Kingdom. For those of us in the church today, do we reach the righteous standard of Noah—or far better, the Kingdom-heroic standard of Abraham?

Kass observes that there are no recorded questions from Noah, just simple obedience. At one level, this is impressive. But then we remember that many of the Bible's most prominent heroes had significant flaws and wrestled heartily with God. Moses questioned his commissioning; broke the stones on which the Ten Commandments were written; disobeyed by hitting the rock in the Wilderness (Num 20); and repeatedly wrestled with God over Israel. Habakkuk, Job, and the Psalmists question how God is

---

9. Sacks, *Covenant and Conversation*, 46.

running His universe. From David and Jeremiah to Peter and Paul, the men after God's heart often displayed far more than mere obedience.[10]

Abraham, the next "hero of the faith," doesn't ask any questions or cause any trouble in his commissioning. But as we'll see, he makes up for it later. In any case, it falls to Abraham to change the world. Where Noah stands out in a nasty world, Abraham will show much more: the courage to leave behind his life in Babylon and go to an unknown land; God blessing him so he can be a blessing to others; his repeated interactions with the world (albeit with mixed results); his amazing hospitality with Lot and the angels; using his 318 trained men responsibly; his willingness to advocate for strangers with God; and his willingness to sacrifice Isaac rather than argue with God about what looks like his own family's preservation.

In some ways, this is analogous to being satisfied with pulling weeds, when God wants us to plant flowers. In Ephesians 4, Paul talks about the "old man" behaviors and attitudes to be jettisoned, along with the "new man" virtues and blessings to be added. We certainly admire Jesus for the sins he did *not* do. But what makes his earthly life even more remarkable is what he *did*—how he handled extremely difficult situations with exquisite style and substance: the perfect word with the perfect tone; touching the leper and talking with the Samaritan woman; exhorting his disciples and messing with the Pharisees; dealing with the vulnerable through grace, dignity, and compassion.

Putting it another way, God doesn't want us to be a thermometer, adapting to the room we've entered. And when change is possible, he doesn't want us to leave a room that is too hot or cold for something more comfortable. He wants us to be a thermostat—able to change the temperature of the room. It's not enough to be nice in a cold room; it's not ideal to flee a hot room. It's not sufficient to stay above the waters and survive the Judgment of the Flood. God wants us to make a difference in this world.

WRAPPING UP . . .

At least in worldly terms, political greatness is defined by effective and ethical responses to crises or significant challenges. Think of Winston Churchill

---

10. The only religious "innovation" we see from Noah is his sacrifice. God seems pleased enough with it. But we're not sure why Noah does this, since it was not commanded—and we might worry that it was done out of superstition or manipulation rather than thankfulness.

in World War II. Or Lincoln and Washington in early American history. Among American presidents who started serving within the last century, only Ronald Reagan rises to this level.[11] He dealt with the worst economy since the Great Depression, the "malaise" of the country during the Carter years, and the Soviet threat during the Cold War. Reagan's economic policies were impressive; the country returned to optimism; and his military policies led to the break-up of the USSR soon after he left office. Amazing for our times: Reagan worked with Tip O'Neill and a strongly Democratic House to accomplish these results. And unbelievable for our times: Reagan won 49 of 50 states in his 1984 re-election bid.[12] Vision, policy, execution, and leadership—a phenomenal combination.

In Biblical terms, greatness is often recorded with the same criteria through the direct and indirect help of God. Moses leading the people out of Egypt and through the Wilderness to the verge of the Promised Land. Joshua and Caleb's faith as spies to Canaan, their courage with the rebellious people, and a generation later, their leadership across the Jordan. Daniel's early days of training and his faithful, effective work for government within exile. Mordecai's tenacity in standing against Haman and his ingenuity in working with Esther. Nehemiah overcoming obstacles to rebuild the wall in Jerusalem. Peter's leadership among the disciples and then in the Early Church. Paul's perseverance through staggering trials and his work in evangelism, church planting, and discipleship.

But other times, the greatness of people in the Bible is too small to be measured in worldly historical terms: the courage of Rahab, the initiative of Ehud, the loyalty of Ruth, the charity of Boaz, the prayers of Hannah, the perseverance of Jeremiah, the grace of Hosea, the resolution of Habakkuk, the invitations of Andrew, the faith of the Centurion, the tenacity of the Canaanite woman, the repentance of Zacchaeus, the martyrdom of Stephen, the leadership of Titus.

The big characters in history and the Bible impress me. But the biblical "little people" inspire me and give me hope that I can be great in the little things of God's Kingdom. My dad was a great man of this sort. My parents separated after 17 years of marriage, divorcing six years later. Mom could

---

11. Many people would put FDR on the list, but his record on civil liberties was troubling (see: David Beito's *The New Deal's War on the Bill of Rights*); he didn't honor Jesse Owens after the 1936 Berlin Olympics; and his economic policies were abysmal. In the 6th year of the New Deal, the unemployment rate was still 19%!

12. Reagan lost Minnesota—the home state of his opponent Walter Mondale—by only a few thousand votes.

be a handful and Dad was a good guy, but that wasn't sufficient to make the marriage work. Some good news for me and my two siblings: We *learned* that being a good guy wasn't good enough to handle challenging people and tough circumstances.

Dad stayed in touch and usually got along well enough with Mom. Many years later, they started dating again and remarried 23 years after their separation. In the meantime, he had become a disciple of Jesus. Their oldest grandkids were five years old—when conversations and holidays would have started to get really awkward. When they put things back together, the only divorce we've had in our family was healed.[13] Their marriage still struggled, but it was much better the second time. Dad could have gone other directions, but he pursued Mom instead. Dad was a hero—and the sort of hero that all of us can be. Dad moved *our* world—and as a result, he moved *the* world.[14]

---

13. See Johnston et al., "Divorce, Family Arrangements, and Children's Adult Outcomes." They find that earlier divorce has a greater impact on kids.

14. For a podcast discussion of this story, listen to Solid Steps Radio, "#16 Marriage."

3

Leave and Go

COMPLETE TEXT: GENESIS 11:10–12:9
RECOMMENDED READING: 12:1–9
POTENTIAL MEMORY VERSES: 12:1, 12:3

DURING MY LAST YEAR of undergrad at George Mason, I had a spiritual awakening prompted by Maxie Burch teaching through the book of Romans in Sunday School. It was the first time I can remember being challenged by Christianity. Understanding Romans required a lot more thinking than what I had experienced through sermons and teaching. The Bible hadn't seemed to provide or require all that much intellectually.

When Maxie covered Romans 12:9–21, I was convicted that the Lord wants us to strive for a life that was far beyond me. Sure, I was "a sinner saved by grace" and "fell short of the glory of God." But in practical day-to-day terms, it had seemed as if the Christian life was something relatively easy to achieve. From my parents, I knew this might not be enough to have a good marriage. But it was the only plan I understood: good guy and family man, strong career and solid citizen, Sunday School teacher and a deacon. Looking back, I had repeatedly heard the same high calling through the Sermon on the Mount about life in the Kingdom. But God used the freshness of Romans 12 to get my attention about the ethics of the Christian life.

The same year, I was applying to grad schools. I was rejected at the three top-tier schools where I applied (likely because of the academic struggles I described in chapter 2). I was accepted at Duke, but not offered enough money to graduate without debt. So, the decision came down to Ohio State and Texas A&M. They were comparable in terms of academic rankings. I figured it'd be Ohio State, since it was closer to Dad in Northern Kentucky. I had lived at home with Mom for my undergrad years; living near Dad for my grad years made sense. Plus, Ohio State was much closer to my friends in Northern Virginia and my relatives in Louisville.

But with my burgeoning faith, I decided to commit the decision to the Lord in persistent prayer—the first time I had done this. After visits to both campuses, it seemed clear as a bell that I should go to A&M. Texas was—literally and figuratively—a thousand miles away from anything I had known; I left a lot behind and it was a strange place to me. It turned out to be the best six years of my life, setting up virtually everything that would follow. The Lord could have worked through circumstances at Ohio State, but I am convinced that the decision "to leave and to go" to the Lone Star State was what God wanted for me.

Texas was certainly different—the culture and the accent, the weather and the football, hats and boots, wide-open terrain and pickup trucks, what was valued and what was considered funny. My first-ever roommate brought his furniture to our apartment in a cattle trailer. I quickly learned to love Tex-Mex, especially at hole-in-the-wall restaurants. I grew to enjoy country music and got really good at two-steppin'. The Lord opened doors for me to be active in music, including a studio for violin lessons and two part-time stints as a public school orchestra teacher. Through music, I met people who stretched my faith and I led my first Bible study with the concertmaster of the community orchestra. (We chose I Samuel since she and her husband had a daughter named Hannah.)

At A&M, my teaching style ("flipped" and "Socratic") was greatly informed by the Gillette brothers. I was profoundly influenced by Bob Reed, my dissertation advisor—both professionally and personally. He taught me how to do research; he mentored me in the faith; and when I got married, Tonia and I modeled our family after his in terms of adoption and hospitality. And I was deeply impacted by Dwight Edwards, the preacher who awakened my passion for the Bible in general and the Old Testament in particular. When I first attended Grace Bible Church, he spent the entire academic year on Joshua. I couldn't imagine how this was possible, until I heard his first sermon!

Not everyone has a dramatic story of "leave and go." But all of us are called to move along at some point—and it's often a significant challenge. Not everybody answers the call—at least initially. Some guys get stuck in their mom's basement—working part-time, playing video games, smoking weed, surfing the Net, and watching porn. Kids often leave home for college, but live on their parents' dime and fall prey to the freedoms of unsupervised dorm life. Still others leave, but don't go anywhere great—for example, shacking up and joining the rat race at work.

GOD'S NEXT PLAN

Adam and Eve embraced rebellion in the Garden of Eden. And then things got really ugly in the generations to follow. A fresh start with Noah looked promising, but he manifested subtle and obvious problems. And for all of the effort in the Flood and the Ark, the world looked about the same after Noah's life. Now what? God's next plan was to work with one man and his family—and then to extend this work through generations into a nation devoted to Him. (Spoiler alert: This plan wouldn't work well enough either, leading to Christ, the Cross, the Resurrection, and Pentecost—the disciple-making and miracle-working ministry of Jesus, the New Testament, the New Covenant, and the indwelling of the Holy Spirit for believers.)

And so, Genesis moves from the last episode in the universal human story (Babel) to the first episode in a new story as God teaches His ways to a particular people. The narrative shifts from thousands of years for the entire world to four generations of one family. From the new world of Creation and its unimpressive post-Flood sequel to a new man and eventually, a new nation. From "the whole world" and an ethereal rainbow to a sliver of Promised Land for Israel—a certain people situated in place and time.

The catalysts for all of this were the gracious election of a loving God and the bold choice of faithful Abram (whose name will later be changed to Abraham). In this light, Abram's response to the Lord's call in Genesis 12:1–3 is a watershed moment in Biblical and world history. And it has tremendous applications to our need to leave things behind in order to follow a good and great God.

THE CALL TO LEAVE AND GO

Let's look at the Lord's concise two-part speech to Abram in detail. God gives the command and then adds a seven-fold promise. The promise is presented in a 3-1-3 pattern, centered on "you will be a blessing." The punchline: Abram is blessed—with many things—to be a blessing. So too with us. We are given grace upon grace to extend grace upon grace to others. Abram will be given what Babel worked so hard to achieve: name, fame, power, and renown—but all in and through God's will. So too with us. We can have greatness in the Kingdom through faith in God and obedience to His good and perfect will.

The Lord's command has two key verbs: to leave and to go. (As you might imagine, the relevant Hebrew phrase, *lekh lekha*, is huge in Jewish thought.) The verbs are repeated three times here for emphasis. This is not just a trip to the grocery; it is a moment of ultimate—personal and universal—importance.[1]

The Lord specifies leaving certain things: country, people, and his father's household. "Country" represents the land with its climate, topography, and crops. It points to Abram's sense of patriotism and nationalism—as well as the need to emigrate to a new place. "People" stands in for friends, society, and cultural influences. Think of neighbors, peers at work, and things you do for fun. His "father's household" is comprised of family and non-immediate family—closer relationships, with all of their influence and resources. The list becomes more personal as it proceeds—from physical and social to familial. Like Abram, we are shaped by our context—from social forces we scarcely understand to family backgrounds whose impact we may or may not comprehend.

What else does Abram leave? His business contacts, his reputation, his favorite foods, his comfort zone. Abram was middle-aged, seemingly prosperous and settled, presumably living the good life by any worldly standard. Think how hard it can be to change when things are so comfortable! But Abram is about to move from cultural mecca to rural backwater, from urban stability to a nomadic lifestyle, from knowns to so many unknowns. In a word, he's leaving all that's familiar and ending most of his worldly attachments.

---

1. The word "go" will reappear in Abraham's climactic act of faith in Genesis 22.

LEAVE AND GO

THE NEED TO LEAVE AND GO

What else could God have done? Why not start with Abram in Babylon as a faithful follower of God in the most powerful society in the world—and spread Abram's influence and God's Kingdom from there? It doesn't usually work this way. To be a "new man" will require a new place. To even attempt to be a holy people, Israel will require a set-apart-ness from the peoples around them. Of course, a new man in a new place also underlines God's election, grace, and glory. But by leaving and going, Abram will be better able to forsake idol worship (Josh 24:2–3) and follow after the One True God. Abraham is to become the father of monotheism—and thus, Judaism and Christianity. He would be set apart in holiness, feeling special and acting differently—as bad influences were removed and new God-centered tendencies were added.

In this, it's much like the Christian life. Repentance and a second birth (John 3:3). Buried in baptism, arising to new life (Rom 6:3–4). The old man and new man of Ephesians 4:22–32, with Paul's litany of behaviors and attitudes that change in this newness. Dead to sin and alive to God (Rom 6:11); from instruments of wickedness to instruments of righteousness (Rom 6:13). Crucified to the sinful nature and the worldly systems (Gal 5:24, 6:14). "If anyone is in Christ, the new creation has come; the old has gone, the new is here!" As such, we are in exile from the World, but are now ambassadors of God's Kingdom and ministers of reconciliation (II Cor 5:17–20). In Acts 2, Peter presents the Gospel and instructs his audience to leave "this corrupt generation" and join the unified, beautiful community of the early Church (Acts 2:40–47). Leave and go.

Even as believers, it can be difficult to understand how our background has shaped us. And it's even more challenging to imagine how our culture impacts us. Can the goldfish understand water? Our family worships in a non-denominational church, but for various reasons, we sent our children to Catholic schools for many years. For one thing, we wanted them to have exposure to another form of Christian culture. I smile now, remembering how the boys complained about kneeling during Mass. I asked them why Catholics do this, before concluding that maybe we should be kneeling more.

When Kurt Sauder and I take teams to train on how to make disciple-makers in Africa, we wonder how our cultural context influences our perceptions—for good and for ill. The bad news is that we're outsiders—unable to understand easily. But the good news is that we're outsiders—able to see things they cannot. We worked with one leader in Ghana whose church practiced church discipline aggressively. After a period of being ostracized, profligate sinners were allowed to return, but had to sit at the back of the church in red chairs. As an outsider, we were able to gently ask questions about whether this form of probation was ideal. Of course, if the leader came to America, he might reasonably ask why we don't practice more rigorous church discipline!

All of this is one more reason to travel internationally and to participate in mission trips. In Romans 1:12, Paul speaks of mutual encouragement. We often imagine that we're going there to help them—and we probably are useful to them, if the work empowers them and the trip is done well.[2] But the larger gain is usually for those who travel—in gaining a perspective they cannot have unless they get outside of their fishbowl.

WHEN THE GOING GETS TOUGH . . .

This was a huge, concrete step of faith for Abram. Such new situations often yield independence from worldly things and dependence on God. As Eugene Peterson put it: for Abram, this "is a rejection that is also an acceptance, a leaving that develops into an arriving, a no to the world that is a yes to God."[3] Abram is told to go to Canaan, but is given no detail beyond this. It is a region where he will wander. It is the exact opposite of his Babylon life: settled, known, and secure. In sum, he is to leave *and* to go—where God tells him to go. He will exchange familiar for unfamiliar, security for insecurity, comfortable for uncomfortable.

We're amazed at the faith of Abraham, especially here and in Genesis 22. Usually, great steps in faithfulness start with obedience in small steps—and God's mercy in encouraging us through various trials. Sometimes, God asks for larger steps to set up smaller steps—as Abram here and as in the case of Gideon. In Judges 6, the angel (or preincarnate Christ) tells timid Gideon to tear down his father's idols. Dad was the leader in the community, so this was a call to bold opposition against his father, the community, and their gods. Mark Twain reportedly said that if you have to swallow two frogs, then swallow the bigger one first. This was a huge frog for Gideon—and anything after this should seem small by comparison.

---

2. Often, mission trips are more enabling than empowering. For a provocative book on the tensions within this tough but important topic, see: Corbett and Fikkert's *When Helping Hurts*.

3. Peterson, *Long Obedience*, 105.

Leave and Go

Whether God calls us to something small or something large, it's really all the same from a divine perspective. In I Corinthians 10:13, Paul writes that God will not tempt us beyond what we can bear. But the promise holds here too: Whatever God calls you to do, He will enable you to do it in His strength. In Philippians 4:10–13, Paul says that he had learned the secret of being content in every situation—that he could do all things through Christ who gave him strength. There's an experiential learning process in play here. Whenever you feel prompted by the Spirit, follow Him. (If you're not sure the prompting is from the Holy Spirit and the prompting seems like it might be sinful, then seek godly counsel!)

The narrative of Abram's decision to follow is amazingly understated for such a pivotal moment—both for Abram and for world history. "So Abram went . . . " Three words and one remarkable sentence! More than a thousand miles and three-plus months given all their livestock. Blink and you'll miss it! But the upshot is that Abram is the epitome of both initial faith and its capacity for development (which peaks in Genesis 22 with the binding of Isaac). Abram asks no questions here. One can see this as wonderful compliance or an ominous silence that echoes Noah and back to Adam. But as we'll see later, there's much more to Abram.

"By faith Abraham, when called to go to a place he would later receive as his inheritance, obeyed and went, even though he did not know where he was going." (Heb 11:8) "Against all hope, Abraham in hope believed and so became the father of many nations . . . " (Rom 4:18) As a result, Abraham is "the father of all who believe." (Rom 4:11) And "those who rely on faith are blessed along with Abraham." (Gal 3:9) We should follow in the faith-filled footsteps of Father Abraham. Leave and go.[4]

The same thing—albeit in less grand and historical terms—is available to all of us. We can leave Babel and Babylon behind—in order to go, following God and walking in faith. What does this look like for you? Turning aside from parents who are a mess. Starting to support your church financially (try 1% if this is a new discipline for you), extending your giving

---

4. I like how Leon Kass sums up the calling of Abram and his response: "God does not merely command Abram. He also appeals directly to Abram's situation and to Abram's likely longings and ambitions . . . land . . . the aspiration to be a founder of a great nation . . . and a great name . . . The voice addresses him, not only personally but knowingly and with concern: marvelously, from Abram's point of view, the speaker has seen directly into Abram's heart . . . What kind of being is it that speaks but is not seen and—more wondrous . . . can see into my invisible soul, to know precisely what [I want]? Let's take a walk with this awesome voice and see what it can do . . . [So] Abram completes the rejection of Babel and heads off . . . " (*Beginning of Wisdom*, 241–42, 256–57).

sacrificially, or finding other organizations and individuals to help. Limiting your social media, your golf, your shopping, or your video games. Joining a small group and investing more heavily in your discipleship with Jesus through the Scriptures. Offering sacrificial hospitality to strangers, orphans, and widows. Serving at church and with another non-profit organization. Leave and go.

WHO IS ABRAM?

A discussion of Abram's initial faith reasonably centers on the details in Genesis 12:1–3. But the surrounding context tells us quite a bit about the man, his early days, and his character. In Genesis 11:10–32, we see his historical, cultural, and familial background. Of greatest importance, his wife Sarai is barren. This is crucial from a worldly perspective, especially within that culture and in that time. But it's also problematic in a biblical worldview, following the mandate to multiply, to be fruitful, and to exercise increasing dominion (1:27). And we're left wondering how Abram could possibly move God's gracious story forward.

We can also imagine the impact of her barrenness on their marriage. Abram stays married to her (and only her) despite this deficiency. Is it because of her beauty (12:11,15; 20:2)? Perhaps. More likely, it's an early hint about his piety and faithfulness. Of course, her barrenness later becomes the occasion for God's grace and election: His preeminent role in establishing this new people. God will again bring a "new humanity" into being—a new Creation of a sort—through the future-fertile womb of Sarai. As such, Abram follows Adam and Noah as fathers of the fallen human race—and as an attempt by the Lord to restore broken relationship with mankind.

It's interesting that Abram and his extended family initially head to Canaan, but stop in the city of Haran for a time.[5] We're not sure whether God's call to Abram happens in Babylon and the extended family tags along until Haran—or whether Terah leads them out of Babylon (11:31) and then Abram is called to move from Haran to Canaan. If the call was received in Babylon, the response doesn't seem ideal. They *leave*. (Success!) But they "settle" in Haran initially and Abram is still with his "father's household." (Hmm . . .)

---

5. In English translations, the city has the same name as one of his brothers. In the Hebrew, the names are closely related but not identical.

Leave and Go

God's will is often revealed and accomplished in stages, so perhaps this was all part of the plan. Maybe Terah was ill and seemed near the death recorded in 11:32. Haran was different from both Canaan and Babylon, so it may have been a convenient way-station to smooth a rough transition between where they were and where they were going. But if Abram initially settled for less by staying in Haran, this serves as a picture of the temptation to compromise within the Christian life.

We see a similar picture in Israel's deliverance from the bondage of Pharaoh's slavery—having the faith to get *out* of Egypt. But then they fall short, lacking the faith to get *into* Canaan in Numbers 13–14, resulting in the 40 years of wandering in the Wilderness. They leave but they do not go. Ian Thomas develops this theme in his excellent book, *The Saving Life of Christ*. Even when we are delivered from sin and bondage, we may settle for Wilderness living, instead of the fruit and fight of God's promised land in Canaan (as I detail in my book on Joshua, *Inheriting Our Promised Land*).

In part, Abram is the product of his parents—and in particular, his father's influence. Kass argues that "Terah was a radical . . . [who] set the example for Abraham's own radicalism. Cultural discontinuity was part of the cultural teaching on which Abraham was raised."[6] Of Terah's three sons, Haran dies early and Nahor stays in Ur, but Abram travels with his father—and eventually completes the full move into staggering faith and obedience.

In Genesis 12:4–9, we see a handful of small but telling actions. Abram journeys through the land. He constructs altars at pagan worship sites—as elements of true worship and godly memorials to the one God. And he calls on the name of the Lord, invoking the powerful Name who had called him, building the relationship to which he had been invited. God has promised land and descendants. But as Abram travels, he sees the opposite: his childless wife and a bunch of Canaanites on "his" land. In the divine economy, Abram owned but did not possess the land; the Canaanites possessed but did not own the land. Both were sojourners of a different sort!

Then again, who else but the Canaanites would be in Canaan?! Well, Abram! Yuval Levin is helpful here: "God must put a non-Canaanite into the land of Canaan, to get away from the simple natural way of things. To be a Canaanite in Canaan requires no effort, no action, no thought. To be a Hebrew in Canaan will require attention and exertion . . . God's new way would not succeed among a people who simply let things be as they are;

---

6. Kass, *Beginning of Wisdom*, 298–99.

it demands a people willing to become what they have not always been."[7] The same is true of us. The lure of cultural Christianity is omnipresent; the tension of being in but not of the World is universal. I Peter 2:12 tells us to "live such good lives among the pagans," requiring us to stand apart *from within* the World around us, rather than a focus on fleeing or closeting from its influences.

Finally, we're told that Lot went with Abram—and that Abram took Lot with him: two different angles that give credit to both of them. How old was Lot? If Haran died when Lot was young, then this is equivalent to adoption, with Abram admirably committing to raise his nephew as a son. Did Abram disobey the Lord by bringing Lot? After all, he was supposed to *leave* his family! Was the Lord's command to be taken literally or figuratively? Maybe childless Abram saw Lot as "heir insurance"—the "descendant" he could have in light of Sarai's barrenness. In any case, this is the first sign that Abram is willing to do more than simply obey. It would have been more convenient and more strictly obedient to leave Lot behind. But Abram exhibits greatness and expresses grace by bringing along the orphan Lot.

WRAPPING UP . . .

It's one mistake not to leave; it's another to leave and have nowhere good to go. Think of the Prodigal Son and his jacked-up older brother in Luke 15. The prodigal leaves as a mess and makes a much bigger mess. But the older brother stays home as a different kind of mess, growing resentful toward his station in life. Ironically, the prodigal leaves—on a sad and painful detour—before truly going. The older son fails to leave and looks obedient, but his heart is actually hard. Maybe he needed to leave before he could go.

Paul critiques those who were not working in Thessalonica (I Thess 4:11–12, II Thess 3:6–13). They thought they were leaving with Jesus who was coming back any day, so why go to work? But this left them dependent rather than independent, helpless rather than helpful, failing to contribute and taxing others. If you have a burden you can't carry, get help (Gal 6:2). But make sure to carry your own load (Gal 6:5). Mooching off others is not permissible in the divine economy. If you're not working and are capable of work, get a job. Parents: If you're enabling your adult children to be bums, then insist on making a plan for them to work, take care of their bills, and

---

7. Quoted in Kass, *Beginning of Wisdom*, 271–72.

pay rent—or to move out. (The rent payments are probably for them, not for you.) Help them leave and go.

In marriage, we're called to "leave and cleave." But how many spouses struggle with a failure to (really) leave one's parents, letting their (direct and indirect) influence wreak havoc in their marriage. In parenting, we're called to nurture and wean, as Hannah in I Samuel 2. Failure to nurture is one thing. But especially if you've nurtured conscientiously, how do you let go and move from parent to coach and even friend? Leave and go.

As I wrote the first draft of this chapter, our second son Brennan had just returned from a "vision trip" to Japan—to consider full-time foreign missions there. After graduating from college, he completed a rigorous two-year residency program at our church and had plans to go into standard forms of ministry. It's too long of a story to tell here, but it suffices to say: If you know Brennan, you'd expect foreign missions to be way down the list of likely paths. But in short order, God put together a string of remarkable providences in rapid succession. And so, foreign missions moved from off the stove to the front burner. Leave and go.

What will happen in the future? God knows, but we don't know yet. Was this for the trip itself—for Brennan or for others who would see him or hear about the journey? Was it about a willingness to go, but he won't ultimately be called to go to Japan or even overseas? Was it to stretch or re-direct him? All we know (so far) is that he is walking in faith, trying to discern how to leave and where to go. And if he does this, we know he will bless God and others, as God continues to bless him.

4

Lies vs. Truth in Love

COMPLETE TEXT: GENESIS 12:10–20, 20:1–18, 21:22–34
RECOMMENDED READING: 12:10–20, 20:1–15
POTENTIAL MEMORY VERSES: 20:6, 20:9

M. Scott Peck is most famous for his best-selling book, *The Road Less Traveled*. But he wrote another book that had more influence on me: *People of the Lie*. There, he makes a case that lying is the most devastating sin. I've usually heard pride described as the deadliest of "the seven deadly sins." Going our way instead of God's way is at the heart of every transgression. It was a key part of Adam and Eve's problems in the Garden. And even Peck's preferred pick certainly stems from pride.

But here's Peck's point: Lying and deception frequently accompany other sins, as an attempt to cover-up, rationalize, and save face. (We saw this with both Adam and Cain.) Lying to others makes you less prone to correction by others. Beyond that, if you lie to yourself, how are correction and repentance even possible? Whenever I could be convicted by my conscience or poked by others, my response would be to deny the truth of what is being said. When I lie to others and myself, I'm engaged in deception and self-deception, promoting confusion and a false reality, aligning myself with the deceptive Serpent of Genesis 3.

Perhaps because he was a psychologist, Peck connected lying to narcissism. And we can see the link. Self-absorbed, an inflated image of self,

Lies vs. Truth in Love

living in a fantasy world. The character trait and the related personality disorder are named for the mythical Narcissus who fell in love with his own reflection, rejecting the love of others to embrace the love of a fiction. Whether one fully agrees with Peck, it's clear that lying has the potential to be a serious problem.

Years later, I read a book by the behavioral economist Dan Ariely, *The (Honest) Truth About Dishonesty: How We Lie to Everyone (Especially Ourselves)*. He argues that everyone lies—not the bald-faced whoppers which get most of our attention, but the little lies that range from cheating at golf and inflating expense accounts to exaggeration and going soft with our words when we're trying to be nice to people. We want to see ourselves as honorable and truthful, but we also benefit from stretching, fudging, and hedging. It's been said that "we're all in sales." As such, all of us are tempted to lie as we sell ourselves to others—and even, to ourselves.

Ariely describes some of the literature's experimental work to tease out the extent of our lying and the conditions under which it is more likely. One finding I've incorporated into my on-line courses: Research shows that putting an honor code at the beginning of a test tends to reduce cheating, while an honor code at the end is ineffective. This says something about the impact of reminding us about the value of truth and integrity. Externals prompts may be helpful, but dependence on the Holy Spirit holds even more promise for believers to have increasing victory in this area.

Reading Ariely, I became both more and less concerned about the problem. Lying and cheating are more prevalent than I had imagined, but it can't be *that* bad or we'd all be a bunch of criminals and psychopaths. I think Peck and Ariely would have disagreed about the seriousness of lying. But both acknowledge its dangers and both adhere to the biblical concern about a false approach to life. For Jordan Peterson, revelation about his own lying was a turning point in his spiritual journey: "I came to realize that almost everything I said was untrue."[1] When reality is perceived as unbearable or when we can manipulate others successfully, lying becomes an especially dangerous temptation.

I wonder if men are any more tempted than women to lie. For what it's worth, I'd guess that the ways in which men and women lie—and the things we lie about—are different. But does it matter all that much? In any case, we worship a God who is called "Faithful and True." (Rev 19:11) And we are opposed by Satan, "the Father of Lies." (John 8:44) What are the

---

1. Peterson, *12 Rules for Life*, 205.

practical and ethical problems with lying? What does it look like to be an effective truth-teller in God's Kingdom? More broadly, how can I stay out of trouble with my tongue and use it as "an instrument of righteousness" (Rom 6:12–13) in this world?

ABRAM AND PHARAOH

In the first half of Genesis 12, we were excited to see the emergence of Abram (who will later have his name changed by God to Abraham). He exhibits a visionary faith and looks like someone who can walk well with God and promote His plans for the world. Abram's level of trust is amazing, but we're also impressed with his courage and willingness to sacrifice comfort and familiarity in Babylon for change and uncertainty, the challenges of his trip to Canaan, and a nomadic lifestyle in the Promised Land.

This optimism is soon replaced in the narrative by the surprising and sobering events in the second half of Genesis 12. Abram leads his household to fertile Egypt in the face of a severe famine. (This is ominous if you know the history of Israel and Egypt in the next book of the Bible, Exodus.) But he's worried about the locals killing him to take his wife Sarai. He's (quite reasonably) concerned about a might-makes-right approach in Egypt, especially with respect to foreigners. Abram cites her beauty. (Isn't that romantic?!) But she's 65 years old at this point. Did she have other attributes that were attractive? Or is he just worried about people taking something (or someone) because they can?

Whatever the case, instead of trusting the Lord to take care of them, Abram takes matters into his own hands with a half-truth. He tells the Egyptians that he is Sarai's "brother" and omits that he is Sarai's husband! As her "brother," he could remain in control of the marriage process if someone courted his "sister," since he would be responsible for arranging a dowry from potential suitors. The truth is they are *half*-siblings. (We learn their family history during the reprise in 20:12.) This reminds me of the phrase "too clever by half"—a reference to someone who is a little too clever for their own good. As we'll see later, Abram and Sarai aren't exactly allergic to manipulating a situation to achieve their goals. The sadly-similar sequel (Genesis 20) and their use of Hagar as a child surrogate (Genesis 16) illustrate that this is (or becomes) a pattern for them.

Now, one can imagine a powerful rationalization for Abram: I'm responsible for a lot of people, so sometimes you do what you gotta do. And we can cut him some slack. This is a *really* difficult situation. (For example, imagine the tensions that go with encountering corrupt customs agents in a less-developed country.) And he is a "relatively new believer." For example, given the popular religious views of the time, it's not clear that he would know whether God had any power in Egypt. Still, this seems to fall (far) short of the ideal for God's new man and new plan.

Sarai turns out to have a surprise suitor: Pharoah, the king! We're not told why he's interested. Maybe she *was* as pretty as Abram said! Maybe she was really good company. Maybe he wanted to add an exotic outsider, looking to boost the multi-cultural flavor of his harem. In any case, Pharaoh preempts Abram's plan by taking her first and paying later. (Hey, at least Pharaoh paid—and ponied up handsomely!)

Abram has underestimated how much Sarai would be sought and now he has a real dilemma on his hands. Even if he can get an audience with the king, how could he say no to the marriage offer? Leon Kass puts it this way: "either he can try to save his own life at the expense of his wife's honor, or he can risk his likely death, after which his wife will also be taken. Thinking about God's promise of his becoming a great nation, Abram may well reason that it depends on his own survival even more than it depends on Sarai's fidelity and marital chastity."[2] Ouch!

Abram is powerless here, but the Lord intervenes with a set of plagues.[3] Pharaoh figures out cause and effect (maybe by asking Sarai) and sends for Abram. Pharoah's response seems measured but frustrated—likely not wanting to mess with Abram's "god." Pharaoh sets them free, allowing them to keep the earlier gifts. It's ironic that this probably included Hagar who will play a big role in their story, starting in Genesis 16.

Even with the "happy ending," this is a sad story. In pursuit of sustenance and safety, Abram almost lost his wife. Others bear the consequences of his sinful decisions. The impact on Pharoah's household and Sarai are relatively obvious. It's possible that Lot is impacted by Uncle Abram's failures here. And his sin of lying and deception will reappear in the future. Lot's daughters will deceive him (Genesis 19). Abram repeats this strategy years later (Genesis 20). Isaac exactly emulates his father in this sin (Genesis 26). Grandson Jacob deceives Isaac about his identity to get the preferred blessing from his dad (Genesis 27). And ten of Jacob's sons fib about

---

2. Kass, *Beginning of Wisdom*, 273.

3. As an aside, catch the wonderful parallels and foreshadowing for events in the book of Exodus.

Joseph's fate (Genesis 37ff). Instead of being a blessing to all (12:3)—as was God's plan—Abram brings trouble to Pharoah and a curse that extends for generations in his family.

ABRAHAM AND ABIMELECH

Years later, Abraham pulls the same stunt with Abimelech in the roughly equivalent story of Genesis 20. But this seems far worse than the episode with Pharoah. There is no famine and thus, no desperation. God has recently promised him that Sarah (the new name God gives to Sarai) would become pregnant with the promised child—and yet, Abraham takes this risk! (Notice that God clearly and quickly intervenes here, avoiding any questions about who's the father of Isaac!) And in the epilogue to the sequel (21:22–34), it's sad but understandable that Abimelech needed a vow from Abraham for assurance. This points to the lasting effects of sin, especially dishonesty, in damaging our credibility and our witness.

By this time, Abraham's faith should have been stronger after spending so much more time walking with the Lord. Then again, how frustrating is it for us when we stumble again, despite knowing better? And sure, we hope to learn from our mistakes. But it's often easier to sin the second time. (The best way to avoid sinning the second time is to not sin the first time!) Worse still: Abraham describes this as an ongoing strategy (20:13)—or maybe he's just lying again.

In the Genesis 12 account, God had not explicitly told Abraham this was wrong—and things had turned out well enough. In this, we see an inescapable dilemma within God's grace. When He bails us out, it's more likely that we'll stumble into sin again and hope for (or even come to expect) more grace. As Paul puts it in terms of our salvation: When sin increases, God's grace increases all the more (Rom 5:20). We want grace, but grace and the promise of grace can tempt us to fall again.

I find great comfort (and humor) that God calls Abraham a "prophet" here (20:7) and then tells him to intercede for Abimelech in prayer. Abraham is the first to receive this title—which means "truth-teller"—a terrific irony since he has lied or at least shaded the truth here. But despite the mistake, God still grants him this status—to intercede for others, even those he has harmed. Why? We understand the heart change that comes from Jesus' injunction to pray for our enemies. What happens when we intercede for others we have harmed, especially when they are more righteous than we are? Again, God has said that Abraham will be a blessing to all nations. This is part of Abraham's identity, even when he didn't fully live up to it.

There are other lessons here. First, like King David later, Abraham's heart is with God, but the actions don't always follow. The mistakes reasonably get our attention—and they're a big deal—but the bigger issue biblically is always our relationship with God. Second, it's noteworthy that this episode follows God's election of Abraham, his great display of faith initially, and God's abundant promises. Being among the chosen is a privilege, but it is also a burden with the potential for pride and other problems. Third, God allows a lot of free will and messy stuff to happen for our testing and His own purposes. Likewise, God uses these strange circumstances and Abraham's bad decisions for His own ends (Rom 8:28). God didn't let one man's foolishness ruin His plans.

Finally, notice the kindness of Abimelech to Sarah, treating her better than her own "brother" and husband. One hopes and suspects that all of this is convicting to Abraham. In chapter 7, we'll talk about God working on Abraham as a father; here, God is working on Abraham as a husband. Related: It's encouraging that Abraham is both saint and scoundrel. Perhaps his pagan background brought baggage or this was just a stubborn character flaw. And it's noteworthy that the Bible describes its heroes, warts and all. We should aspire to greatness in the Kingdom, but be sobered by how far the great ones can fall.

FALSE TESTIMONY, LIES, AND LYING LIARS

"To be honest" (#TBH) is a phrase that grinds my gears. Sometimes I'll say what I'm thinking: "Are you saying that you're not *always* honest with me?!" What people *mean* is "to be candid"—as in, I'm going to be more transparent than usual about what I really think. Maybe I'm just a crank about this, but many of us have problems with honesty (as well as candor and transparency). Why should we practice saying that we're not always honest, without being troubled by the phrase at all?

Here's another pet peeve of mine: people who think the 9th Commandment is "Do not lie." Instead, it's "Do not bear false testimony." What's the difference? Well, the latter is lying about someone, to do them harm, especially in the context of testifying within a court system. False testimony is *always* a problem—both in the sense of slandering the individual (it's always "against" someone) and undermining the integrity of a vital social institution.

Telling a lie is often a problem, but not always. For one thing, it's more difficult to define. When does marketing devolve into fraud? When does careful wording on a resume descend into deceit? Lies can be by omission or commission. But what should we say in response to nosy or difficult questions from strangers or gossips? Or more broadly, when is (complete) honesty "the best policy"?

There are also too many examples of "good lying" to condemn it out of hand. A few key examples? In Exodus 1, God commends and blesses the midwives for lying to Pharaoh about the Israelite baby boys. In Joshua 2, Rahab lies to the king's messengers. In Judges 4–5, Jael deceives the enemy Sisera, putting herself in a position to drive a tent peg through his temple. In the first half of John 7, Jesus misdirects the disciples about going to a festival to avoid danger and to keep his ministry under the radar. There are interesting historical and contemporary examples too: hiding Jews during World War II; tactics to expose what happens in Planned Parenthood facilities through audio and video; pulling off surprise birthday parties; and so on.

All that said, lying is certainly not a good general practice. And being a *liar* (as a matter of character or identity) is terrible—what the Scriptures call "a lying tongue." (Prov 12:22) Lying as an event is one thing; as a lifestyle, it's another. It's the last character trait mentioned in the list of sinners in Revelation 21 and 22. It's consistent with Satan's nature and activity as "the Father of Lies." (John 8:44) It often hurts others and hides sin. It often harms us and acts to sear our consciences. If caught, it is damaging to one's reputation. And it can be devastating if it becomes a pattern.

COMMITTED TO TRUTH-TELLING IN LOVE

Ephesians 4:29 is one of my life verses. There, Paul writes: "Do not let any unwholesome talk come out of your mouths, but only what is helpful for building others up, according to their needs, that it may benefit those who listen." Unwholesome talk of certain types gets a lot of attention in the Church. Most notably: Don't cuss or yell; don't be mean or vulgar. But harmful talk comes in many other flavors. We've already talked about lying and false testimony. But a good list would also include slander and gossip, gaslighting and breaking promises, flattery and boasting. Sticks and stones will break my bones, but words will never hurt me? Wrong!

Lies vs. Truth in Love

In James 3:1-12—a great description of the power of the tongue—the apostle compares our words to a ship's rudder, a horse's bit, and a bit of fire. Think of the impact of a small object like a rudder and a bit—to turn a ship or a powerful animal. So too, our words can move mountains. Likewise, we know that "it only takes a spark" to get a fire going; consider the damage that a single match and a single word can do. More important, the standard in Ephesians 4:29 is not just avoiding sinful words, but making sure to say all the words we should—and to say them well. As always, it's not just sins of commission, but sins of omission which should get our attention. We remember how Jesus spoke—not just that he avoided cussing when He hit His thumb with a hammer, but for saying the perfect thing perfectly in each context. Paul says to use our words to "build others up." Is my speech constructive, destructive, or just treading water? Do I have the wisdom and courage to be effective with what I say? Do I (really) want the best for other people? Would I want someone to say this to me? These are useful metrics for evaluating our words.

But Paul also offers two important caveats. First, he says it's "according to their needs." This implies that I have the discernment to know their needs and the wisdom to speak ably to their needs. It implies a depth of relationship that allows me to know what to say and how to say it to that person. It implies a courage to say difficult things at times, the perseverance to get better at this difficult skill, and the humility to apologize when I err. What I should say—and how I should say it—will depend on the person, their temperament, their past, my relationship with them, etc. All of this is made far easier through the indwelling of the Holy Spirit.

Second, Paul says "that it may benefit those who listen." It's not up to us. Even if we communicate perfectly in terms of style and substance, the recipient must still decide what to do with it. This relieves the pressure on us and should make it easier for us to muster our courage. As with the "watchman" of Ezekiel 33, success is defined as faithfully fulfilling what God has asked us to do and say.

In Ephesians 4:15, Paul exhorts church leaders to train their people to grow in maturity, including our ability to "speak truth in love." This serves to emulate Jesus, who was "full of grace and truth." (John 1:14) We can certainly relate this to evangelism. Peter exhorts us to "Always be prepared to give an answer to everyone who asks you to give the reason for the hope that you have. But do this with gentleness and respect . . . " (I Pet 3:15) But it's a lot broader than that. As such, let's give Paul the final biblical word here: "Let your conversation be always full of grace, seasoned with salt, so that you may know how to answer everyone." (Col 4:6)

WRAPPING UP...

As a professor, I often get to speak with students. Of particular relevance here, I have many opportunities to "build them up"—to encourage and challenge them. Sometimes, the conversations are easy—for example, encouraging a tentative student who has given a great answer in class or an emerging student who has improved on a test score. Even so, it's tempting to be lazy and miss these opportunities.

More difficult but also important: opportunities to challenge students who are not living up to their potential; who speak well but don't write well; who are sharp but don't prepare for tests; and so on. In each case, I want to build them up—to exhort them with words that will encourage them to grow as a student and as a person. In these cases, it's even more tempting to avoid a potentially valuable but difficult conversation.[4]

Other times, something seems "off," but I don't know what it is. Again, I have a choice—and I believe it's better to err on the side of saying too much. These conversations are more tentative and still riskier, since there is no clear context for my approach—as I prayerfully poke and prod at something unknown. Occasionally, my sense is way off—and other times, the attempts don't seem to work. In these cases, it's a bit uncomfortable. Fortunately, the students always seem to at least appreciate my concern. But sometimes, it pays off big-time.

A few years ago, I felt prompted by the Spirit to come alongside one of my students after class to ask how she was doing. She didn't say much to me at the time and the encounter seemed somewhere between ok and awkward. But later, she told me that my effort was life-changing. We eventually talked about a sexual assault she had experienced at another university. After the semester, she joined our college-age Bible study and really began to grow in her faith. It was an immense pleasure to mentor her in faith and her professional life—and to attend her wedding a few years later. All of

---

4. For an excellent example from football, read about Chris Petersen encouraging Sean McVay out of the blue: Rodrigue, "How a Phone Call." From basketball, read about the impact of Gregg Popovich as a "master of tough conversations": Devlin and Jenks, "Gregg Popovich Is a Coaching Legend."

this stemmed from my obedience to the Spirit in an awkward moment that seemed to bear little fruit.

In all of the above cases, who would criticize me for not saying something, especially in a context where it seemed risky? Well, I would! And I believe God wants that from me and for me. As per Ephesians 4:29, I am called and committed to build others up according to their needs that it may benefit those who listen. You may not be in the classroom, but you have similar opportunities—at work, in the home, and in everyday encounters. And most of us should be more courageous and more helpful with our tongues.

Pray for the Spirit to inform and empower you with the right words, at the right time, in the right tone, and through the right spirit. (Also pray that the listener will have ears to hear and will understand what you're trying to communicate.) Never lie about others and avoid shading the truth in ways that benefit you. Commit to apologize when you sense that you've harmed someone. Work diligently for clarity in communication. Avoid both passivity and damage with your words—back to the silence of Adam and the violence of Cain—both what you say and how you say it.

Beyond merely not engaging in slander or gossip, work to stop it. Double-check accusations and tactfully tell people when they're spreading a lie.[5] When you hear gossip, say something nice about the person on the receiving end of the attack. This usually stops it! Or when someone says, "You know, I probably shouldn't tell you this . . . ," then jump into the conversation, smile, and say "Then don't." Abraham was a great man of faith who walked with God but struggled at times with his tongue. In this chapter, we've seen him shade the truth with Pharaoh and Abimelech. In chapter 7, we'll see him fail to speak courageously with his wife and Hagar. Let's work to emulate Abraham's overall faith and walk with God. But let's work to exceed Abraham's faith and righteousness as people of wisdom, courage, and integrity in our words.

---

5. For public rumors, you can check Snopes.com and TruthOrFiction.com.

5

Magnanimous and Mighty

COMPLETE TEXT: GENESIS 13–14
RECOMMENDED READING: 13:5–17, 14:11–16
POTENTIAL MEMORY VERSES: 14:14, 14:23

IN 2000, AL GORE ran against George W. Bush to become President of the United States.[1] Gore had been Vice President for the previous eight years under Bill Clinton. The Clinton scandal with Monica Lewinsky wasn't helpful, but the country and the economy were doing well. So, Gore should have been in good shape to win the Oval Office. But he wasn't nearly as likeable as Clinton; Al was a technocrat while Bill was folksy. Al was also in his early years as a crusader on global warming (later relabeled "climate change"). And Al's wife Tipper was viewed as a prude and a scold for setting up congressional hearings to complain about album lyrics.

Voters also learned that Al and Tipper were skinflints in terms of charity. The Gores released their tax returns (a long-time tradition for presidential candidates) and the public found out that they had only donated $353 to charity in 1997—on an income of almost $200,000. The funny thing: Al was fond of using government taxation to use *other* people's money to help the less fortunate, but Al and Tipper were not willing to use their own money. Not cool!

---

1. Remember Florida and the "hanging chads"? If not, look it up. It's a wild story!

Or consider the story about the two Russians who were bitter enemies. Both were dragged before the court after an incident between them earned the attention of the police. The judge imagines that he's using Solomonic wisdom as he explains his decision: The court will give one man whatever he wants, but award twice as much to his enemy. The judge asks one of the men for his decision—and he replies: "Put out one of my eyes."

Nobody likes a stingy person, but it's still tempting to be stingy with others. It's sad to see someone hold a grudge, but it can be alluring to savor our bitterness. Everyone admires grace and wants to receive it in everyday life, but giving it can be much more difficult. As C.S. Lewis said: "Everyone says forgiveness is a lovely idea, until they have something to forgive."[2] But stinginess and unforgiveness are utterly incoherent for Christians. We have been lavished with God's amazing grace—forgiven and otherwise blessed, even though undeserved—and so, our natural response should be to extend grace, forgiveness, and blessings to others.

In Genesis 13 and 14, we're given two memorable stories about Abram and his dealings with his nephew Lot. In the first story, we'll see the remarkable generosity of Abram, even when it would have been easy to make excuses for being stingy. In the second, we'll revisit the idea of "might makes right." We'll learn that Abram has put tremendous resources into a sizable militia. What will he do with his power? How will he handle a family member who has distanced himself? Will Abram use his resources to be a blessing to others, even those who have made less-than-ideal decisions?

RESOLVING PROBLEMS WITH GRACE AND WISDOM

Early in Genesis 13, we might wonder about the dynamics of Abram's family. Sarai is not named, but we're reminded that she is Abram's "wife." (We might not have been sure that the marriage was going to work out at the end of Genesis 12!) And Lot is set apart in the text. One wonders if he's an integral part of the family or more of a third wheel. Soon enough, we learn that he's ready to range out on his own.

The family is moving around and both men have become quite wealthy. Despite their nomadic lifestyle, the land is getting too crowded for their households and their livestock. They have too much of a good thing—and whether too little water or pastureland, their shepherds begin to quarrel. There's also a passing mention about the locals (13:7), as if

---

2. Lewis, *Mere Christianity*, Book 3, Chapter 7.

they're seeing and watching the disunity. For one thing, it's a bad look—for a man who is supposed to *attract* others to believe in God. For another, the disunity may present an opportunity for outsiders to exploit a weakness in a might-makes-right world.

In this, we see one of the burdens of wealth and the trouble that it can bring to families—whether an inheritance, marital money problems, or joint business ventures that go sideways. With the distribution of an estate, I've seen a handful of times when everybody had seemed cool with money and possessions. But then somebody gets obsessive about a treasured item or the appearance of a sudden financial opportunity reveals another side of their character. Two frugal spouses make money matters relatively easy, but anything else leads to tension between different approaches or a tight budget with little generosity. Wealth is a blessing, but a decidedly mixed blessing given the complications it brings. What does Abram do here?

First, Abram's response is proactive. Instead of waiting for trouble to arise between him and Lot, Abram works to resolve the emerging problem before it bubbles over. He anticipates a likely crisis and takes initiative to fix the issue. To do this, he must have humility, vision, and courage—as he displayed in his momentous leave/go decision in Genesis 12. How easy this looks, but how difficult it can be to do! How many times do we fail to see trouble brewing that should have been easy to imagine? How often do we see problems emerging, but we procrastinate, hoping it will go away—or pray that it will be resolved, while failing to act? Abram is a model here of resolving disputes before they get rolling.

Second, Abram's offer is generous. We'll see this again in the next chapter when we discuss his impressive hospitality in Genesis 18. The proposal to Lot entails personal sacrifice for Abram, but he puts family peace over personal well-being. (If he was driven by greed at all in Genesis 12, it's not an issue here.) He recognizes that to be united, sometimes one needs to split. And he grants Lot the first choice—a decision that will be purely voluntary: no force, paternalism, or persuasion. In fact, Abram is looking to empower Lot by allowing him to make his own decision—and hopefully, the right one. When Lot chooses, his later problems are his own fault, not Abram's. There is great wisdom in this: When we give people freedom, they lose the ability to (credibly) blame others for bad outcomes.

Third, Abram's plan is magnanimous—especially amazing since Abram is an older family member in a position of authority. More specifically, he had probably been like a father to Lot. So, Abram takes charge by engaging in servant-leadership, putting others first. Lot has not been promised anything by the Lord. Abram could have excluded him. Instead, he starts to be the blessing to others that the Lord has prophesied over him. Contrary to Cain, Abram is his "nephew's keeper," working for Lot's best interests. Maybe Abram is eager to hear Lot's choice as a reflection of his character. Remember that Abram may be wondering whether his promised descendants will come through his "adopted" nephew.

Fourth, Abraham's approach may be the best for his own sake. He might prefer the second best—or at least be happy with it—because it will prevent him from focusing on the wrong things (as turned out to be a problem for Lot). I've seen this principle in my career, where I had opportunities to move up the ladder, but was quite productive where I was and content to stay in my context. Another application: There's nothing wrong with negotiating for higher pay with a job. But when you push for more, expectations will be higher. None of this is a call to complacency or settling for mediocrity, but we should still wisely recognize the trade-offs at hand.

What are Abram's motives here? One can read this as people-pleasing, but this seems to sell him short. He wants to avoid conflict, especially when surrounded by potential enemies, so the move is wise. He wants to preserve family unity, focusing on what matters rather than temporal material concerns. He is concerned about the people in both households, wanting them to see what walking faithfully with the Lord looks like. As such, this is a great example of servant-leadership, putting others first, and seeking to be a blessing with the resources and choices available to him.

From what the narrative will convey about Abram throughout his life, this decision seems to be made through an abiding trust in the goodness of God and His faithfulness. Abram's faith allowed him to be largely indifferent to Lot's choice. With an eternal perspective, a vibrant faith, and the memory of God bailing him out with Pharaoh, Abram knows that the Lord will deliver on His promises—whatever Lot decides. Walking faithfully with a good and great God, such decisions look amazing, but turn out to be relatively easy.

GO EAST YOUNG MAN?

In 13:10–13, we read about Lot's choice and the basis for his decision. This is the first time we get a good look at him; we didn't know a lot about Lot before this. We know he's Abram's nephew; he's riding along on Abram's coattails; and he has been influenced by Abram's faith and character. We don't know about his relationship with the Lord—other than an educated guess that it is less vibrant than Abram's and considerably more robust than the faith of an average pagan.

Lot "saw" that the land to the east was "well-watered"—the original "grass is greener" story. The reference to "look and see" is a bad sign—that he is walking by sight rather than by faith, focused on temporal and material angles rather than an eternal perspective. The description of the land's desirability brings to mind both Eden and ominously, Egypt. It's a reasonable decision from a worldly view, but it does not seem concerned with God's will. It's selfish ("Lot chose for himself" in 13:11), rather than putting Abram first. It ultimately fails to match Abram's humility, character, and faith. What should Lot have done instead? Thank Abram for the offer and then insist that his uncle choose first!

The parenthetical reference to Sodom provides eerie foreshadowing—and Lot doubles down on this by pitching his tent among the "great sinners." The decision seems naive or blind to the temptations and problems that will emerge. Because of his choice, he'll face a crisis in Genesis 14. But ultimately, Lot's Genesis 13 moment will become a Genesis 19 moment in Sodom—as he finds himself immersed in sin, judgment, and destruction that he did not anticipate. From the narrative's overarching perspective, it has also become clear why Abram and Lot need to separate—and why Lot cannot be "the son of promise."

As with the climax of the Pharaoh debacle, God intervenes—this time, explicitly rewarding Abram for his faithful approach here (instead of bailing him out of a bad decision). Notice that from Abram's perspective, the seed *and* land promises have just been threatened. He seems to have lost the "best land," his only kinsman, and his only potential "son" at this point. But God responds by reiterating His promises in both realms.

Three other little details. First, it seems noteworthy that the Lord shows up after the potential disunity is gone and the noise has subsided. Often, we are unable to hear God in the midst of churn and turmoil. Second, Lot looks and sees on his own, but Abram is told to look by God. Lot is driven by his own agendas; Abram is waiting on the Lord. Third, it's cool that Abram gets to "walk through" the land (13:17). He gets to enjoy and experience it. (It's as if God is excited to give Abram a preview of the gift!) It's another picture of God's provision but also Abram's participation. By walking through the land, he's (figuratively) exerting dominion and authority over it, as a form of symbolic property rights. But it's also a signal that all of this belongs to God, His promises, and His Kingdom.

I like what Allen Ross says to summarize this story:

> Hardly any other chapter in the Bible describes faith [that] so marvelously . . . functioned in a conflict. Lot, walking by sight, chose on the basis of what appealed to him. His choice was self-seeking and self-gratifying. But such a choice became dangerous and short-lived, for all was not as it appeared to be on the surface. Abram, on the other hand, walking by faith, generously let Lot choose first. Abram was unselfish, trusting God. He had learned that it was not by his own plan that he would come into the possession or by jealously guarding what was his. He acted righteously and generously. One who believes that God is pledged to provide for him is not greedy, anxious, or covetous.[3]

PRAY FOR PEACE BUT BE READY FOR BATTLE

In Genesis 14, we have the Bible's other story about Abram and Lot—also remarkable, albeit for different reasons. A decade later or so, Kedorlaomer is the head of a four-king alliance out of Babylon which has power over five other leaders of city-states in Southern Canaan, including Sodom and Gomorrah. Eventually, the latter rebel by failing to pay tribute. This elicits a successful military response to punish the rebels and restore the status quo.

Lot is in a lot of trouble; his earlier choice has backfired. (He went east, but things went south!) Notice that he's "in Sodom" now (14:12), when he had started "near Sodom." (13:12) We'll have more to say about this later. For now, let's simply note that Lot's desire for material prosperity and more control has cost him his freedom. He had taken himself out of Abram's protection, if not God's will—and things are not going well. More broadly, we're given a picture of chaos, the abuse of power, injustice, etc.—again, a might-makes-right sort of world—into which Abram will step forward and take action.

Informed of the battle and Lot's predicament as a hostage, Abram solidifies an alliance of local kings and pursues the victors. He has "318 trained men" with him—an indication of his wealth and a picture of him effectively bringing all of his resources to bear. In I Timothy 6:17–19, after

---

3. Ross, *Bible Knowledge Commentary*, 52.

warning about the potential dangers of money, Paul exhorts the rich to be rich in good deeds—and Abram does that here.

Abram is prepared for battle; he has stewarded his resources effectively; and he has empowered others to be successful in this mission. He is ready but not eager for battle; he is hoping for the best but ready for the worst.[4] Despite having an impressive militia, no other military engagements are recorded, underlining that this is for justice rather than power, for grace rather than greed. He doesn't take the land God has promised him, but waits for God's timing and His will.

His servants follow along agreeably, indicating their respect for Abram. In spiritual terms, it's a picture of a church leader training their laypeople to be effective as disciple-makers, fulfilling an oft-overlooked top-tier mission of the church (Eph 4:11–16). Abram uses a divide and conquer strategy, surprising the opponents at night. There are no losses recorded; he achieves a great victory against superior numbers. This is standard military strategy—an impressive combination of their participation, but still God's miraculous provision. Abram rescues Lot and others as well, extending grace and restoring them to their previous position and possessions.

Abram is courageous in battle. He has no over-riding fear of death, as had been the case in Egypt with his wife Sarai. With the promises of the Lord fresh in his mind, he is able to risk his life to do the right thing. As in Genesis 13, and unlike Cain, Abram is very much his nephew's keeper. He doesn't hold a grudge against Lot; there is no passive/aggressive delay; there is no "I told you so" and letting Lot bear the consequences of his earlier decision. Instead, Abram takes aggressive, costly, and risky steps to bring Lot back. Sadly, Lot doesn't benefit in the long run, returning to live in Sodom with the consequences that follow. As an application, it's interesting to consider when we should intervene aggressively in the lives of others, rather than letting natural consequences teach them truths about life.

In the postlude, the king of Sodom comes out to meet Abram—and to ask for his people and possessions in return. The king offers Abram wealth, but he refuses, making clear that his efforts are purely voluntary—an act of grace. Why? He wants all credit and glory—current and future—to go to God. Abram wisely avoids worldly entanglements and obligations to

---

4. Joshua 22 has a similar story between the Western and trans-Jordan tribes of Israel. You can hear my coverage of this on my podcast, *The Word Diet* ("Joshua 22's Failure to Communicate").

others—both their reality and their perception. This contrasts with his decision in Egypt to accept the gifts, indicating that his faith is maturing.

We also get to read about the mysterious Melchizedek. He is the righteous king of Salem (which means "peace" and is a precursor to Jeru-salem). He's also the first priest in the Bible. He offers bread and wine—an ordinary meal that refreshes the troops and parallels Communion. He blesses Abram, attributing his victory to intervention by "God Most High." And Abram responds by giving Melchizedek one tenth of the spoils of battle (the first biblical reference to a "tithe"). This underlines Abram's humility after the victory and the blessing of God.[5]

Genesis is primarily personal and familial. But it's also political and cultural—the history of four generations of one family that becomes a great people. Looking forward to the political establishment of national Israel during the Exodus, the narrative provides "pre-political" hints with Abram's Egypt story in Genesis 12 and here, a strong dose of "international" politics. How will Israel govern? Hopefully, like Noah: personal righteousness and obedience to God. But beyond that, like Abram: a concern for justice, a disposition toward holiness, a willingness and an ability to be effectively involved in a messy world.

WRAPPING UP . . .

Abram's graciousness with Lot and the land in Genesis 13 is impressive. In Genesis 14, we learn that Abram has trained a small army and springs into action to save his nephew. Considering the rest of Abram's story, we realize that he does not use the army again—unwilling to act as a might-makes-right man, to take what he wants from those in the world around him, to push God's timing with respect to the Promised Land. And notice how much spiritual growth he has exhibited since the end of Genesis 12!

Are you and I so magnanimous with those who rate below us by the world's standards? Do we have the foresight to train and prepare for a difficult moment in the future? Do we have the willingness to help or even rescue those who have gone a different way or harmed us in some way? Do we exercise restraint with our power, position, and possessions—our blessings from God? Abram is good with others—both family and strangers.

---

5. David and the writer of Hebrews use Melchizedek to prefigure Christ and *His* "priesthood" under a "new covenant." See: Psalm 110:4 and Hebrews 7.

He follows God. He's engaged well with society. And all of these together? What a combo!

Andrew Carnegie started work as a 13-year-old "bobbin boy" at a cotton mill and eventually launched the U.S. steel industry. He sold Carnegie Steel Company to J.P. Morgan for $480 million and became the richest person in America. By the end of his life, he had given away $350 million, with plans to give the rest away after he died. In addition to his staggering business success, social influence, and financial might, Carnegie's philanthropy is legendary—arguably the greatest in history. His funding—and his love for education and music—led to more than 2,500 free public libraries and 7,500 church organs. He founded what became Carnegie Mellon University and the educational pension fund TIAA-CREF. He anonymously financed "Manhattan Music Hall," but people didn't want to attend a "music hall," so it became "Carnegie Hall."

Carnegie was charitable, but not for its own sake. He criticized ineffective and indiscriminate charity that fostered bad habits. If charity is not effective, what's the point? He valued charity, but also championed the free-market system that made his wealth and economic growth possible. Today, like Al Gore, many people will vote to use other people's money to help others. But are they willing to provide help themselves? Beyond money, many people need our time, energy, and expertise to make progress. Are we stingy with what they really need?

One of Carnegie's maxims was to divide life into thirds: Get all the education you can; make as much money as one can; and then, give it all away. Of course, we have much more to offer than money—the time, talent, and treasure we have, the spiritual gifts we've been given, and the Gospel we can offer. Carnegie stands as a passionate man who blessed all sorts of people with his resources. Like Abram, Carnegie was blessed by God and became a tremendous blessing to God and others.

In October 2006, a milkman in rural Pennsylvania killed five Amish schoolgirls and injured five others before killing himself. In a time before mass shootings had become more common, the tragic story became famous as a staggering example of mercy and grace. The Amish community announced their forgiveness, came to the killer's funeral, hugged the widow and her family, and donated money to support the family. Their commitment to the concept of forgiveness had been longstanding, allowing them to reflexively extend forgiveness to the killer and grace to the killer's family.

Magnanimous and Mighty

This Amish community not only professed the value of forgiveness, but practiced the principle in exceedingly difficult circumstances. They have embraced grace from God, but also fervently extend it to others. They don't believe that forgiveness eliminates wrong or releases the killer from subsequent consequences. They don't ignore the possibility that grace and forgiveness will be abused. They don't downplay the role of counseling or stoically imagine they are untouched by tragedy. But they refuse the right to hold a grudge or to retaliate. This allows the possibility of restoring relationships—and even, as appropriate, to reestablish trust. On one hand, their forgiveness and grace are amazing; on the other hand, they are merely the way of Jesus' Kingdom.

Perhaps the strongest example of magnanimity in the Bible is the Father in the Parable of the Prodigal Son (Luke 15). The younger son requests his portion of the estate before its time, implying that he's eager for his dad to be dead. The son is certainly excited to be rid of his father and whatever requirements and restrictions would come with being in his realm. The son is a knucklehead and probably headed into trouble. But the dad consents to his request—and apparently, begins to pray and to hope. Finally, after the son's resources have been exhausted and his options have become ridiculously unsavory, he "comes to his senses" and returns home.

We often focus on the younger son. And the older son is a different sort of mess. But the hero of the story is the faithful and gracious father who uses his resources well and loves those around him. Unlike the Prodigal, Lot gets in a rough patch and does not return—as we'll see, going even deeper into trouble. Instead, may we use our resources, power, and opportunities well, following in the faithful footsteps of Carnegie, the Amish, Abram, and the Father.

6

In vs. Of the World

COMPLETE TEXT: GENESIS 19
RECOMMENDED READING: 19:1–29
POTENTIAL MEMORY VERSES: 19:29

I'VE ALWAYS LOVED JOHN Stott's commentaries. But my favorite Stott line is his definition of "rabbit-hole Christianity"—when the only contacts with the world are mad, brave dashes from one Christian event to another. This approach can stem from legalism, imagining that holiness and righteousness come primarily through separation and abstention. Or it can derive from fear, as if we're rabbits continuously avoiding threats and enemies. Instead of a healthy dose of "take your stand" in our daily life, the predominant verb is "to flee." Biblically, the Pharisees come quickly to mind. To some extent, they were preserving power and status from the threat of Jesus' ministry. But their opposition to Jesus and their aversion to "sinners" was also driven by legalism and fear.

That said, moral and spiritual compromise is a valid concern—a universal problem with specific temptations that are particular to each of us. Biblically, Samson, Peter, and Judas are strong examples. With his supernatural gifting and Rambo-like military victories, Samson is emblematic of someone who lets success go to his head (or hair). He saw himself as invincible and played with fire until he got badly burned. Peter was the leader of the disciple pack, but denied Jesus three times despite being warned by

Jesus. Judas seems to have had good intentions at the onset, but his different agenda for the Messiah eventually led to theft, treason, and treachery.

In Genesis, Lot is a notable compromiser—and contrasts strongly with Uncle Abraham, who was able to be active in the world without much compromise. What can we learn from Lot's failures as we look to emulate Abraham and especially Jesus—interacting well with the world, avoiding both rabbit-hole Christianity and the slippery slopes that lead to increasing temptation and regrettable compromise?

GETTING INTO A LOT OF TROUBLE

Sprinkled throughout the Abraham narrative, we see a handful of big choices by Lot. In Genesis 12:4, he makes a huge move to leave Babylon and travel with Abram's crew to Canaan. We don't know any of the particulars, but his decision to leave his former life behind is at least somewhat impressive, especially since he did not have Abram's direct revelation from God. The next key moment is the fateful decision about how to separate from Abram in Genesis 13. Both men had grown wealthy—and so, a small area of land was insufficient to handle both of them and their prodigious herds. Offered a gracious choice by his uncle, Lot didn't refuse the first choice, took a long look, chose "for himself," and located near Sodom. Not good.

If Lot's choice and relocation were a movie scene, there would be sad and ominous music playing in the background. Sad because the family is dividing. A bit ominous because we sense that Lot's choice is not coming from a good place. And really troubling for those who know where the story goes and are painfully aware that it will not end well. Soon enough (in the narrative), Lot is captured by locals and then rescued by Abraham in the military adventures of Genesis 14. But this turns out to be only a blip on Lot's radar and a rough but memorable day on his calendar, as he settles back into his comfortable life near Sodom.

From there, we don't read anything more about Lot until the terrible events of Genesis 19. As this narrative opens, we find him sitting at the city gate of Sodom—indicative of his prominence in the city. He's gone from *moving toward* Sodom to *living near* Sodom to *leading in* Sodom—a powerful picture of compromise. With Abraham, Lot, and Sodom, we see a great man outside the city, a "good" man inside the city, and a really messed-up society.

SODOM AND GOMORRAH

Genesis 19 is preceded by two amazing vignettes in Genesis 18 (and Abram's name change in 17:5). The first story shows Abraham's impressive hospitality toward "three men" (revealed soon to be the Lord and two angels). God reiterates the promise of a baby for Abraham through Sarah (initially made in 17:16) and then pins down the timing of the baby's birth (in about a year).

In the second story, Abraham argues with the Lord about the fate of "the righteous" in Sodom, after the two angels head there "to see how bad things are" and presumably to render judgment. God allows the picture of Him "bargaining with" Abraham—and they settle on ten righteous people as the minimum to save the city. With that settled, the reader wonders: Will enough righteous people be found there? Either way, what will the Lord do? And what will happen to the angels when they visit Sodom?

The narrative in Genesis 19 starts to resolve these questions almost immediately. The two angels arrive and find Lot at the city gate, eager to offer hospitality. He shows respect, speaks kind words, extends a gracious invite, and offers to wash their feet. They decline and Lot forcefully (and nervously?) insists until they accept. He preps the entire meal, rather than relying on a servant, his daughters, or his wife. Curiously, he offers them "bread without yeast"—a quicker recipe that points forward to the Passover meal in Exodus 12 as Israel abruptly exits Egypt. Then, with more foreshadowing, he says the guests should leave "early in the morning."

If this was a movie scene, you can imagine the music moving from foreboding to a jump scare over the next few verses. The men of Sodom show up at Lot's door, with the ultimate lack of hospitality. Extremely rough stuff: a mob at night ("all the men" in 19:4 is probably hyperbole, but still!); the threat of homosexual rape to vulnerable travelers (really?!); and just hours after they arrived (word traveled quickly!). The moment quickly illustrates the rank immorality of Sodom's men. This isn't just a few kids stealing a couple of apples.

Credit to Lot for his courageous attempt to quietly reason with the mob. (Can you picture the moment?) He calls them "friends" (literally, "brothers"). Maybe it's just artful rhetoric, but later events and Lot's life as a whole indicate that they're closer to him than one would hope. Then he offers a contemptible compromise to the malicious mob: his two daughters. Maybe he thought this would reveal the insanity of their demands. But the men's reply is reprehensible: ridicule, xenophobia, and more threats of violence. Zero respect for Lot or his guests. If he had any authority as a city leader, it only lasted as long as he did what they wanted!

But now, the angels come to the rescue. The shut door of Lot's house reminds us of God shutting the door of the ark, as the judged are left on the outside. The men are also blinded—a practical punishment, frightening and debilitating. It's a fitting picture of their ironic impotence and their spiritual status. As Matthew Henry put it: "Justly were those struck blind who had been deaf to reason."[1] It also allows time for Lot to identify others who should escape judgment; for Lot and Co. to get out of town before the judgment; and even, for the evil to potentially repent.

Lot's crew leaves with dawn approaching. (Did anyone sleep that night?!) The timing is perfectly just: before strangers would enter the city; only the townspeople will be destroyed. It also allowed judgment to be visible—and figuratively, provides a picture of the dawning of a new day. The angels urge Lot to leave, but he hesitates. This parallels Genesis 3, when Adam and Eve doubted God's goodness, His word, and His judgment. The angels grasp Lot and extend mercy to him. In Jude 22–23, it says we should "Be merciful to those who doubt; save others by snatching them from the fire; to others show mercy, mixed with fear—hating even the clothing stained by corrupted flesh." As we avoid compromise, who are we snatching from the fire?

Why was it so challenging for Lot to leave and go? It was difficult to get Lot out of Sodom, because it was difficult to get Sodom out of Lot. He wasn't sure where he was going. He was leaving what had become his "comfort zone." Mix in some materialism and worldliness, leaving behind possessions and position. He had chosen this area for its fertile land. Now, the same opportunity for prosperity had become a snare. His willingness to leave Babylon had evolved into an unwillingness to leave Sodom.

The angels' instructions to "flee and not look back" are literal, but they're also a wonderful picture of passionately repenting and completely rejecting a flawed approach to life. Through God's grace, we can largely leave our pasts in the past—the sins if not the consequences. Similarly, in Philippians 3:13–14, Paul encourages us to leave things behind so we can run the race well. Lot's response is telling: He says "I'll die." Often, a new approach to life feels like death—and it always involves death at some level: the Flesh and the World crucified through Jesus (Gal 5:24, 6:14), a dying to self.

---

1. Henry, *Commentary*, 99.

Finally out of Sodom, Lot then begs for a shorter trip. Again, the angels extend mercy, acceding to his request and offering a concession—to stop at a village, instead of going to the mountains. Is Lot looking for a semblance of "civilization"? Has Lot grown soft physically and emotionally, unable to make the trip in contrast to Uncle Abraham's vigor? Both are called to leave and go. Abraham responded with faithful obedience, while Lot second-guessed God. Abraham bargained passionately for others, while Lot's efforts are tepid and focused on himself.

The judgment itself would have been staggering to witness, but the recap is terse. What starts as just another day—comes to a sudden end. The outcome is complete: utter devastation of all life and vegetation. Ironically, the fruitfulness of Sodom that initially attracted Lot is withered by flame, turned into scorched earth, replaced by salt and sterility.

THE SIN OF SODOM?

It's common for theological conservatives to infer that Sodom's sin was homosexuality and for liberals to argue that Sodom's sin was its lack of hospitality (not wanting to condemn homosexual conduct). But one doesn't need Genesis 19 to identify homosexual conduct as sin; that case (literally) ranges from Genesis 1 to Revelation 22. And inhospitality is certainly problematic, but presumably not enough for God to fire-bomb a city!

In any case, the matter is more complicated than either position. First, God had decided to destroy Sodom in Genesis 18:17, before the events of Genesis 19. Second, we're not given a reason for the destruction in the narrative. But 18:20–21 and 19:13 provide a hint, describing "the great outcry against" the people of Sodom. Voluntary behaviors don't usually result in outcries; more likely, it was someone using force or injustice against others—say, murder (as Genesis 4:10 with the ground "crying out"), rape (as the narrative unfolds), or other types of oppression and injustice. In other words, the sort of behavior you see in a might-makes-right world.

Third, in the Bible's other 18 references to Sodom, only Jude 7 mentions sexual improprieties. (They "indulged in sexual immorality and pursued unnatural lust.") But *every* passage uses Sodom as a point of comparison—ten times to Israel, and four of those times to describe Israel as *worse* than Sodom.[2] If the Israelites did not engage heavily in homosexual

---

2. Two of these four comparisons were made by prophets (Lam 4:6, Ezek 16:46–50); the other two were made by Jesus (Matt 10:15, 11:23–24).

conduct, but were judged more harshly than Sodom, homosexuality could not have been the primary sin of either.

Thankfully, Ezekiel 16:49–50 gives us the direct answer from God about the sin of Sodom: They were "arrogant, overfed and unconcerned; they did not help the poor and needy. They were haughty and did detestable things before me. *Therefore* I did away with them . . . " Why was Sodom destroyed? Obviously not because its sins were the greatest, but to make it an example—the first judgment against a city. Sodom was the *first* city to receive judgment, not the *worst* city in history. (This follows Genesis 6–8's worldwide judgment example—the Flood. As such, Noah and Lot stand in as pictures of mercy within God's overwhelming and perfectly just judgment.) It's simplistic to chalk up Sodom's destruction to homosexuality or hospitality. Instead, looking into the mirror of Ezekiel 16's definition of Sodom's sin should be sobering for all of us.

LOT IN SODOM

The details on Lot in Genesis 19 are fascinating and applicable. First, let's reconsider him at the city gate—likely as a leader in the city. When you're in a difficult situation with potential for compromise, it's important to consider when you should "stand" or "flee"—with work, at church, or in relationships. What if you have the opportunity to lead in a difficult situation? Can you fix it or at least improve it? If our good and great God is known for one thing, it might be "redemption." Created in His image, we want to redeem. Fitting his design for our lives, He wants us to redeem. But when, practically, is this a utopian pipedream, a practical problem, or a beautiful possibility?

Second, consider Lot's hospitality to the two guests. From what follows in the story, his example would shine like a candle in the darkness. He had seen strong hospitality modeled by Abraham and Sarah—and emulated it. Whatever Lot's other flaws, there remained an impressive desire to care for the stranger and the vulnerable. In II Peter 2:7–8, he's labeled a "righteous man." One wonders if this is as a point of comparison to the Sodomites, the relative strength of his character in a terrible situation, or simply because of his impressive hospitality in hostile circumstances. In any case, by practicing robust hospitality, we can love our neighbors and illustrate the Gospel to the world around us.

Third, we see a number of compromises from Lot and his wife as they flee. He hesitated to leave. He complained that the mountains were too far and the angels allowed him to stop at a small nearby town. And then, his wife infamously looked back to Sodom and was turned into a pillar of salt. One imagines it was a longing look, but it doesn't last long. There is no mercy here, implying a limit to God's patience. Why does God draw the line at this point? For one thing, she disobeyed a direct command (19:17). Maybe she looks back out of curiosity, trivializing God's judgment into a spectator sport. What's clear: She had a strong inclination to return to Sodom, even with recent events. She had a passionate and unfortunate attachment to Sodom, despite its injustice, unrighteousness, and evil. James 1:6-8 warns about being "double-minded"—something that plagued Lot and his wife.

Fourth, after the intervention of the angels, they plan to leave town early the next morning, before the promised destruction. But a small detail in the text reveals a lot about Lot. The angels offer to bring others with them. However, when Lot tells his sons-in-law-to-be, they think he's joking (19:14). How little respect they must have had for Lot! Was he a hypocrite or just not holy enough to get their attention? If I took a message from God to people at work about imminent destruction, they might not know how to respond, but I'm confident that they wouldn't think I was joking. Similarly, when the men of the town come to Lot's door, they start by looking for his cooperation—as if that might actually be possible!

A PATHETIC ENDING

The story ends with Abraham seeing the devastation. There is no recorded response from him, but presumably, it's awe and dread. He may presume that Lot is dead and may feel responsible. God ultimately shows mercy to Lot. But at least for now, the lessons for Abraham are the utter righteousness and deadly serious justice of God.

Meanwhile, Lot and his two daughters end up settling in a mountain cave (ironic after 19:19's request). Why doesn't Lot go back to Abraham? (Or why doesn't he go back to Haran—as Abraham did for Isaac's future wife in Genesis 24?) It can be difficult to limp back after an embarrassing failure. It would've been a great choice to go back to a gracious man, but pride got in the way. Lot is, in essence, a Prodigal Son who never returns. Like his wife, he's still looking back and has no hope for a way forward. Can we put aside pride to return, repent, and be redeemed? And are we sensitive enough to people who might be trying to leave their caves?

It's ironic that there wasn't enough room in the land for the prosperity of Abraham and Lot, but now Lot is broke and confines himself to a hole in the ground. It's also ironic that Lot has moved from being "in the world" to utter isolation. Maybe Lot had inklings of the troubles to come, but he may have never seen it coming at all. The chronology of sin usually ranges from A to Z, but often we only point to the X and Y that directly lead to Z, failing to see the long trail of decisions that got us there.

C.S. Lewis has a great quote on these themes: "Good and evil both increase at compound interest. That is why the little decisions you and I make every day are of such infinite importance. The smallest good act today is the capture of a strategic point from which, a few months later, you may be able to go on to victories you never dreamed of. An apparently trivial indulgence in lust or anger today is the loss of a ridge or railway line or bridgehead from which the enemy may launch an attack otherwise impossible."[3]

Lot probably thought he was just living his best life—and then one day, he wakes up in a cave. But then it gets worse! His daughters see no path forward either: stuck in a cave with a father paralyzed by guilt or fear. So, they get him drunk (twice!) and he gets them pregnant. Lot may be a compromiser, but his daughters are children of Sodom, willing to rape their own father! In all of this, Lot is a lot like Noah after the destruction of the Flood: drunk, naked, and disgraced. The behavior in this episode isn't directly condemned, but the results speak for themselves. Moab becomes the Moabites; Ben-Ammi becomes the Ammonites; both will be bitter enemies of Israel in the future, providing an analogy to the long-run consequences of sin.

Thankfully, Lot's story does not end there. The beautiful story of Ruth opens in the dreaded Moab, where one of their sons is married to a local named Ruth. This troubling start is powerfully redeemed by the resurgent faith of Naomi, the loyal love of Ruth, and the compassion of the Christ-like kinsman-redeemer Boaz. Amazingly, the child of Boaz and Ruth turns out to be an ancestor of David and Jesus Christ. Ruth is even listed among the four women in Christ's genealogy (Matt 1:5)—all amazing stories of God's inclusiveness and redemption. In a word, the story of Lot ultimately ends with how much God loves to redeem!

3. Lewis, *Mere Christianity*, Book 3, Chapter 9.

WRAPPING UP...

Lot's life is a warning against compromise, slippery slopes, and becoming increasingly immersed in "the World"—the systems of life and thought that run in opposition to God. It's tempting to view such things as a binary 0/1. A common example of this is marital infidelity or a marriage otherwise gone south—as if they occur in a single fateful moment. But the reality is that the marriage may not have started all that well—or more likely, that it started well enough but faded over time—with *both* parties responsible for much of the decline. Here's another great C.S. Lewis quote on this topic:

> Every time you make a choice you are turning the central part of you, the part of you that chooses, into something a little different from what it was before. And taking your life as a whole, with all your innumerable choices, all your life long you are slowly turning this central thing either into a heavenly creature or into a hellish creature: either into a creature that is in harmony with God, and with other creatures, and with itself, or else into one that is in a state of war and hatred with God, and with its fellow-creatures, and with itself.[4]

For better and for worse, every choice matters. Consequences often remain. But every sin can be covered by repentance and grace. And every mistake can be reversed, recovered, and redeemed.

Part of this relates to how we can best engage our culture today. Some advocate "the Benedict Option," emulating St. Benedict in drawing away from the world. This is not to closet ourselves into "rabbit-hole Christianity," but to strengthen our institutions through purposeful discipleship and then, to return into the world. Others advocate "the Boethius Option," staying as engaged in the world as possible to do the good that we can do in the moment. Both approaches have their merits—and what's best for one person may not be best for another. As a specific example, what should Christian parents do with K-12 school choices for their children: standard public schools, charter schools, private schools, or homeschooling?[5]

The wisdom and impact of these choices have changed over time because culture has evolved. In his book, *Life in the Negative World*, Aaron Renn describes the general trend in America from a "positive world" (where

---

4. Lewis, *Mere Christianity*, Book 3, Chapter 4.
5. Related: I have a little book on the broader question of what to expect from college, *College 101: What Students and Parents Should Know About Universities.*

In vs. Of the World

Christianity is highly respected) to a "neutral world" (where it is treated pluralistically as one legitimate approach among many) to a "negative world" (where it is treated with skepticism or even hostility). All of these have challenges. For example, a positive world creates a setting where many more people imagine they're Christian because the culture is Christianized.

We see a similar pattern in the Old Testament. Israel struggled repeatedly in the Wilderness, before its ultimate act of rebellion in Numbers 13-14. Later in its history, Israel stumbled repeatedly into idolatry. Despite warnings from God over time through Moses and an array of prophets, they repented at times, but generally devolved into worshipping gods other than Yahweh who had revealed Himself to them and saved them from Egyptian bondage.

In Revelation 18, John calls believers to come out of Babylon, representing worldly powers and systems. (In this, we see parallels with Abram leaving Babylon and going to walk with God in Genesis 12.) In Revelation 2:1-7, the church at Ephesus is commended for its good works, but told to return to its "first love"—apparently, a series of choices that were impressively moral, but increasingly driven by duty rather than love of God and others. In Luke 17:28-33, Christ used Lot and his wife as a catalyst for people to leave Jerusalem before the destruction of the Temple in 70 AD and maybe again at the End of Time.

We can also look to the Scriptures to see interesting examples of this with respect to government power. As we'll see later, Joseph is tempted to "Egyptianize," trading the holiness of Israel for the power and perqs of Egypt. In I Samuel, we see the temptation of power for Saul—as he transforms from someone who has absolutely no interest in being king to someone who jealously guards his power against David. In I Kings 3-11, Solomon is the wisest man in the world, but was also a decidedly mixed bag as a king. Daniel is our most hopeful Biblical example: refusing to bow to idols and power, focused on faithfully following the God of Israel.

Jesus is known for what he did more than what he did not do. He was both radically "in the world" and decidedly not "of the world." He didn't commit any sins, but his method was not avoiding the world and "sinners," but engaging them perfectly through the Scriptures, empowered by the Spirit, on mission for the Lord. May we be alert to the temptations and compromises around us, standing and fleeing as necessary, making a difference in the world without becoming of the world.

7

Patience vs. Pushing

COMPLETE TEXT: GENESIS 15–18, 21:1–21
RECOMMENDED READING: 15:1–6, 16:1–17:5, 17:15–19
POTENTIAL MEMORY VERSES: 15:1, 15:6

ONE OF MY FAVORITE *Saturday Night Live* skits is based on the frustration of having a great line, but delivering it a few seconds too late. Rather than getting a big laugh, delivering a potent zinger, or offering a meaningful observation, the listeners don't understand because they've already moved on. Instead of you being perceived as funny or insightful, your friends are somewhere between confused and annoyed. And then, do you just let it go or try to explain the context (which usually doesn't help as much as we hope)?

We've all been troubled by bad timing and missed opportunities. In the skit, science has developed a pill that moves the clock forward by the few fateful seconds. Suddenly, bewilderment turns into laughter or respect. Thanks to modern medicine, now the joke hits; the line lands. The remark improves the conversation instead of stopping it. As in other parts of life, it can be all about the timing.

One definition of sin is "missing the mark." In this, we're quick to identify sins of commission over sins of omission. It's relatively easy to identify imperfect words or deeds that miss the target. However, it's not so easy to identify imperfect motives and poor timing. But time is a big deal in God's economy. The already and the not yet of His Kingdom. The temporal and the eternal. Faith that looks back and hope that looks forward. Not just love as an abstract concept, but actually loving people in the time and place we inhabit. Not simply the ability to exhibit character and integrity for a moment, but the ability to persevere over the years.

And then, there are our two big questions to God when we're questioning His ability to run the universe: Why and how long? The "why's" of life can be annoying. But the "how longs" can be extremely frustrating. How long will my son continue to act like a knucklehead? When will the cancer go away? How many months until I get a better job?

The Christian life is, in part, a call to patience that reminds us about God's amazing patience with us. He was patient with those who have now become His children—from objects of wrath to trophies of grace. But now that we are children and heirs to the King, how much more patience does it require for Him to tolerate our continuing stumbles? Jen Wilkin notes that "We allow the most the most trifling annoyance to test our patience: the way someone chews, the dirty dish left on the counter, the forgotten turn signal . . . But God, against whom we have committed and continue to commit actual sins both small and great, bears with us patiently in the full knowledge of every single one of our offenses."[1] How can we have the patience of God with the people in our lives and the circumstances of our lives?

It's often tempting to try short cuts that won't work. Sure, it's important to work smart as well to work hard—and all things equal, sooner is better than later. But overlooking red flags to continue dating someone because you're desperate to get married? Fudging an expense account or otherwise nibbling at the edges of ethical violations at work to make a quick buck? Imagining financial opportunities with big rates of return without much risk in investment decisions? All of these are likely to take you places you don't want to go. Wait for and look to work within God's timing.

ABRAM'S CONCERNS

Abram can teach us a lot about timing and patience. When we read his narrative, it's easy to overlook the reality that these events unfolded over decades. God had promised him so much, but it was all in God's timing. This probably explains the surprising opening in Genesis 15. Last we saw, Abram had just won a tremendous military victory. "After this" (probably soon afterwards), God proactively appears in a vision to encourage Abram

---

1. Wilkin, *In His Image*, 112.

not to be afraid, telling him that the Lord is his shield and his "very great reward": to defend and bless; to protect and prosper; to provide security, safety, and sustenance.

The "reward" part of this is cool, since Abram had declined post-battle booty from the King of Sodom (in Genesis 14) and given Lot the first choice of the land (in Genesis 13). But Abram is already a wealthy man by now. What reward does he need? Stranger still: Why is he afraid? He just whipped a bunch of pagan kings to rescue Lot. Maybe he had a "brush with death" in the battle. Perhaps he's worried about reprisals from the vanquished. But one suspects that he has other concerns on his mind. God has promised him a Promised Land. Sure, I have my tents, big herds, and a nice militia. But I'm surrounded by people with really different values, many of whom are hostile to me or wouldn't mind having my stuff. God, what's the plan—the actual detailed plan?

God had also promised him a great nation and as many descendants as the dust of the earth. OK, sure, but how? Sarai and I are apparently infertile. And Lot just left, so adopting him looks out. God, what are you doing here? This is where Abram takes the conversation. Notice that he's asking good questions here: no demandingness—simply expressing legitimate desires based on God's promises. He's honest with God, rather than complaining or whining. After all, what's the point of a reward or a legacy without children? What good is the promise of land without the delivery of an heir? He proposes adopting his servant Eliezer, a common practice which also reveals that Lot is not a worthy heir. But God has other plans.

Genesis 15:4 is the first appearance of the phrase "the word of the Lord came to"—key prophetic language in the Bible. And it's well-placed, given the encouragement in this conversation between friends. The answer to Abram's idea about Eliezer is "no"—and then, the promise that the baby will come from Abram's body. (Note that Sarai is not yet specified!) God reiterates the promise of innumerable offspring (fulfilled literally in Israel and spiritually through all believers), switching the metaphor from dust to stars. This elicits a great statement of faith from Abram in 15:6—a line that is quoted powerfully by Paul: "Abram believed the Lord and it was credited to him as righteousness." (Rom 4:3)

Then, God addresses the specifics of the land. Abram questions this and God responds by setting up a sacrifice within the vision. Among other details, God promises 400 years for Abram's descendants in Egypt, including slavery and oppression. It's not just Abram who will need to be patient

PATIENCE VS. PUSHING

with the unfolding of God's will, judgment, and sovereignty! In all of this, God does not lay out tons of detail, but He does reiterate His promises and provide more information.

TAKING MATTERS INTO THEIR OWN HANDS

As Genesis 16 opens sometime later, we're reminded that Sarai had borne no children. She suggests her maidservant Hagar as a surrogate "wife" (a common cultural practice) so Sarai could "have" a child. With God's promises echoing in Abram's head—that he would father a son (with no mention of Sarai)—he probably sees this as a providential opportunity: a willing wife, a fertile female, and a potential route to the promised child. Maybe Abram and Sarai are both wanting to run a science experiment on whose plumbing was faulty. (Notice that Sarai says "perhaps" in 16:2!) Will each be happy with the research results, however it turns out?

There are fascinating parallels with their trip to Egypt in Genesis 12. Abram's child would be born to an Egyptian woman—as Sarai's child would have been born through an Egyptian father (Pharaoh). Abram imitates Pharaoh in starting a harem. Abram and Sarai both ask the other to compromise the marriage to accept another partner. (Interestingly, the first two occasions for adultery-like behavior in the Bible stem from calculation rather than lust.) Abram was in charge in Genesis 12; Sarai is in charge now; neither is doing a great job in their marriage. And ironically, Hagar was probably part of their Egypt-gained wealth.

The key here is that they knew God's general promise, but not His method or His timing. It's been ten years since the initial promise in 12:4—and they probably expected it to be fulfilled sooner than later, given their ages. Lot had not worked out and Eliezer had been vetoed by God. They had been promised a son, but not necessarily through Sarai. God had been silent since then, presumably in the face of Abram and Sarai making petitions to Him. Interestingly, God does not approve, condone, or interfere in this episode.

To cut them some slack and to apply this to us: Waiting does not imply complacency, apathy, laziness, etc. In the face of God's silence and our uncertainty on how to proceed, when do we act and when do we wait? The big "spiritual" answers here are gratitude for what we have; focus on what we do know about God's will; prayer to receive insight and revelation; and learn from our mistakes. But there are other concepts in play as well:

cultivate patience through small moments in everyday living; be careful about the temptation to use worldly methods; and avoid reliance on our own strength to reach God's goals.

Still, in practice, it can be difficult to define "our (ideal) participation" within God's provision. You can imagine them rationalizing that this sounded like a good idea, especially given God's promise of a child. And if not, God would probably step in to prevent damage, right? And look how things turned out: Hagar conceived, so this must be a blessing from God!

A few other principles emerge here. First, the temptation grows as the trial lengthens. I'm sure it was awesome for Abram to have the experience in Genesis 15, but then "reality" returns—and stays—until we get to the beginning of Genesis 16. Likewise, Sarai succumbs to this temptation through her increasing biological hopelessness; her circumstances fade and her character flaws are revealed. Second, their temptation was related to their past struggles. Hagar was acquired on their trip to Egypt. And after Abram's scheme in Genesis 12, it was more difficult for him to refuse Sarai's plans here. More broadly, past failure can damage future credibility and make it easier to relapse in the same area.

Third, temptation comes from Abram's wife, as Adam with Eve. Sometimes, trouble can come from our closest friends and family. Fourth, getting more specific, as with Adam and Eve, temptation arises from an aggressive wife in the face of a husband's passivity. Until Sarai's offer, there is no prior record of Abram wanting another wife—as was customary with infertility or just pursuing polygamy for kicks. Why no apparent hesitation here? (Was there even a "pregnant pause"?) Fifth, although tempted, Abram is still responsible for his actions. It's easy to second-guess him here, but it should also be easy to empathize with their struggles and their decision.

HAGAR'S PERSPECTIVE

As an aside, we might wonder what Hagar thought about all this. One can imagine anger (seeing this as a form of rape), charmed (out of love and respect for Abram), or most likely, seeing this as a great opportunity for improved status. In any case, she is used as a means to an end by Abram and Sarai. She also becomes a "wife" (16:3) and will emerge as a person to whom God grants immense dignity. In the meantime, she doesn't handle her "success" well. Hagar conceives a child and then despises Sarai. Abram

PATIENCE VS. PUSHING

and Sarai hope to build up their family, but instead, this strategy causes a lot of trouble.

In the first husband/wife dialogue recorded in the Bible, Abram and Sarai blame each other (as in Genesis 3). Ironically, both are correct; there's plenty of blame to go around. But one would hope to see them hold up a mirror to see their own sin instead of proudly pointing a finger at the other. Ultimately, Abram goes passive (again, emulating Adam's silence) and fails to be a peacemaker. Sarai then mistreats a vulnerable pregnant woman, taking out her frustrations on Hagar.

Soon, Hagar runs away—in some combination of bravery and desperation. She's on her way back to Egypt when an angel of the Lord stops her in her tracks.[2] He calls her "servant of Sarai" and "mistress" instead of "wife of Abram," instilling humility, revealing her purpose, and already pointing to her proper response. Amazingly, God reveals Himself to a foreigner, a woman, and a slave here—and appears to her before Sarai! He makes promises to her—even as one who is "not chosen." And she even gives God a name before Abram does.

Abram does the right thing upon her arrival—without being told directly—convinced and convicted by her return and her testimony. (Interestingly, he listens to Sarai to start the trouble and he listens to Hagar at the end to resolve it.) As per 16:12, Ishmael's descendants have been a thorn in Israel's side ever since. The bottom line is that doing things even with good intentions, but without God, can complicate matters immensely.

THE CENTRALITY OF CIRCUMCISION—AND FATHERHOOD

Like many men, Abraham was strong at work (Genesis 13), at war (Genesis 14), and at church (Genesis 15), but not at home (Genesis 16). God will use Abimelech to teach Abraham a lesson about marriage in Genesis 20. But God has something for Abraham as a father in Genesis 17. The narrative opens with God giving Himself a new name: "God Almighty" (*El Shaddai*). This title highlights His power and provision—and here, it signals something big to be revealed. He also changes Abram's name to Abraham—from "exalted father" to "father of a multitude." And He lays out an "everlasting covenant" centered on obedience to God in general and to circumcision in particular.

---

2. Most likely, this is the pre-incarnate Christ from what we see in 16:10. If so, His appearance to Hagar is the first in the Bible!

It's been 13 years since the Lord spoke to Abraham and it's apparently time to initiate Ishmael into manhood—perhaps through circumcision (as practiced in other cultures) and other rites of passage. God pronounces circumcision as the *key* rite for Abraham's descendants. But here's the kicker: It would be done at one week of life instead of at 13 years old. In other words: Dad was to be deeply involved in the training of his sons—in matters of faith and life—from the beginning, not just when they were "ready to become men."

Why circumcision? First, it required the shedding of blood, foreshadowing what would be required in the sacrificial system—and ultimately, with Jesus. Second, it had health benefits, especially in those days. Third, it implied a deep concern with sexual ethics. Fourth, it points forward figuratively to intimacy with God. Later, idolatry will be described as adultery—infidelity in one's relationship to God. Fifth, it would be helpful in forming and maintaining a nation—a rite of passage that would instill unity among the people. Sixth, it resembles baptism for New Testament believers as a form of obedience and a sign of belonging to God's people—as if putting on "the team uniform." Seventh, it is an external that points to an internal. Paul runs with this in Romans 2:25-29a and 4:11-12, but the idea was introduced in the Law (Lev 26:41, Deut 10:16, 30:6). It's a picture of self-sacrifice, a cutting away of the Flesh, a crucifixion of the Sin Nature (Gal 5:24), and a dying to self.

But circumcision was often used by pagans as well. We see God redeeming its practice here—and modifying it to something done near birth. For pagans, it was useful as a male rite of passage into society and it pointed to the youth's new sexual potency. But for Israel, circumcision will have a quite different meaning: Manliness is vitally expressed as paternal duty regarding the male newborn, celebrating procreation and perpetuation of the faith rather than sexuality *per se*. It is an early reminder that bearing a child is a lot easier than the more important task of raising the child well, starting with circumcision. And in all of this, the father will have a vital role to serve.

SARAH'S PREPOSTEROUS PREGNANCY

The 13-year gap between God's visits is also another 13 years of infertility for Abraham and Sarai. They imagine that Ishmael is the promised child. God hasn't said otherwise—until now. Don't let this slip by you too quickly:

Patience vs. Pushing

For 13 years, they thought their method with Hagar was the chosen path! Sure, times were tough soon after Ishmael was born, but things seem to be rolling now.

Instead, God reveals another way forward. Not only will the promised child come through Abraham, but through Sarai as well! Abraham will not be the father of many peoples unless Sarai is the mother of those peoples. Sarai gets a name change too—to Sarah. Interestingly, it's given to Abraham to give to her—as God's dominion is transferred to Abraham in the form of leadership within the family. Now, Abraham's name for his wife will be "princess," emphasizing their marriage and her dignity.

When Abraham hears that Sarah will be a mother, he falls down with laughter. In the next chapter, Sarah will also laugh when she receives the news. But God responds differently to each, implying that the laughs are coming from a different place. God will correct Sarah's cynicism, but apparently shares the laugh with Abraham. After all, this is really funny! Continuing the inside joke, the son's name will be Isaac which means "laughter."

I like what Frederick Buechner said about this: They "laughed at first because they didn't believe; they laughed at the sheer impossibility of it. They laughed because they were told they would have a son when they had reached an age when they didn't even dare to buy green bananas. And after the child was born, they laughed because they did believe. They laughed that when Sarah went to Wal-Mart, she was the only shopper to buy both Pampers and Depends. They laughed that both parents and baby had to eat the same strained vegetables because nobody in the whole family had a single tooth."[3]

Genesis 18 opens with Abraham's tremendous hospitality toward the Lord and the two angels. He's "sitting at the entrance of his tent," perhaps anticipating an opportunity to serve. He "looked and saw"—and then responded, dropping everything and allowing his schedule to be interrupted. The narrative tells us that he hurried (three times) and that he ran. Cooking a lavish meal then was a slow process (no microwaves!), but he did what he could do quickly (with some delegation to Sarah). He offered water and "bowed low," showing respect and establishing himself as their servant (instead of eating with them). And all of this, despite his age, earthly wealth, and divine position. The details may seem trivial, but it shows us that Abraham can be a blessing to all nations. No xenophobia or injustice toward the alien and the stranger. Treating all people with dignity and respect.

---

3. As paraphrased by Ortberg, *Life You've Always Wanted*, 211.

Abraham asks that Ishmael also be given a blessing (17:18). It's noteworthy that Abraham asks, but not surprising given his relationship with God. And it's significant that Abraham wanted to ask—a sign of how much he loved Ishmael, instead of blowing him off for Isaac. God affirms the blessing and promises the new baby in about a year.

Fast-forwarding to Genesis 21, Ishmael "exits stage right" after some sort of an episode. The key verb is a word play on Isaac's name. So, it could be that they were merely playing and Sarah over-reacts. Perhaps Ishmael was "laughing" at Isaac. Or perhaps he was "Isaac-ing"—i.e., trying to play Isaac's role. In any case, Sarah doesn't like it, so Ishmael and Hagar are banished. God will once again minister to Hagar and Ishmael, but the table is set. Hagar is gone and Sarah is Abraham's only wife now. He separates himself from the young man Ishmael and now faithfully relies on his toddler Isaac to be the vessel of the promise and the inheritance.

WRAPPING UP...

Patience is an everyday temptation and opportunity. A traffic jam or someone driving "too slow" in front of you on a two-lane road. A slow-moving checkout lane or someone who tells painfully long stories. A student who is slow to learn or a colleague who runs an inefficient meeting. We often seem more patient today because of technology. Long lines and traffic are easily overcome with entertainment delivered by the computer in our pocket. But this also implies that we have less opportunity to develop true patience. And when difficult times come and our phones can't soothe our anxiety, to what or to whom will we turn? How do we grow in patience and kindness, exhibiting the love of Christ?

When I was in grad school, my dissertation advisor felt convicted about his lack of patience and began to pray for more. The next morning, a brand new grad student showed up from China and ended up at Bob's office—with no idea what to do next. Bob spent the rest of the day helping him find an apartment, navigate a Walmart, and equip himself for the beginnings of life in America. Bob went home frustrated that he hadn't "gotten much done" at work, before realizing that his prayer had been answered: He was able to work on his patience for most of the day!

But often, what looks like patience can actually be complacency and procrastination. The opposite of taking things into your own hands is laying back in a hammock and hoping that things resolve or at least work out well enough. (Actually, by omission, that's taking things into your own hands as well!) The standard of perfection here is the right word and right deed, the right motive and the right strength—in the proper timing. Anything less is missing the mark.

I've talked about the second half of Genesis 18 twice earlier—Abraham "bargaining" with God about the fate of "the righteous" in Sodom. Abraham was decidedly far from complacent there, arguing with God about the way He was running the universe. Abraham is a hero of the faith, in part, because he aggressively intercedes on behalf of complete strangers. He is patient within the "negotiations," but he presses God instead of settling for passivity.

The timing in that case was obvious, since God showed up to talk about imminent doom. But the other two narratives take us back to the question of how we can know the perfect timing. When God doesn't speak to us, as he did to Abraham, we're left with God's word, wise counsel, and the Holy Spirit who informs and empowers us. Still, this does not clear up nearly everything. Let me give you two principles to close out: First, your decision may not matter all that much in the divine economy. So, relax and just make a decision. The example I like to use here is a ham or turkey sandwich for lunch. Does God care which you choose? Maybe sometimes, but generally not. So, pray if you want, but just decide and keep moving.

Second, it's reasonable to infer that God wants us to have a bent toward taking action. Two great stories: In I Samuel 14, Jonathan isn't sure whether to attack the Philistines. He lays out a providential fleece that leans toward taking action, knowing that God could intervene if He didn't want Jonathan to proceed. When God doesn't stop him, Jonathan and his armor-bearer whip the Philistines in a skirmish. And when David wants to build the Temple for the Lord, Nathan the prophet goes along with the plan. But then the Lord intervenes. There's no rebuke, but he says that David is not the man and the task will fall to his son. Similarly, we should err on the side of "fighting and building," but be open to the Lord telling us "no."

Aside from the stories, there are good reasons to expect that a bias toward action is desirable. For one thing, sins of omission are more subtle than sins of commission—and Jesus' ministry calls us to deal with the often-overlooked subtleties of sin. Jesus is better known for what he did than what he didn't do. So, let's do the same. Finally, remember the Parable of the Talents (Matt 25): the praise for the two who risked what they were given to steward and the condemnation (as "wicked and lazy"!) for the one who buried the talent. The punchline: At the margin, if you're not sure, then say or do something. Timing still matters, but don't let this paralyze you into inaction, silence, and passivity.

8

Faith and Reason

COMPLETE TEXT: GENESIS 22:1–25:18
RECOMMENDED READING: 22:1–18
POTENTIAL MEMORY VERSES: 22:5, 22:8, 22:12

I ADMIRE THE CLEVER title of a good book on apologetics by Norm Geisler and Frank Turek: *I Don't Have Enough Faith to Be an Atheist*. The title alone makes a number of points. We can't prove (or disprove) the existence of God. Thus, faith is a necessary part of the gap between reason and our inferences about the Divine. And the extent of this gap will differ between individuals. So, we would expect to see relatively blind or well-reasoned faith—both among those who believe in God and those who say they don't.

My cheeky comment on this topic is "I don't believe in atheists." I'm confident that there are many agnostics. Really, all of us are agnostics, since we don't *know*. (The term is derived from *a-gnosis*, meaning "without knowledge.") But people who are fully persuaded (or even confident) that there is no God? I believe they're rare and only exist through willfully blind faith. As per Romans 1:20, nature testifies to God's existence. There is nothing close to a comprehensive explanation for the origins and development of life *without* God. What other narrative is more compelling than a Creator God who used evolutionary mechanisms to some (debatable) extent?

And as per Romans 2:14–15, our consciences testify about right and wrong—and our many violations of a Standard that transcends. This latter point is the foundation of C.S. Lewis' fabulous book, *Mere Christianity*. Paraphrasing one of Lewis' arguments: If you encounter someone who claims to be a Moral Relativist, you can punch him in the nose and watch him change his tune. We all believe in right and wrong—at least when it's done to us—and thus, Someone outside of that Standard who established it.

In *Orthodoxy*, G.K. Chesterton discusses key paradoxes of life which are best explained by Christianity. For example, it turns out that the last really *are* first; and it's actually true that we gain life when we lose it. In John 6:68, Peter expressed his faith through a rhetorical question to Jesus: "To whom shall we go?" Because of reason, logic, and what he had seen, Peter believed that Jesus had "the words to eternal life" and had faith in Him. A bit paradoxically, Christians are called to both greater reason and greater faith about things that are true.

People can also have faith in things that are false. This is one way to understand idolatry. We can believe in things that are not even real, ironically giving those things power over us. (Isaiah 44:9-20 is hilarious on this point!) For example, some people believe that the number 13 has supernatural powers; invoking it will supposedly cause "bad luck." And so, the *objects* of our faith are crucial. In contrast, from Genesis, Abraham had an eminently reasonable faith in the good and great God he had experienced (Heb 11:8-19).

Throughout Genesis, we've seen faith in action. Adam and Eve have faith in the Serpent's claims over the goodness and competence of God. Noah has the faith to obey and build the Ark. Lot has the faith to go with Abraham, but not enough faith to stay with Abraham or to stay out of Sodom. Abraham has been back and forth: amazing faith in leaving Ur for Canaan, rescuing Lot from the five kings, arguing with God for the righteous in Sodom, and so on. But he also took things into his own hands with Pharaoh, Hagar, and Abimelech—lacking (or misunderstanding) the faith required to follow God in obedience.

In Genesis 22, we'll see Abraham's most famous and staggering example of living by faith: the binding and "sacrifice" of Isaac. But as the narrative continues to unfold, we'll also see more mundane acts of faith—as Abraham buries his wife and takes steps to find a wife for Isaac. What does faith look like—in the extraordinary and the everyday? Abraham has much to show us here.

FAITH AND REASON

THE AMAZING FAITH OF ABRAHAM

With Ishmael's exit in Genesis 21, the stage is set for the climactic event of Abraham's life. This is the last recorded time that God speaks to him, rounding out a set of seven visits from the Lord. And the structure of the narrative brackets this story with his other amazing display of faith early in Genesis 12. (Both feature the idea of "leave and go"!) Abraham's story begins with leaving behind his father's house—and now, he will leave behind his son as well. He had let go of his past—and now, he will let go of his future.

This is an incredible display of faith from the Father of Faith—and thus, a difficult story to fully comprehend. (If it were easy to understand, it wouldn't take as much faith!) Soren Kierkegaard's *Fear and Trembling* is a classic treatment of this passage and how to understand Abraham's faith. Kierkegaard notes that his faith is not fatalism, stoicism, or apathy—counterfeits that can look like faith. For Christians, the easiest powerful angle of the story is the way in which it points forward to Christ. But what can Abraham teach us about faith?

The narrative graciously opens by warning the reader that this is a "test." (The story is still gut-wrenching, even with the warning!) At least in English, a test implies something where the tester hopes for success; a temptation implies something where the tempter hopes for failure. Here, God wants to *test* Abraham's faith—for Abraham, Israel, and us. A test can also refine or develop our faith—and surely, this is God's hope for Abraham (and for us) as well. Given Abraham's impressive faith, the test can't be too easy—or it's not a test. For example, if I give you an hour to do 50 problems of single-digit addition, that's not a test; it's a nothing burger and a nuisance. The bottom line: If God gives this as a test to Abraham, it's something that he and his faith can handle—as wild as this seems to us.

God calls out to Abraham, whose name ironically means "father of multitudes." Some translations obscure the Hebrew meaning in 22:2. But God requests (rather than commands) Abraham to offer his son to Him as a sacrifice. In a word, within His relationship with Abraham, God asks him to exhibit free will in this amazingly difficult and faith-filled matter. Abraham gives the textbook response for an obedient servant: "Here I am."[1] This is the same phrase he will say at the climactic moment in 22:11—in both cases, the simple, succinct, submissive reply of one who is ready, able, and willing to serve.

---

1. See: Isa 6:8, Exod 3:4, I Sam 3:4,6,8.

Isaac is more God's son than Abraham's anyway—and what God gives, He can reasonably take away. This also serves as an exclamation point that Isaac and Israel's beginnings are completely born of God's grace and sovereignty. Likewise, the children we receive from God are God's. We hope to raise them figuratively as "holy and living sacrifices" (Rom 12:1), dedicated to living and passing on what is right, holy, and gracious.

The instructions are terse and sobering. Moriah is where Jerusalem will be founded. It's a three-day journey, underlining another connection to Jesus' death, sacrifice, and resurrection. The sacrifice is to be a "burnt offering"; Abraham is being asked to kill and then burn his son. This indicates the extent of the dedication God wants from Abraham and us. The facets of the trial are staggering: losing any child, losing one's only child, losing the child of promise, and being asked to kill and destroy that child! How could one do this? Hebrews 11 tells us that Abraham reasoned that God would resurrect Isaac to fulfill his earlier promises. His faith is based on hope rather than mere resignation or stoicism.

What's missing in the text? There are no questions, feelings, or pleadings from Abraham. (Remember that Abraham had lobbied for the Sodomites earlier, but here, he does not argue for his own son!) There are no reassurances, explanations, or promises of reward from God (as He had done repeatedly earlier). Abraham must be perplexed and troubled, but he will pass the test with flying colors. In an odd way, God is also being tested by Abraham! God, you promised this; I will follow you; how will you make this right?

Another indication of Abraham's faith: They leave early the next morning. No snooze alarm or leisurely breakfast; he immediately gets to the task ahead of him. There is a lesson here: When we face difficult moments, don't procrastinate or delay; don't look for excuses or rationalizations. Can you imagine the trip? The others in the travel party aren't sure what's going to happen, but surely Abraham was sober, impacting the mood of the others. There are no recorded words. What would one say? "Man, it's hot today." Or "How 'bout them Cowboys?" Many times, talking about difficulties is helpful; other times, not so much.

It's one thing to *claim* faith and trust; it's another to *actually* trust. Do we believe or do we *believe*? In the 19th century, people were amazed when the "Great Blondin" walked with a wheelbarrow on a tightrope over Niagara Falls with 100 pounds of weight. But then, he asked to transport someone's child the same way—and nobody would take the offer. C.S. Lewis said it's one thing to trust a rope and another to trust that rope when you're hanging off a cliff.

Abraham takes the wood with him (a practical step) and cuts it personally (bearing the costs). The 50-mile trip gave plenty of time for solitude to reflect and wrestle. When they got to the mountain, they left the servants behind—perhaps to avoid interference. But really, it's not theirs to experience anyway. (Did you catch "we" in 22:5, indicating that Abraham expects to return with Isaac?) Here, we get the first biblical references to three key words: obedience (22:18), worship in tandem with the idea of sacrifice (22:5), and one of the Hebrew terms for love (22:2). All of these concepts are connected: love, obedience, sacrifice, and worship. You can't have some without the others—without bearing (or at least a willingness to bear) great costs.[2]

THE BINDING OF ISAAC

Everyone focuses on Abraham's faith, but what about Isaac's? He's a "boy," but the Hebrew term is flexible on age. He's old enough to reason (22:7) and carry the wood (22:6). Maybe he was 13 to emulate Ishmael's circumcision? In any case, he's old enough for this trial to require his submission to old man Abraham. He is a quiet but active participant in this moment, with courage and faith that is arguably more impressive than his father's. (He hasn't heard the voice of God!) With the wood on his shoulders, Isaac looks like Christ with His cross, submitting to the Father's will.

Isaac has a question for his dad, seeing that something is missing for the sacrifice. Hopefully, Abraham's answer was reassuring: "God himself will provide." Abraham uses Isaac's trust in him to encourage his son's trust in God's providence. But there is still no reassurance from God and they travel on together. Abraham builds an altar and Isaac agrees to be bound. Abraham moves to sacrifice—and then, finally, God intervenes through the angel of the Lord (likely, the pre-incarnate Jesus again).

A small but cool detail: the angel calls out to Abraham *twice*, signaling the urgency, but also implying Abraham's commitment to the sacrifice. Again, Abraham says "Here I Am." Perhaps it's said with a sense of "What now?!" But more likely, it's tinged with eagerness and hope. Can you begin to imagine this heart-pounding moment? God says "Now, I know"—not

---

2. II Samuel 24:24 is excellent on this, when David insists on paying for the oxen for his sacrifice.

a statement against God's omniscience, but a literary tool that reveals Abraham's complete obedience and faith. More to the point: now *Abraham* knew, now *Isaac* knew, and now *we* know!

The word here is usually translated as "fear." But the Hebrew term is more robust than our narrow sense of the word—flavored by reverence, awe, respect, and devotion. And that's what we see from Abraham: He loved God more than Isaac. For one thing, this underlines monotheism and crushes idolatry. Nothing should compete with God in our lives. Isaac certainly knows that he's not #1 in Abraham's life. This is important for us as well—that God comes before all, even ahead of our spouses and children. This also tells us that (biblical) faith is not merely intellectual or passive. What we do with our faith is a close reflection of what we *really* believe.

Abraham "looked up" (as he did in 22:4) and accepts the gift he had reasoned prophetically: a "ram caught by its horns" for the sacrifice. Provided by God's grace—not just a ram, but an easy catch. (Imagine him having to chase it down instead!) The idea of substitutionary atonement debuts here—as later, the Passover Lamb for Israel (Exod 12) and Christ for us (I Cor 5:7). It's also interesting that it's a ram rather than a lamb. When Abraham expected to sacrifice a child, he instead sacrifices an adult—a picture of his own death to self in this fateful moment and more generally, in his relation to God.

Abraham names the place *Jehovah-Jireh* which means "the Lord will provide." This interaction between fear and provision leads Abraham to action rather than paralysis or fatalism. At least looking forward, if the most prominent theme in the story is the transmission of faith in Yahweh to the next generation, it's noteworthy that good parent/child relationships are also known for provision and reverence of authority.

The conclusion is magnificent: repeating the covenant based on Abraham's obedience; reiterating the amazing legacy and blessing that he will have; and now promising the conquest of the Promised Land in the future. What's also clear from this narrative: God is not at all interested in human sacrifice—and not interested in *any* sacrifice, as much as reverence, trust, obedience, etc. This was a big deal in Abraham's historical context where child sacrifice was common. We don't sacrifice our kids to God or gods these days—well, except for career, various pleasures, and living out our dreams vicariously through our kids. This serves as a warning (especially to fathers) about prioritizing God over family—but then, family over all else.

BURYING SARAH

After the binding and near-sacrifice of Isaac at Moriah, Abraham comes down the mountain with the servants, but not Isaac. Is this part of the rite of passage? Does Isaac need some time away from Dad after the heart-stopping moment? Do father and son want solitude to develop their relationship with God? No other words are recorded between Abraham and Isaac—and although Isaac grieves his mother (24:67), he is not present at her burial. For better and perhaps for worse, Abraham's relation with God continues to dramatically affect Isaac.

My wife and I wonder about this with our own children. Biblically, the concern is the rarity of vibrant faith moving between the generations in the Scriptures. We want them to have a close walk with the Lord. But we don't get to make that decision—and our walk doesn't need to look like theirs. We tell them this, but do children really understand such distinctions—even if they're as interested in apprenticeship with Jesus? Church attendance and moral conformity are relatively easy; robust discipleship with Jesus is another kettle of fish.

What about Sarah? At the time of her death, she's in Hebron, about 30 miles away (23:2). Why? It's certainly reasonable to wonder whether all of this was too much for her! If we are faithful, there can be times when family and friends do not understand what we're doing in our walk with God. Jesus talked about pearls before swine (Matt 7:6) and said we might have to put God above friends and family (Luke 14:26). Gideon destroys his dad's idols. Saul doesn't tell his uncle what Samuel had revealed about his future kingship (I Sam 10:16). If we obey God in contexts where others (especially non-Christians) will find it difficult to understand, we may end up sacrificing closeness in certain relationships.

From here, the narrative moves from the climax of Abraham's story to winding up his affairs and transitioning to the next generation. In Genesis 25, we read about Abraham's later children and his death. In Genesis 24, Abraham arranges for Isaac's wife. And for most of Genesis 23, we read about Sarah's burial.

With Sarah's passing, Abraham needs to acquire land for a burial site—an ironic problem for someone who has been promised a promised land. The purchase is a deposit of sorts on that pledge and putting down some roots. The bargaining process with Ephron is interesting—what looks to be relatively standard negotiations in a way that we can't understand fully today. The final price is exorbitant (ten pounds of silver). But at the end of the day, Abraham can't care much about all of this. He's in mourning and it probably all seems trivial. He's wealthy, so why haggle? As he did with the king of Sodom years before, Abraham does not want a pagan to get glory that should go to God. And he has a long-term perspective; he knows that all of this land (and much more) will belong to his descendants.[3]

MARRYING ISAAC

The marriage of Isaac is the longest chapter in Genesis. Granted: It's a really important part of the story. How can Abraham's line move forward unless the promised child can marry and extend the family tree? But it's surprising that God saw fit to give it so much space, especially when we would love to have a lot more information about other parts of the narrative! Why so much detail here? One likely reason: Since Isaac is a precursor of Christ, then his wife is analogous to the Church—a special bride indeed!

The servant is unnamed, but is usually assumed to be Eliezer from Genesis 15:2. (His anonymity allows us to avoid distraction in the text.) This is an "arranged" marriage, but it is accomplished by a vibrant combination of God's providence and human effort. The servant takes an oath by placing his hand on Abraham's inner thigh—near his femur (the strongest bone in the body) or on his "family" (connecting this to sex and procreation). Not wanting a Canaanite wife for Isaac, Abraham looks to distant relatives for an appropriate spouse. Even though this part of the family presumably was not walking closely with God (if at all), it was an improvement over the local options. The 500-mile trip communicates the seriousness of Abraham's concerns.[4]

Why doesn't Abraham make the trip himself? He's an old man and this is a long, difficult trip. (Then again, he does crank out a bunch of other children in Genesis 25!) Why doesn't he send Isaac? In 24:6–8, we see that he's worried about Isaac remaining there and abandoning the promised land. And maybe he has greater trust in the older servant's judgment about such things. After all, in matters of love and marriage: older, sober, and wiser can easily trump younger, excited, and naive.

---

3. This angle is quite similar to Jeremiah 32 when the prophet buys land in Jerusalem while Israel is in Babylonian exile.

4. This reminds me of the song by The Proclaimers. The servant walked 500 miles and then "walked 500 more" just to get Isaac a wife before he probably "fell down at [Abraham's] door."

The servant brings camels, indicative of wealth and the need for many people to (safely) make such a grueling and risky trip. He prays wonderfully for success and grace—and asks for a sign. He prays for wonderful attributes in Isaac's wife-to-be: hard-working, going the extra mile, humility, hospitality to strangers and even animals, and a heart to serve. In other words, this is about character (and hopefully faith) at least as much as kinship. As we instruct our children in seeking spouses, we want them to find the right kind of person—and more important, to *be* the right kind of person. "Faith" is one important aspect, but there are others.

God answers the servant's prayer quickly with an amazing providence. A grand-niece of Abraham responds to the call. She has everything that the servant requested—and she's beautiful to boot! Rebekah's response is fetching at many levels—in word and deed, in diligence and speed. She gives water to the servant, but goes above and beyond by caring for the animals too. Long story short: The servant and her brother Laban work out the details; Rebekah assents; and the marriage is on. (Laban will play a big role in the next generation too. Stay tuned!) As her father-in-law-to-be, Rebekah will also "leave and go," entering God's plans for the patriarchs—and ultimately, the lineage of Jesus Christ. In a nutshell, the marriage is arranged through Abraham's preparation, his servant's execution, and Rebekah's willingness—all directed by God and motivated by faith. It is another great example of God's provision and their participation.

With this key task completed, Abraham exits the stage early in Genesis 25—an "old man, full of years," buried by both Isaac and Ishmael, as the brothers reunite. But ironically, Abraham lived another 35 years after Isaac's wedding. Abraham made his plans as if he was in his last days, but his last days lasted a long time. It's easy to remember the pivotal historical events in Abraham's life. However, these decades underline the importance of persevering faithfulness. Most of us have key moments in our lives, but most of our days are everyday. May we be found faithful in both the mundane and the momentous. Prepare for the great things that may come your way—and be faithful in the little things.

WRAPPING UP...

The concept of faith goes far beyond "religious" belief and is a surprisingly common aspect of life. One can see it most easily with historical claims, when their past-ness makes them (far) more difficult to assess. We can't prove that George Washington was the first president of the United States. But there's a lot of evidence for it. Did Americans land on the moon? Was Lincoln more concerned about slavery or tariffs at the start of the Civil War? Did Oswald have a co-conspirator when he shot JFK? We also see this play out in the scientific realm—where we're in the present tense, but matters are complex. Is the earth flat? Did Covid-19 begin in a Chinese lab? Does the flu vaccine help much? In moderation, are dark chocolate, red wine, and coffee good or bad for my health?

What about the miraculous—for example, in the Bible? Did God unleash ten plagues against Egypt to make Himself known to Moses, Pharaoh, Israel, and Egypt—and to set His people free from bondage? Did a big fish swallow Jonah? Did Elijah and Elisha perform miraculous deeds through the power of God? Did God resurrect Christ from the dead? Here, we see a combination of the historical and the highly unusual. Some people have a bias against the supernatural—and so, are predisposed to discount or disbelieve miracles. And when the events are historical, the evidence becomes less powerful. But what are the alternative explanations and are they any more compelling?

Finally, there are elements of faith in everyday matters. Are hand sanitizer and soap effective against "invisible" germs?[5] Will the bridge support my car as I drive across it? Will these leftovers make me sick? Will my spouse love me 'til death do us part? Will diet and exercise make me healthier? Will spiritual disciplines such as giving, serving, and praying really help to transform me into Christ-likeness?

In all of these things, logic, reason and evidence are all desirable. But it's actually rare when we can prove or know something with 100% certainty. In such cases, examine the evidence; avoid credulity; use the mind God gave you; and make the necessary moves through faith to the most reasonable inferences. In the case of theology, the most compelling conclusion is to believe in a good and great God who knows what's best and wants what's best for us. The amazing faith of Abraham helps us see the goodness and greatness of God.

---

5. I like the joke about "anti-bacterial" soap: "I thought anti-bacterial was already part of the deal."

9

Passion vs. Apathy

COMPLETE TEXT: GENESIS 25:19–28:9
RECOMMENDED READING: GENESIS 25:19–34, 27:1–28:5
POTENTIAL MEMORY VERSES: GENESIS 25:23, 25:28, 25:34

WE CAN BE APATHETIC about things that should get our passion. We can invest too much in silly or marginal things. We can be lazy, despite having much to offer. We can be zealous with little knowledge. We can be passionate about the wrong things. Matt Emmons is a world-class American shooter with a world championship and three Olympic medals. But he is best known for hitting the bullseye of the wrong target and blowing a huge lead on his last shot, missing out on another Olympic gold medal in 2004. Even perfection if aimed at the wrong target will not allow you to reach the desired end.

In the Old Testament, pagans chase false gods and Israel fails to be holy, idly following pagans into idolatry. Kings depend on their military strength rather than God. So far in Genesis, we've seen a version of apathy and passion in the silence of Adam and the violence of Cain; a passion for evil in the times between Cain and Noah; zeal from Abraham and Sarah to pursue the promised child with Hagar; and apathy from Lot with respect to the problems of Sodom. Do we care about the right things for the right reasons—and pursue them rightly?

Passion for the wrong things will often take you to a dead end or a cul-de-sac where you can turn around. But apathy will take you nowhere—and since it often doesn't look as bad, it can be easy to settle there. Still, we see the downsides of apathy in everyday life. Who wants a tepid drink? Who doesn't recoil from a limp handshake? Who enjoys people who are (too) nice—who never have an opinion or a passion? Elie Wiesel is often credited with the quote that "the opposite of love is not hate, but indifference." In contrast, Theodore Roosevelt said, "Far better it is to dare mighty things, to win great triumphs, even though checkered by failure, than to rank with those poor spirits who neither enjoy much nor suffer much, because they live in the gray twilight that knows neither victory nor defeat."[1]

Why is cold often better than lukewarm in the divine economy? Apathy is a counterfeit for certain virtues, but leaves little to work with. Lukewarm often looks more respectable, but usually results in hypocrisy and devolves into other problems. Lukewarm avoids prospects for change. If you're cold, you're more likely to move toward the heat. It's easier to restrain a fanatic than to resurrect a corpse. This speaks to the downsides of "cultural Christianity." In contrast, think of those who convert after trying to disprove God and the Bible (e.g., C.S. Lewis, G.K. Chesterton, Lee Strobel). God wants fire or even ice over tepid.

We see this in Scripture. Consider Joshua and Caleb in opposition to the ten spies in Numbers 13–14; the ministry of John the Baptist; the prodigal son and the older son in Luke 15; the prevalence of profligate sinners in the ministry of Christ; Paul and Peter in contrast to the respectability of Judas; Job, Habakkuk, Moses, and the Psalmists in their passionate wrestlings with God; Christ saying that he will vomit out the lukewarm Laodiceans (Rev 3:16).

Now, we revisit apathy and passion through two famous stories from the narrative of Jacob and Esau: the birthright in Genesis 25 and the blessing in Genesis 27. The birthright includes the leadership and spiritual parts of the inheritance—for Abraham's descendants, an opportunity and a responsibility to live out God's calling to their grandfather. The blessing is the material part of the inheritance—a double portion of the wealth to be carried into the following generations. Both were typically granted to the oldest son. But as we've already seen in Genesis, the Lord rarely favors the firstborn, working against social norms. Cain and Ishmael were firstborn; Seth, Noah, Abraham, and Isaac were not. What will happen in this generation?

---

1. This quote is attributed to Roosevelt from a speech ("The Strenuous Life") delivered to the Hamilton Club in Chicago on April 10, 1899.

PASSION VS. APATHY

In between these two stories, Isaac will repeat Abraham's chief sin in the first half of Genesis 26, lying about his wife to a king. The patriarchs' penchant for deceit will continue the sins of father Abraham through Isaac, his wife Rebekah, and their two sons. Isaac will also exhibit passivity with his sons, falling far short of God's plans for fathers—as per Abraham and circumcision. And Isaac will introduce a new sin that will bear bad fruit in this generation and the next: parental favoritism. Hey, it's not all bad news about Isaac. In the second half of Genesis 26, he will exhibit perseverance and work as a peacemaker in working with the locals.

MY TWO SONS

We're introduced to twin brothers Esau and Jacob in the "account" that begins in 25:19. The story opens with 20 years of barrenness (25:20,26)—a long period, as with Abraham/Sarah in the previous generation and Jacob/Rachel to follow. Isaac prays for his wife and there are no recorded complaints from Rebekah. (This contrasts with Abraham's lack of recorded prayer, noisy complaining by Sarah and Rachel, and the use of concubines in the other two generations.) From the narrative, the prayer seems to be answered quickly. As with Abraham and Sarah, it was clear to Isaac and Rebekah that the fruit of the womb was a matter of God's provision and their participation.

The twins jostle in the womb—a foreshadowing of the wrestling to come. (It's a pre-natal version of the sibling rivalries that dominate the narrative in Genesis!) The rumbling in her belly is unusual enough to evoke Rebekah's prayer—whether out of concern or curiosity. She asks a personal question about the present and receives a political answer about the future. (Abraham received revelation in the previous generation, but Rebekah receives it here.) The interpretation is that the twins will represent two nations—with the younger as the stronger. (Again, God does not choose the older child.) What sort of strength? It's not clear here—and as it turns out, it won't be determined by the usual worldly metrics.

Is this predestination for her to understand as life continues—or is this counsel that she is to pursue through her own means? Did she talk to Isaac about this? If not, why not? (Is this "the silence of Rebekah"?) If so, why didn't Isaac listen? For one thing, it is often challenging to handle indirect revelation given to others. ("Hey, God told me X, Y, and Z." Uhh . . .) But Isaac already has some experience with this in relationship with

God and his father! As the story unfolds, it can be easy to use hindsight to critique Rebekah (as with Abraham, Sarah, Hagar, and the promised child). But Leon Kass is helpful here: Rebekah "knows, from her troubled pregnancy, that something is up . . . she seems to hear, 'Look, you face a difficult choice, between two alternatives: only one of your two sons will be right for the task. A choice must be made, whether you like it or not, and *you* are the one who is going to have to make it.'"[2]

Esau is hairy and "red" (a Hebrew term related to the earth). Both imply that he's born like a man—at least in a worldly sense. But of course, that's not a good sign biblically. He will become "a man's man" who is uninterested in the things of God—not a good fit for transmitting the faith to the next generation. He looks stronger, seeming to exhibit physical strength by emerging first. But Jacob is ambitious and manipulative. He is in pursuit of the firstborn's blessing from the beginning, grasping Esau's heel—as though struggling even to be out of the womb first!

Their differences widen as they get older. Esau is a hunter; Jacob is a momma's boy. Not surprisingly, parental favoritisms and loyalties emerge, probably encouraging the differences. As we'll see, Isaac prefers the wrong son for bad reasons. But Rebekah's motives are not explained explicitly. Is it bias since Jacob helps around the house? Is it based on her divinely-revealed knowledge of who *would* inherit the birthright/blessing from the prophecy? Likely, it stems from her belief that Jacob *should* inherit them, given the character of both sons.

TRADING THE BIRTHRIGHT FOR A BOWL OF SOUP

In the story of the birthright, Esau is famished and willing to trade something of eternal significance for some bread and a bowl of soup. We're told that he "despised his birthright." (25:34) Matthew Henry compares the food problems of Esau and Eve: "As dear a morsel as ever was eaten since the forbidden fruit."[3] Fittingly, in Hebrews 12:16, Esau is described as "godless"—uninterested in the things of God. The birthright was determined by God's sovereignty and announced by God's prophecy, but here it is also achieved through Jacob's effort and Esau's apathy.

We'll see later that Esau seems to be more moral than Jacob—a "good guy," but in combination with independence from God and apathy toward

---

2. Kass, *Beginning of Wisdom*, 380.
3. Henry, *Commentary*, 125.

Passion vs. Apathy

God. (In 26:34–35, Esau provides more evidence of the latter, marrying two pagan women and bringing grief to his parents.) We see this a lot in our world: "good people" who are indifferent to God. Why would such people *expect* to go to Heaven? They cannot be good enough to merit salvation and eliminate the need for God's grace and justification through Christ. Why would such people *want* to go to Heaven? If they're uninterested in worship and being with God's people now, why would they want an eternity of that? Sounds like that'd be Hell for them!

And how are such people able to be "good"? Because of God's grace in their lives—by temperament, genetics, good parenting, etc. As such, how can they take credit for what they've largely been gifted? In this, C.S. Lewis compares the Gospel to toothpaste. He notes that a toothpaste company would never promise that all users would have whiter teeth than those who don't use it. It would merely promise that using its toothpaste would make your teeth *whiter* over time. Some people are born with whiter teeth—through no credit of their own. The same is true, to some extent, with character and behavior.[4]

Meanwhile, Jacob receives something of great value to him. As an economist, I get excited about this example of "voluntary, mutually beneficial trade"—the norm in economic markets and everyday behavior where both parties exchange something of lower worth (to them) for something of higher value (to them). One might argue that Esau was facing monopoly power since he was hungry, but he exaggerated his hunger; he had options (with a bit of patience and work); and he never expressed any regret about the trade. One might critique Jacob for not being more charitable. But the larger reality is that Esau is simply not interested in a thing of great value in the divine economy.

Don't miss the other good news here: This problem is resolved without violence or fratricide. Abel and Cain didn't do nearly as well—and Joseph will be badly mistreated by his brothers in the next generation. The bottom line: Eyeing God's promised blessing, Jacob takes action and obtains the birthright. This may illustrate why Jacob is the better fit, but it clearly shows why Esau is not the primary son to carry the faith and the promises of God into the future.

---

4. Lewis, *Mere Christianity*, Book 4, Chapter 10.

Gen Men

DECEPTION TO GAIN THE BLESSING

In Genesis 27, the second shoe drops, but this is a more challenging story. We're reintroduced to Isaac—now old and blind: a foreshadowing of Isaac's inability to discern in the narrative. Worried about dying soon (although he will live another 40+ years), he decides to give his chief blessing (along with the double portion of his material wealth) to Esau. Isaac sends Esau out to get fresh game—to look for an excuse to have a good meal and commemorate the moment. (This is also a great literary device that builds tension!)

Compared to Abraham, none of the players seem impressive, but God will work with flawed people to move His sovereign purposes forward. Where's Jacob? Traditionally, he would be blessed at the same time, albeit receiving less. And if Jacob has the birthright, he should receive the primary blessing. Does Isaac not know about the prophecy to Rebekah? Does he know that Esau sold the birthright for a pittance? Is this a cultural reflex from Isaac or a function of his affection and bias for Esau?

Isaac can't see, but Rebekah can hear and is privy to his agenda. Her favoritism and/or divine perspective will trump his blindness. She devises a plan to cook a meal and get around Isaac's plan. What to make of this? Is she pursuing God's best but inappropriately—working for what God has already promised (as we saw with Abraham, Sarah, and Hagar)? Or is this a bold, decisive, courageous thing that must be done when no other good choices are seemingly available?

The narrative does not include editorial comments from the Lord, leaving us to wrestle with this vital question. What does it look like to depend on the Lord, to live with God's provision and our participation—neither laying in a hammock nor doing things in our own strength? The ends never justify the means, but what were her other choices? Silent submission, prayer, and waiting on the Lord? Try to persuade Isaac about God's plan; tell him about Esau's trade with Jacob; and remind him of Esau's character? Is she taking "reasonable" steps in a patriarchal society with a blind husband who favors the son not favored by God—in response to the prophecy she has received?

Jacob submits to his mom's plan and then plays a starring role in this heart-pounding drama. (Dressed in his costume, this is the first recorded Halloween outfit.) We don't see Jacob feeling any guilt; his only fear is getting caught. (If you're worried about getting busted, it's wise to reconsider your actions and your motives!) Jacob's name means deceit and grasping

PASSION VS. APATHY

the heel. With his first recorded lie, he deceitfully makes a grab for the blessing, with a big assist from mom.

Isaac is suspicious, but is ultimately overcome by the ruse and his own limitations. He is deceived by four of his senses and not trusting his fifth sense (hearing) or relying on his "sixth sense" (his faith in God—no prayer is recorded). The difference between Jacob's voice and hands (27:22) is a good picture of hypocrisy: Say one thing but do another. (Jacob's kiss and betrayal are also types of what will happen to Jesus with Judas and Peter.) Isaac's blessing to Jacob is comprised of prosperity, power, and position, but there's nothing on land, descendants, covenant, or Abraham—and there's only a generic reference to God (*Elohim* instead of *Yahweh*). Not an impressive effort from the promised son of the faithful father Abraham, but it will be enough to move the ball down the field of faith and family.

Esau returns, prepares the meal, and gets ready for the big moment. (He does all of the work, while Jacob only plays a part.) But the truth is soon revealed. Isaac can't rescind the greater blessing. His anger is interesting: Is he merely upset at being defrauded? Is he kicking himself for not taking his suspicions more seriously? Is he frustrated with his own blindness and ignorance? He offers Esau a good but lesser blessing instead; Esau is blessed but not "chosen." And Jacob has lived up to his name. He's not much of a man at this point, but he does want the things of God—and God can work with that passion much more than with Esau's apathy.

NOW WHAT?

The aftermath is sobering. Where sibling rivalry was quelled with the birthright trade, it is stoked here with the blessing fraud. In what looks like a sequel to Cain and Abel, Esau threatens to kill Jacob—and to seize the birthright and blessing by force. We wonder if the faith of Abraham can indeed be perpetuated. Rebekah hears about this and goes back to work on Isaac, providing good advice and pointing her blind husband to a good solution—the Bible's only reported words between the couple.

Her idea: Jacob needs to go back to the homeland to find an appropriate wife. He should leave for "a while"—a term meaning a few days. But it will turn out to be 20 years! (In a sense, Rebekah sacrifices a son.) Isaac agrees. Ironically, he wants Jacob to get a wife like Rebekah—even after this (or maybe, because of this)! Meanwhile, Esau's wife choices are unfortunate, but also provide more evidence that the divine path forward is better with Jacob.[5]

On his way out of town, Jacob receives an even better blessing from Isaac—perhaps because he knows that Jacob is receiving the blessing this time and he wants to encourage the perpetuation of the faith. This blessing is more extensive and God-centered—with a reference to God as *El Shaddai* (as well as the more-generic *Elohim*), promising prosperity and population, mentioning the promised land, and echoing God's covenant with Abraham.[6]

Although Jacob gets the blessing, the costs are huge. It tears up the family; his brother wants to kill him; he will never see his mom again; he flees home and is exiled for two decades; and he will endure some painful and ironic deception by Uncle Laban. In many ways, his life will parallel Moses: a decisive and morally-murky moment that changes everything, but also points to future greatness in the Kingdom.

Again, what to do with all of this? God wants faith. But here, we have Rebekah and Jacob using their senses, strategies, and human strengths to inappropriately pursue the blessing. Was the Lord happy with any of this? Surely, He was pleased enough or He would have intervened. The right man has the birthright—and Jacob is a mess, but he is zealous for the things of God. Jacob has a long way to go (geographically and spiritually), but the process can continue. In any case, God's providence continues to be in control and His plan keeps moving forward—within the exercise of their free will.

ABIMELECH II AND DIG ANOTHER WELL

The first episode in Genesis 26 occurs before the birthright story in Genesis 25.[7] The story also establishes a parallel between Abraham and Isaac, since Abraham used the same strategy twice, including once with Abimelech (probably this man's father and perhaps a dynastic title like Pharoah). It also invites comparison between Abraham and Isaac on the "world stage."

---

5. Esau will improve his harem a bit in 28:8–9, marrying some women from Ishmael's line.

6. Isaac's last recorded word is his father's name.

7. Having the twins with them would have made the deception far more difficult—and they're not mentioned at all. So, this is probably placed here as a literary tool to stretch out the resolution of the tension created by the birthright story.

Passion vs. Apathy

The arc of God's story with Abraham and his descendants is never meant to be purely personal, but to impact the world—here, through "international" politics. Compared to Abraham, Isaac is a lesser man; he only has this one chapter of Genesis devoted to him; he never leaves Canaan; he has no great adventure; he tries to imitate Abraham here and fails. But Isaac still flourishes and ultimately succeeds personally, politically, and in perpetuating the faith.

Food continues to play a huge part in the narrative—both in the sense of tying this to Abraham's similar adventure (12:10,13) and in linking this to poor food choices in the surrounding stories (Esau's hunger in 25:30 and the pivotal meal in Genesis 27). God intervenes to prevent Isaac from leaving—the first time that God addresses Isaac. (Abraham did the same by arranging for Isaac's wife in Genesis 24. It's interesting that Abraham and Jacob both end up in Egypt, but this is apparently not a good idea for Isaac!) To his credit, like Abraham, Isaac submits with unquestioning obedience to God.

God reiterates the now-familiar promises: His presence, descendants, land, covenant, and being a blessing to others. (It's always good to remember God's faithfulness and promises during trials!) After this, we're perhaps a bit surprised to see Isaac try the sister/wife gambit. This provides a good picture of the impact of a father on his children, as this sin goes generational. Interestingly, the lie is deepened here—from a half-lie about a half-sister to a full-blown lie about someone who is no sister at all.

Perhaps Rebekah and Jacob "learn" lying from Isaac. Out of this family background, Esau will emerge as godless but moral; Jacob will emerge as a believer with baggage. Is this cause and effect—or just correlation? When do our sins and behaviors impact others, especially within families? (Abimelech handled this much better in Genesis 20 than his son does here. Should we draw the same lesson from both families?) Did Abraham (and Sarah) share their failures? Or maybe Isaac thinks that this worked out OK for Dad, so why not? In any case, to cut Isaac some slack: It does become much more difficult to do the right thing when you perceive that your life is on the line and it's so tempting to take things into your own hands!

But Isaac is not careful in concealing the fraud—affectionate with his wife in broad daylight, in front of the king—and Abimelech catches him in the lie. The narrative again depicts Isaac as driven by strong physical appetites that he doesn't control well. Abimelech confronts him but is merciful. The Lord seems to immediately bless Isaac, as if He was waiting until the sin was in the open. In any case, Isaac's renewed prosperity allows him to return home.

Unfortunately, Isaac's success leads to jealousy and the locals harm him by filling in the wells that his father had dug.[8] They don't ask to share or buy the water; they don't want to learn how to dig a well; they don't tell him to move along and steal his wells. They just fill them in! Passive-aggressive and child-like, but also a serious act where water was such a crucial issue. Jonathan Sacks sees all of this as the origins of anti-Semitism—persecution of a successful minority group, driven by envy, deepening into hate and even violence.[9]

Abimelech asks him to move away. Isaac assents, digs more wells, and continues to deal with opposition. In each case, he never protests and just moves on until he's not being bothered anymore.[10] Is Isaac acquiescing or a peacemaker? This is certainly different than Abraham's willingness to fight when necessary, his diplomacy with leaders, and his "bargaining" with God over Sodom. In any case, Isaac's persistence, his faith in God, and his turning the other cheek are all commendable. Like Christ (again), Isaac didn't resist when his own rights had been violated.

A FEW MORE THOUGHTS ON ISAAC—AND US

There are five narratives in the Bible with Isaac as a key player: his faithful cooperation in the binding and near-sacrifice (Genesis 22); God leading Abraham's servant to find Isaac's wife (Genesis 24); Isaac's reprise of the sister/wife deception with Abimelech (first half of Genesis 26); his peaceful and persistent response to the recurring problems with the wells (second half of Genesis 26); and his largely passive role in the Isaac/Esau brouhaha (Genesis 27–28).

Isaac is the product of his parents and God's grace. He's not as sharp as his father, but he is ultimately able to pass on his father's faith to the next generation with some help from his wife. He is duped in the climactic story, but he finishes the episode well. He was faithful in his love for Rebekah and his persistence with the wells. Jonathan Sacks says that Isaac "represents

---

8. Given Abimelech's oath in 21:31–32, this provides useful foreshadowing of Egypt forgetting Joseph and abusing the Israelites later.

9. Sacks, *Covenant and Conversation*, 160–162.

10. Paul Overstreet has an old country song on this called "Dig Another Well." Check it out!

the faith of persistence, the courage of continuity . . . So it is with all great achievement: one part originality, nine parts persistence."[11]

In this, Isaac is a lot like most of us. We might aspire to the greatness of Abraham, but we might not have it in us—either by temperament or by context. Still, we can always strive to be faithful. Ultimately, Isaac was honored through a frequent title for God in the Old Testament: "the God of Abraham, Isaac, and Jacob." We're told in Hebrews 11:20 that Isaac acted "by faith." The application for us? Faith does not mean perfection, greatness, or a lack of blindness. God graciously works with all abilities and levels of success. He wants our trust, our love, and our perseverance.

If Isaac is a mixed bag in terms of faith and life—and if Jacob is a work (very) much in progress—then Esau represents those who may be impressive by worldly standards, but are ultimately uninterested in the things of God. We can be passionate for the wrong things. We can be passionate for the right things but pursue them improperly. We can bumble and fumble our way through life. But in the divine economy, our highest priority should be to avoid apathy toward God. Life is too long—and the prospects of eternal life are too great—to treat a good and great God with indifference and a loving Savior with a wave of the hand.

When Elijah challenges the prophets of Baal in I Kings 18, he calls on the people to get off the fence, to make a choice, to commit to God or the available idols. Despite the evidence, they are unwilling to voice a decision. As frustrating as mistakes can be, as ridiculous as profligate sinners and rampant pagans can be, as troublesome as evil can be, there is a strong case to be made that lukewarm mediocrity is the biggest problem of all. Let's be zealous in avoiding apathy and pursuing the things of God properly.

WRAPPING UP . . .

From the field of "Public Choice" economics, we know that all people are "rationally ignorant and apathetic" about politics and public policy. Most people have very little knowledge about either; a few people know quite a bit about a few topics. Voting is based on political party, a candidate's popularity (through yard signs and advertising), or support/opposition for a policy or two. But all of this ignorance is completely rational. Why would one invest much time and energy into something where one has so little to offer: a vote and maybe a bit of money to support a candidate?

11. Sacks, *Covenant and Conversation*, 164–65.

Related to this: Few people have a coherent political philosophy. As a result, there are few (real) liberals or conservatives. These may be convenient labels for political purposes or as a simplistic way to describe a complex world. But they have little consistent objective basis. For decades, few "conservatives" have vehemently opposed massive federal government spending and debt. And in recent years, there have been few "liberals" who care much about free speech and oppose military interventionism.

Ironically, rational ignorance about politics is often supplemented by inordinate passion, resulting in what Bryan Caplan has labeled "*irrational ignorance.*" Some people spend time on politics as a hobby—and typically, with a lot of bias. They read views they agree with; they talk and listen in an echo chamber. And they imagine that they know much more than they actually know. As a microeconomist who focuses on public policy, I've thought, taught, and written on public policy for decades. I've run for Congress three times and written a book on Christianity, social policy, and economic policy—trying to marry faith, ethics, and public policy. I know (much) more than most people, but I still know so little—again, out of rational ignorance.

Inside or outside of politics: Knowing we're ignorant is one thing. If so, we'll proceed with appropriate humility. *Not* knowing we're ignorant is entirely another thing. Add zeal to this sort of ignorance—and you end up with dogmatism, legalism, and judgmentalism. Folks can imagine that they know much more than they do, castigating the ignorant while being ironically and perversely ignorant themselves.

Thankfully, in our private lives, the costs and benefits of learning and taking action align with more impressive opinions and decision-making—about cars and pizza, goods and services, the material and the spiritual. Since our decisions in those realms impact us directly and significantly, we have a much stronger incentive to invest in knowledge and wiser decisions. For non-Christians, this should result in embracing good theology rather than the inferior theology they hold at present. For Christians, this should be a close walk and obedience to a good and great God, choosing the costs of discipleship over the greater costs of non-discipleship.

10

Cleverness and Perseverance

COMPLETE TEXT: GENESIS 28:10–31:55
RECOMMENDED READING: 28:10–15, 29:15–30, 30:25–31:2
POTENTIAL MEMORY VERSES: 28:12, 29:20, 29:35

Do you have a favorite life hack? It's snowing outside as I write this. We like to use a tarp on our cars and front steps to prevent them from being covered by frost, snow, and ice. In the kitchen? Use your blender to clean itself with soap and water. Use Bloemer's base and Ro-tel to make excellent chili easily. In the home? Store bed sheets inside their pillowcase and use a clothespin to hold a nail you're hammering.

Life hacks range from conventional wisdom to unconventional creativity, from the real thing to wives' tales. Batteries don't last longer with refrigeration. Charcoal doesn't help to whiten your teeth. Using Gatorade and an onion to recharge your phone? Nope. But sometimes the line between truth and fiction is blurry. Did it just work in that one case? Did something else supplement its effectiveness? Will it only help in a certain context?

The attraction to using hacks stems from a legitimate desire to be efficient—with doses of novelty and cleverness on the side. But sometimes, hacks derive from a zeal to be lazy, a passion to pursue short cuts, a desire to avoid the determination that would help us be successful in the long run. Don't use toilet paper rolls to prop up your phone; just spend $5 on a cheap piece of plastic built to do the job. Don't rely on AI to get through high school and college; do the work to build your knowledge, enhance your skills, and learn how to learn. Don't fall for get-rich-quick schemes; watch your budget and put your savings in aggressive but reasonable investments.

Many people finance all of their cars and use 30-year mortgages for houses—and then wonder why it's hard to build wealth. We want to read more often, but we're on our phones rather than in a book after 9 PM. Folks buy $6 cups of coffee daily and then can't figure out why it's so difficult to donate money to church and charities. We don't purposefully invest much in our discipleship with Jesus, but then a decade later, we're somehow surprised that we don't know much more and can't love any better.

The largest part of Jacob's narrative is his 20 years away from home. In these two decades, he deals with his crafty uncle; finds the love of his life (and gets tricked into an extra wife); grows his family (with plenty of drama along the way); and builds impressive wealth (despite Laban's efforts to defraud him). Jacob will become a successful man by worldly standards, while growing in his faith in God. We'll see him exhibit cleverness and practice perseverance—and along the way, we'll look to apply aspects of his life to our own.

CLIMBING THE LADDER

Jacob leaves home to escape Esau and to find a wife in Haran. He goes out virtually empty-handed, in contrast to Abraham's servant who was loaded when he went on his mission to find Isaac's wife. Jacob the schemer will apparently need his wits and wiles to survive and succeed. But what has this approach gotten him so far? He has the birthright and the blessing, but what good are those when you're alone; you're forced to leave everything behind; and someone wants to kill you?

After a long day of travel (40–50 miles), Jacob ends up with a hard bed and a harder pillow. His dreams include a stairway or ladder from Heaven to Earth, with angels going both ways and God standing at the top.[1] Why the ethereal escalator? The movement of the angels was a sign that the Lord would be Jacob's God—not the distant god of deism and detachment, but a personal God who cares for Jacob. Not just the God of Grandpa and Dad, but available to him as well. As Jacob leaves home, his journey is

---

1. It is possible to translate this as God standing beside Jacob. This would change some of the interpretation and applications.

Cleverness and Perseverance

both geographical and spiritual. The Lord was providing a constant means of access and an invitation to communication, counsel, assistance, and protection.

For us, this is a picture of prayer with God. It's also a type of Jesus Christ, with one foot in Heaven and another on Earth—and the only means by which we can have access to the Father (John 14:6, I Tim 2:5). And it's a model for sanctification and ministry. We "ascend" to God and listen to His word, learning what to do—and then we "descend" to the world to do it. There is movement along the ladder, indicative of progress and growth.

Why does the Lord speak to Jacob *that* evening? It immediately follows the acquisition of the blessing from Isaac—despite the thievery and trickery—a quick, gracious, credible confirmation from God. As will happen again 20 years later, these divine moments are on the road and in between pivotal events. Jacob is in solitude, away from standard busyness and distraction. In particular, this is his *first* night away from home. One can imagine his apprehension about the past and the future—what lay behind and ahead. Maybe he is at the end of his rope—desperate, exhausted, vulnerable (especially as a momma's boy). He is away from home, but not away from the Lord; Jacob is by himself, but he is not alone.

Jacob also receives a blessing, reiterating what Abraham and Isaac have heard in the transmission of the covenant: land, descendants, protection, a general grace through him to everyone, and even an allusion to Christ. Jacob learns about the Lord and worships accordingly. He also makes a conditional vow—as if bargaining with God (albeit for himself vs. Grandpa Abraham bargaining for strangers). For now, God is only the God of Abraham and Isaac; this will be remedied later. Jacob will explicitly wrestle with God on his way home—and in between, as he deals with Uncle Laban. But for now, we're reminded that it's not enough to be Abraham's grandson or Isaac's son; Jacob needs a personal relationship with God.

PASSION AND PERSEVERANCE

It's unusual to have a lot of passion and perseverance. And it's sad to see people with neither! One or the other? Sure, that's common. But the temperament that goes with passion often lacks the ability to persevere—and those who persevere are rarely known for their passion. Jacob shows us both in Genesis 29.

After his sweet dream, Jacob continues along, arrives, and immediately starts pursuing a wife—his participation within the population portion of God's gracious provision. He ends up at a well—a common meeting place and one often associated biblically with God's blessings. As in the account with Abraham's servant and Rebekah, God's direct presence will only be implied by what looks like a ton of Providence in this encounter.

Soon, we're introduced to Rachel as she is introduced to Jacob. She is a shepherd—unusual for a woman. Jacob is excited about Rachel, but the sheep are also encouraging as a sign of wealth. Faced with a large stone to protect the well, he engages in a feat of strength and kindness—simply to help, or more likely, to impress her. He follows in his mother Rebekah's footsteps of proactive, energetic service (Gen 24). His kiss is culturally forward but appropriate. Then, he weeps. This might surprise us, until we imagine the joy and relief he must have felt to see anybody, but particularly family—and perhaps to see God's promises being fulfilled so soon.

Uncle Laban hurries to the scene, probably imagining a profitable sequel to Rebekah and Isaac decades earlier. But Jacob doesn't have the goods. Laban makes an ironic reference to flesh and blood—a biological reference to be sure. But as it turns out, he and Jacob are also similar in terms of character and cleverness. In this fateful moment with Rachel and Laban, Jacob has met his match in terms of love and deceit.

Jacob works without conditions for a month. So far, he's probably just paying for room and board—and repaying their hospitality. But then Laban brings up wages. What's the long-term arrangement going to be? Is Jacob more like a servant or family? Is he an insider or an outsider? He can't afford the bride price and he's hooked on one of Laban's daughters. Laban holds the upper hand—and will play it accordingly.

The narrator now describes the women. Leah's name connects to cattle, while Rachel's relates to sheep. Cows are more valuable than sheep—not surprising since Leah is the older daughter. These are not the most flattering names, especially by today's standards. Both names indicate Laban's interest in wealth—and his willingness to treat his daughters like livestock. In terms of appearances, Rachel is "lovely in form and beautiful"—at least subjectively (and blindingly) attractive in Jacob's eyes.

The description of Leah is more complex. The key descriptor is that she had "weak eyes," but it's not clear what the Hebrew term means. It's common to imagine Leah as homely, but she was probably attractive like Sarah and Rebekah—just not as easy on the eyes as Rachel. It's tempting

Cleverness and Perseverance

for moderns to interpret "cow" as a reference to Leah's weight, but this is unlikely given the impending case of mistaken identity. It's more likely that her eyes were the thing you noticed about her—for better or worse.[2] In any case, we're left with a great irony: Her eyes may be weak, but Jacob's (and Isaac's) are far weaker! And it turns out that Leah can see better than her better-looking sister.

Jacob offers to work seven years for Rachel as a dowry. This is double the typical price and a long-term contract—certainly no bowl of soup! Whereas Isaac benefited tremendously from the wealth of his father, Jacob will have to earn most everything. But we're told that the seven years "seemed like only a few days" to him—one of the Bible's most beautiful lines and probably its most romantic. Madly in love, he is blind to both work and time. As Leon Kass puts it: "No poet has ever spoken better of love's power to inspire devotion, to lighten hardships, and to defy the ordinary course of time."[3]

The time comes for the marriage and Laban substitutes Leah for Rachel.[4] How can this be?! Well, too much booze, darkness, sisterly similarities between the two in voice and body, a veil (as in 24:65), and the traditional wedding night silence serve to do the trick. The ironies jump off the page. Isaac and now Jacob are victims of "false identity"; the trickster has been tricked. He had deceived his father about brothers; here, he is deceived by his father-in-law about sisters. He had cheated his brother with his mother; here, he is cheated by his mother's brother. Isaac expected the older and got the younger; Jacob expected the younger and got the older. As Jacob with Isaac, Uncle Laban takes advantage of Jacob's (sexual) appetite and his blindness. Poetic justice and perhaps even divine retribution are achieved through Laban's craftiness. Jacob shouldn't be too upset. But how easy it is for us to be angry at injustices done to us while closing our eyes to injustices we do to others.

Was Leah active or passive in this deceit? Laban presumably instructed Leah—as Rebekah had with Jacob—but all are culpable for their participation (assuming Leah had much of a choice in the matter). Why would Leah do this? Perhaps she was merely compliant to tradition and her father.

---

2. The Hebrew term can be translated as weak, tired, delicate, or sensitive. Leah reveals herself to be sensitive as the narrative unfolds.

3. Kass, *Beginning of Wisdom*, 425.

4. Jacob's failure to name Rachel in 29:21 makes Laban's deception easier to execute and rationalize.

Maybe she thought she could win Jacob's love. Maybe she was jealous of Rachel or worried about ever getting married.

Laban provides a weak explanation. The "custom" was at best, local—and if so, he should have mentioned it earlier! Maybe he thought Leah would have been married off by then, so this became his Plan B. Laban offers a new deal: seven more years of labor for the wife Jacob actually wanted. He is drawn into a dilemma: Stick with the lesser wife or pursue polygamy. Choosing the latter, we can't be too excited about the likely dysfunction of the household-to-be. Two wives would be difficult enough in any case. But here, we know there's going to be favoritism and that can't go well. Granted, the previous generations have struggled to have children. So, two wives might be helpful, but earthly advantages have not been much use in the divine economy so far.

MARRIAGE, FAMILY, AND CHILDREN

With the population blessings to Abraham in mind—and after such a slow start in the previous two generations—the narrative leaps into overdrive with surprising fertility. Appropriately, the focus is on the women. But indirectly, this gives the impression that Jacob is passive as a husband and father. (We'll soon talk about his most significant interaction with his wives in 30:1–2.) And his favoritism toward Rachel will cause damage.

Really, the whole thing reads like a bad sitcom. Hey, watch what happens when Jacob marries two sisters (who are his cousins) and works for their dad! Wacky hijinks are sure to follow, along with canned laughter and eye-rolling moments. Or maybe it's better to imagine this as an intense drama: old Laban vs. young Jacob, a competition between two wives, and sibling rivalry revisited. We can make educated guesses about what this might have been like, but the children's names (given by the moms instead of the passive papa) tell us more.

Leah opens the fertility festivities with the first four sons for the fledgling family. We're told that the Lord opens her womb because she was not loved by Jacob. She is less beloved, but more blessed. Does the Lord prefer Leah over Rachel for character reasons? Is He compensating for her unloved status? Or is He trying to teach lessons to Jacob, Leah, and Rachel? Long-term, Leah's descendants will feature the priests (through 3rd son Levi) and the most prominent kings in the longer-lived faithful Southern Kingdom, including David and Jesus (through 4th son Judah). In all of this,

CLEVERNESS AND PERSEVERANCE

God breaks *His* usual pattern—of breaking the predominant cultural pattern—by choosing to work most with the eldest child Leah! That said, the Lord is still taking a poke at a worldly norm—Jacob's favoritism for Rachel.

Leah names three of the four children after the God of Israel—a very good sign and not entirely expected. A quick read misses her predicament and the poignancy of the chosen names. Reuben's name predicted love from Jacob. But then with Simeon and Levi's names, we see that her prophecy did not come true. With Judah, we see a change of heart "this time"—as she turns to focus on character rather than circumstances, the divine over the temporal—in the first biblical use of the phrase, "Praise the Lord." Leah has changed her focus from Jacob and God (sons #1 and #2), to Jacob (son #3), and finally to God (son #4). Sons #1–3 brought her (temporary) happiness; son #4 brought her peace and joy.

Ironically, Leah was not loving her sons as children, but rather as hopeful means toward the end of acquiring Jacob's love. Self-absorbed, she couldn't have loved or enjoyed the children as much as was ideal. She hopes that husband Jacob will change, but he doesn't. For us, it's funny that wives often imagine that their husbands will change in terms of character, while husbands often imagine that their wives will not change physically. Leah thinks she can win Jacob over, but his heart is elsewhere—an easy application to husbands today, if we put our wives behind our work, hobbies, or an addiction.

WHAT ABOUT RACHEL?

Perhaps because Leah has learned this vital lesson, she has no more children for a while. Meanwhile, Rachel is in agony—in the middle of her 14 years of childlessness (30:25, 31:41). Infertility is difficult enough, but she also chooses to embrace jealousy. It's often legitimate to desire XYZ, but not when desire devolves into demandingness. In part, Rachel is deriving her identity from cultural norms—that her intrinsic value is dependent on her ability to bear children. She's looking to Jacob and children more than God. (There is no hint of prayer from her in the text.) Maybe she's worried about losing Jacob, despite her beauty. But she doesn't seem particularly grateful for her husband's love. And she lacks empathy for Leah's (relatively) loveless marriage. Instead of mutual sympathy, the women compete—the success of both as a source of pain for the other—rather than choosing compassion and mutual comfort.

When we're struggling with jealousy and envy, we should recognize the blessings we have and practice gratitude as a spiritual discipline. We should get busy with giving and serving; idleness is not helpful. We should remember God's grace and that, as sinners, we don't have a right to anything good. We should consider the struggles of the ones we're tempted to envy: the problems that usually come with blessings and whatever other difficulties they face.

Eventually, Rachel lashes out at Jacob. But this is misplaced anger; his plumbing is fine! Moreover, she is his favorite, probably including more attention, affection, and sex. But perhaps her beauty is a curse. She may be used to getting what she wants. With people drawn to her looks, she may not know whether people love her. This is the only meaningful conversation recorded between them—and although she is outwardly attractive, she's inwardly ugly here.

With her screech toward Jacob ("Give me children!" in 31:1), she's provoking him instead of petitioning the God who opens wombs. She's unhappy and kicking the dog to boot. (Often, we're mean and ornery with those we love.) She wants it for "me," not for "us" or to fulfill God's population blessing. She demands children, not just a single child (30:24) and she adds the overly dramatic "or I'll die." Ironically, the birth of her second child *would* result in her death during childbirth (35:17–18).

In his response, Jacob goes from seeming passivity to angry activity. (Had he tolerated a ton of carping before this?) His style doesn't seem superb, but he does ask Rachel a great question. He focuses on God's sovereignty and his inability to do anything; it's out of his hands. (Then again: Would he have been frustrated if Leah had not already borne him four sons?) Jacob chooses Leah in the end, at least in terms of burial (49:31 vs. 35:19–20), but Rachel is still favored at this point (33:2). Do Jacob and Leah mature—or does Rachel's act eventually get really old?

Rachel reaches for a Hagar-like plan, giving her maidservant to Jacob. This yields two sons from the surrogate. The names are Rachel-centered, focused on her vindication and the "great struggle" with her sister. The feelings of victory over her sister must have been fleeting. And what had she won? The scoreboard still says 4–2, even if we count the surrogates. Leah, now struggling with fertility, also seeks the surrogate solution, yielding two more sons. We had hopes for Leah's faith after naming Judah, but this is back-sliding. Rachel tries mandrakes, a cultural superstition connected to pregnancy, rooted in human means and idolatry. Leah gets more time and

CLEVERNESS AND PERSEVERANCE

sex with Jacob who is "hired" as if he's a male prostitute—more passivity from him. She has two more sons and then a daughter Dinah who will play a prominent role later.

Finally, God opens Rachel's womb and she has her first child—the most famous of the bunch: Joseph. God listened, implying her prayers—and with no apparent connection to the mandrakes! Rachel credits God and celebrates that her "disgrace" is ended. She would seem to have it all in this moment, but she names Joseph by asking for another son: a modest desire in a sense, but also a sign that her gratitude and joy aren't what we would hope. Despite all of this—selfish agendas and flawed people—God brings tremendous good: 11 (and soon, 12) sons who will become the tribes of Israel, fulfilling the population promise to Abraham and continuing the pursuit of His plan to rescue us through Israel and eventually Christ.

There are lessons here for every married couple, especially when dealing with difficult circumstances. How do we handle—and how do we relate to our spouse in the face of—disappointment, discouragement, and despair? How do we help each other when one of us despises someone else? How do we deepen—as individuals and as a couple—in the face of challenging contexts and ornery people? How do we handle temptations toward jealousy and envy? We give thanks in all circumstances (I Thess 5:18). We bear with one another in love (Eph 4:2). We accept responsibility for our part of the mess; we repent; we seek to reconcile and restore. In a word: Love God and love others—and help your spouse to do likewise.

CLEVERNESS IN DEALING WITH A TOUGH BOSS

With the birth of Rachel's child, the narrative turns from passive husbanding to active husbandry. As a bargaining ploy or because he'd rather be in Canaan, Jacob asks to go home. (Would it have been difficult to take Rachel away from her dad without her having a kid? Note also that Jacob implicitly believed that he'd be better off near Esau than Laban!) But Laban makes a counter-proposal, bargaining to keep Jacob and his daughters local.

Jacob suggests the black and multi-colored goats, along with spotted sheep. He has good reason to distrust Laban, but this is measurable and they'll be three days apart. (Trust but verify!) Laban immediately agrees, since few of these would typically be born naturally. (Even without knowing anything about animals, we can infer that Jacob's offer was modest or Laban would've bargained for more.) On top of that, Laban rigged the game from the start, removing animals that would have helped Jacob. Did Laban outmaneuver Jacob again? Is Jacob unconcerned, resting in the promises of God and His sovereignty? Or given what follows, is Jacob actually in control, knowing he has another card up his sleeve (31:1-3), and confident that his life hack will work?

The resulting prosperity prompts the crisis point which leads them back to Canaan. As Genesis 31 opens, Jacob is slandered by Laban's sons. Envy and jealousy show up again—a repeated theme in Genesis. Laban gets even more difficult. Maybe Jacob was getting too comfortable there and God stirs the pot. In any case, God intervenes to say it's time to head home and Jacob makes plans to return.

Great news: Rachel and Leah are willing to "leave and go" (as Abraham in Genesis 12) and to "leave and cleave" (as per Genesis 2). Whatever their earlier communication problems, Jacob is effective here, especially on a difficult topic like in-laws. He had reason to worry that they would go—and even to wonder if he could trust them—but they're ready to hit the road too. Their perception is that Laban has treated them poorly and that he has little to offer them anyway. This makes it much easier for them to leave. And they're unified on this! More credit to Rachel and Leah: Often, children find it difficult to leave loser parents behind, even when all of the available evidence and logic points that direction.

They leave and when Laban gets word, he gives chase and eventually catches them—in what sounds like an algebra problem. (The three-day separation with the livestock backfired on Laban since it gave Jacob & Co. a big head start!) God warns Laban in a dream, but he decides to pursue them anyway. Laban utters weak accusations, an empty promise of a going-away party, and a spoken desire to say goodbye. But it's all anti-climactic—except for some drama with his household idol.

In addition to the heart-pounding excitement that ensues, the weird little story on Rachel stealing the idol is provocative. Is this petty revenge, a god to worship, a vestigial souvenir from back home, perceived protection from Laban's attempts to use divination, or a cultural attempt to claim an inheritance later? Jacob's hasty oath ("death to the thief") is understandable but unfortunate, as he is ironically deceived again. And the punchline is hilarious: a powerless idol that can't defend itself and is smothered by a woman on her period. In any case, this episode illustrates that Laban (and likely Rachel) had not escaped the pagan background of their ancestors, underlining the importance of Abram settling away from Haran and Babylon two generations ago.

WRAPPING UP...

The portrait of Jacob is longer (half the book), richer, and more complex than anyone else in Genesis. Kass sums him up: "Less heroic and austere than Abraham, more robust and enterprising than Isaac, Jacob strikes us immediately as more recognizable and familiar—in many respects, not all that different from ourselves. Yet Jacob, though nearer to us, is no ordinary fellow . . . [He] is, first of all, a man of uncommon cunning and cleverness . . . he is also the most passionate. He displays lust for gain and righteous anger, he enjoys big dreams and suffers great sorrows . . . [He] is the first biblical character who clearly falls in love . . . [He] is also tenacious and long-suffering."[5]

In a word, where Abraham seems like a super-hero for our aspirations, Jacob seems like an everyday man with whom we can sympathize and see ourselves in his mirror. In this part of his narrative, we've seen his tenacity, perseverance, passion, and cleverness. Jesus said to be wise as serpents, but as innocent as doves (Matt 10:16). Jacob often had the former covered, if not the latter. Sometimes, we underestimate the value of being clever and creative. In the Parable of Shrewd Manager (Luke 16), Jesus praises those who steward their resources well, even if it's skirting the rules. Maybe we need a little more asking forgiveness than asking permission. Jacob works smart and hard; he deals effectively with difficult people; and he moves the Kingdom forward.

In fact, one usually becomes "great"—in worldly and in godly terms—with the same characteristics. We certainly see it in the patriarchs, but let's consider some contemporary examples. Joni Eareckson Tada dove into shallow water and became a quadriplegic at age 17. Paralyzed and overcoming deep depression through faith, her life has been an incredible testimony about Jesus, perseverance, creative and effective ministry in the face of tremendous challenges.[6]

Cal Ripken was an excellent shortstop for the Baltimore Orioles in the 1980s and 1990s. Nicknamed "the Iron Man," he surpassed Lou Gehrig's

---

5. Kass, *Beginning of Wisdom*, 405.

6. Check out "Joni and Friends" to learn about some of her ministries. Shelbi Shutt and Nic Vujicic have similar stories.

record for most consecutive games, playing every game for more than 16 years. Even without "The Streak," Ripken would have been famous enough by hitting for power (431 home runs) while playing a position then dominated by smaller men. Short and quick seemed like a requirement to play the defense needed at shortstop. But in addition to rigorous physical training, he studied the hitting tendencies of every batter to put himself in a better position to field, creatively making up for his relative lack of agility. Twice, he won a Gold Glove award for best fielder at his position and seven times, he led the American League in "assists" (throwing to another player to get an out). What an amazing combination of cleverness and perseverance!

Few of us will be quadriplegics or Hall of Famers, but many of us will have spouses with chronic illnesses, children who play the part of the prodigal, and difficult colleagues at work. Whatever our circumstances, the call is the same: dependence on God, cleverness as useful, and perseverance to ably run the race to the end.

11

Placate and Wrestle

COMPLETE TEXT: GENESIS 32–33
RECOMMENDED READING: GENESIS 32
POTENTIAL MEMORY VERSES: 32:26, 32:28

SOME PEOPLE WILL WRESTLE at the drop of a hat; others are reluctant to get on the mat. There are times to wrestle—with friend and foe, with ideas and theories, with the application of concepts and principles. And there are times to let things go. Avoid paralysis by analysis and make a decision already. That clever line is not going to work well, so put it away and move on. Don't get in a fight with people who are missing their front teeth. Don't argue with people who already know everything.

And then there's "professional wrestling." Acting and athletic abilities. Drama and gymnastics. Soap operas and suplexes. Noise and flash. Ego and bluster. But none of it "real." People "wrestling," but it's mostly a show. Likewise, some people think they're wrestling when they're not. They quickly give in to temptation. When the going gets tough at work or in relationships, they give up too easily. They imagine that they're earnestly wrestling with ideas, but they only read those who support their current views or they only entertain the worst arguments from the other side.[1]

---

1. In the second year of our discipleship curricula (*Getting Equipped* and *Thoroughly Equipped*), when covering Christianity's thornier doctrinal issues, we expose people to the best biblical arguments for all views within orthodoxy.

In Genesis 32, we'll see some actual wrestling. But in the Scriptures, we see a ton of metaphorical wrestling. Job famously grapples with God—after God allows Job to go through the worst of circumstances. Meanwhile, Job battles with his three "friends" and whips up on them, but without gaining any meaningful victory. God finally shows up to wrestle and Job cries "uncle" (Job 40:4–5) after two chapters of pounding (in Job 38–39). But God goes at it for two more rounds before finally letting Job go—and then declaring him the winner over his friends! Moses, the psalmists, and prophets like Jeremiah and Habakkuk wrestle with God and His people. They don't pull punches; they're vulnerable and candid in their appraisal. They're desperate for an answer; they want relief from their predicament and demand a solution. The response from God is not lightning bolts for their insolence, but a deeper relationship—whether they get the desired answers or not.

At the time of the bout, Jacob is returning home to the Promised Land and we'll see his passion again. Although he picks up wounds of a sort from his 20 years with Laban, Jacob will sustain a hip injury from God that will cause him to limp the rest of his life. But he'll exit the ring as a changed man with a new name and a clearer sense of his identity, his faith, and his destiny.

In the narrative, this wrestling match is placed between Jacob's efforts to placate Esau. We'll be left wishing that Jacob was coming from a better place than his guilt and fear. But at the end of the day, the visit goes well enough: fratricide is averted; sibling rivalry is quelled; and the transmission of the faith and God's promises to Abraham's descendants can continue. Likewise for us: In any given situation, placating may be our best option. When people are ornery or angry, we might hope for full-blown reconciliation, but this may not be achievable. As Paul writes: "Be completely humble and gentle. Be patient, bearing with one another in love." (Eph 4:2) Sometimes, "bearing with" is the best we can do.

We also learn that Esau has turned out to be "a good guy"—likely, a better guy than Jacob. But there's more to life in the Kingdom than basic morality. Esau is still apparently uninterested in the things of God—and so, God's work with Jacob is still the best path forward. Thankfully, Jacob has been growing and will continue to grow. And as we saw with Isaac, God doesn't need much for His grace and sovereign will to proceed.

Placate and Wrestle

GETTING READY FOR THE FAMILY REUNION

As Genesis 32 opens, Jacob is moving from the frying pan to the fire—still between a rock and a hard place—fleeing from thieving Laban to reunite with murderous Esau. Jacob had left home to find a wife and escape his brother. The former has been resolved—in spades! What about the latter? Had time healed the wound from Esau's perspective? Jacob seems to be in (much) better shape in terms of faith. But can they avoid fratricide? Can they resolve this or even reconcile?

On his way home, Jacob has a second encounter with angels—in both cases, between his troubles with Esau and Laban, in times of relative calm and solitude. What an encouragement this would have been—in general and in terms of protection against the impending threat! But not content to rely merely on God's providence and provision, Jacob takes reasonable steps to prepare for his meeting with Esau. He heads to Edom—Esau's territory and south of his ultimate destination. Jacob figures that it's wisdom to deal with Esau on his own terms and in his own timing. Likewise, it's admirable to face our problems (and prospective problems) head on.

To this end, Jacob sends out messengers who act as scouts. Their rhetoric is at least meant to placate, referring to Jacob as "servant" and to Esau as "my lord" and "master." Is this flattery, a cultural courtesy, the start of an effort to bargain, or a sign of personal growth and humility? Practically, Jacob faces a difficult task: balancing strength if Esau wants to go to war with a strong effort to reconcile, including a "pay-off" as restitution. By offering an impressive gift, Jacob is also signaling that he's not a vagabond—and that he's accomplished things to warrant respect. Not surprisingly, worldly people are often impressed by worldly measures of success.

When my step-dad Troy had cancer, my brother and I reached out to talk with him about faith, grace, and salvation. Troy had a lot more respect for me, since I was finishing my PhD and preparing for a career as an academic—while my brother was a mere pastor. (It's funny how church world often overvalues professional ministry, while the secular world undervalues it.) Or in terms of our faith, maybe Troy was impressed that my brother would be paid to be good, but I was good for nothing! In any case, Troy was open to hearing from someone he respected more—and the Lord used me to help bring him to salvation.[2]

---

2. In a letter I wrote to Troy, the Spirit led me to share God's grace toward Samson at the end of his life. Troy thought it was a cop-out to accept Christ at the end of his life. And it bothered him that God couldn't (seemingly) do anything with his remaining days.

PRAY AND PREPARE

The news that Esau is coming with 400 men must have been disheartening to Jacob. It sounds like a showdown and preparation for war. But he's stuck. With his family, he can't move quickly. Laban is behind him and God has called him to return to the Promised Land, so retreat isn't an option. Jacob's only move: Do his best and move forward in faith. As a practical matter, he divides his crew into two groups. Then he prays—the first time it's recorded for him (and the first recorded words of prayer in the Bible). Like most of us, he calls out to God in times of trouble; like many people, he seems to *only* call out to God in times of trouble. This looks like a foxhole faith or a focused faith driven by fear.

We smile as Jacob (nervously and strategically) "reminds" God of His promises and Jacob's obedience. Still, there's a lesson here for us: It is valuable to remind ourselves of God's word, God's promises, and God's goodness, to encourage our faith and the faith of others. Jacob also describes himself as "unworthy"—a huge step, especially for such an independent man. At least on the surface, there is no pride or reliance on his own strength and efforts, and he expresses a limited (and eminently reasonable) agenda. That said, dependence is easy for him in this moment; it is patently clear that this occasion is more than he can handle.

There is no immediate response from God to Jacob's prayer. Again, Jacob takes things into his own hands—or more charitably, does what he can do. In matters of God's provision and our participation, we should pray as if it depends on God and work as if it depends on us. Jacob's next move is to send waves of gifts and rivers of rhetoric to signal his wealth and placate his brother. The gifts are prodigious and practical. Sending many smaller gifts is probably more impressive than one enormous gift. Is this scheming or just appropriate planning by Jacob? Is this a heartfelt plea or just an effort to save his skin? Externally, they would look the same—and we should leave judgment about the internals of others to God and our lightly-held inferences.

Commentators differ on how to interpret Jacob here. Allen Ross says that "Jacob had to learn later that God would have delivered him without such gifts."[3] But Matthew Henry argues that "Jacob having piously made

---

But I told him about Samson's last act—how he killed more Philistines in pulling down their temple than in all of his other adventures. The night after Troy confessed Christ, the blood cleared out of his urine, amazing the nurses and bringing glory to God.

3. Ross, *Bible Knowledge Commentary*, 80.

Placate and Wrestle

God his friend by a prayer, is here prudently endeavoring to make Esau his friend by a present . . . When we have prayed to God for any mercy, we must second our prayers with our endeavors; else instead of trusting God, we tempt him; we must so depend upon God's providence as to make use of our own prudence."[4] I'm inclined to agree with Henry: Too often, we pray, but we don't do our best otherwise.

After the gifts are sent out, Jacob is left alone. Presumably, this is a time for more prayer. He has (purposefully or inadvertently) arranged for the solitude he had experienced at Bethel. Will God respond in a similar way or stay silent? Jacob is again vulnerable, quiet, apart from the noise of family, and at the threshold of a huge moment. Sometimes, we need to face things alone—or at least, with some time alone. In fact, this is the first reference in the narrative to "alone" since Adam in 2:18—and that was decidedly "not good"! But this is different; Jacob chose this. So, too with us. Solitude can be extremely powerful. How often are we alone and quiet? When we're alone, do we experience loneliness and weakness or solitude and strength?

LET'S GET READY TO RUMBLE!

Ironically and fittingly, Jacob has planned for everything except what actually happens. He's covered every base, from strategy to prayer, from word to deed, from rhetoric to gifts. One lesson here: Do what you can, but don't put God in a box. The unknown grappler seems like a man, but more than a man; by the end of the narrative, he seems to be the preincarnate Christ. The mystery man seeks out Jacob that night. With Esau in front of him and Laban behind him, another confrontation was not a priority for Jacob. Good news: At least you're not going to die in a wrestling match!

The supernatural wrestler is real, but he also represents Esau, as well as Jacob's inner wrestling—the inherent problems in dealing with those we have wronged without reconciliation and what follows from living life as a schemer. How can one live in peace alongside deceit and self-imposed turmoil? The darkness underlines the fear and uncertainties facing Jacob. It points to his spiritual blindness and the need for divine light to illuminate his path forward.

As a sport, wrestling is mental and physical; it requires strength and agility; done successfully, it is fueled by passion and perseverance. This contest lasts until daybreak: a long, tough match. It tells us that Jacob possessed

---

4. Henry, *Commentary*, 155.

tremendous natural strength, tenacity, and determination. And it signals the importance of free will—that God allows it to last so long.

And then it suddenly ends at dawn—presumably before too much can be seen. The Man does not exert natural strength to defeat Jacob, but then supernaturally defeats Jacob by wounding his hip. In a word, Jacob could wrestle him successfully, but God could disable him at will. Jacob is a match for any man, but he is no match for the divine. Still, Jacob will not let go—until he receives a blessing from his assailant. Again, we see Jacob's tenacity for the blessings of God. This will be required to extend the faith through a range of difficulties into the next generations. And all of this is in marked contrast to Esau's apathy.

Before being blessed, Jacob is required to say his own name—to admit who he is: a deceiver, a cheater, a fraud. Jacob does not waffle, fudge, manipulate, or lie. He had deceived Father Isaac about his name, but now he owns it. His first blessing had been received through deceit with his earthly father; the second blessing from Isaac was better but still awkward; now, this third blessing is done in honesty with his heavenly Father. Jacob had to admit who he was before he could be blessed. Likewise, embracing the grace of God always starts with acknowledging our sin and our sinfulness.

Then, Jacob's name is changed—from something undesirable to something fitting and beautiful: Jacob would become "Israel" because he wrestled with God and man.[5] The person and the nation Israel will do the same. Likewise, we receive a new identity as children of God, heirs to the promise, and participants in the divine nature. Why is the striving of Jacob rewarded, rather than humility, simple submission, or mere obedience? We can infer from this that God values wrestling and loves wrestlers: the willingness to risk, to get one's hands dirty, moving from broken and wounded to growth and redemption—or in the language of the New Testament, to be an "overcomer." Again, we're back to why Abraham dominates Noah in Jewish identity. Noah was a righteous and obedient man who followed God and escaped the world; Abraham was faithful and mostly obedient, but wrestled with God and changed the world.

Finally, I'm struck by Jacob's limp. Wrestlers bear the marks of their wrestlings. From cauliflower ears to jacked-up joints, grapplers persist and grow, but are prone to wounds and scars. There are consequences despite their successes. And those scars are a memorial of the fight—the victories,

---

5. Leon Kass: "In this act of rebirth, Jacob becomes the first of the patriarchs to acquire a name tied to God's name" (*Beginning of Wisdom*, 460).

the losses, the strength within that makes it all possible. At Peniel, Jacob is crippled and blessed by God in the same moment. As with Paul, God's strength is made possible in weakness and trials (II Cor 12:10).

JACOB AND ESAU: THE LONG-AWAITED SEQUEL

Genesis 33 opens with a recap of the pre-wrestling context: Esau, 400 men, and Jacob dividing his family into additional subsets. Is this more scheming or just the proper formal presentation of his family, especially with Jacob's sevenfold submission to complete the picture?[6] But Esau surprises Jacob (and the reader), running to embrace Jacob. They both weep, presumably out of joy or regret over lost time for Esau, but more likely relief in the case of Jacob. Fans of the Prodigal Son parable of Jesus will see the resemblance here as the repentant returns home to the gracious.

Esau sees the family parade and asks for details. Jacob's reply is encouraging: humility, servanthood, and giving God the glory. (Note that he doesn't identify his wives—a sore spot for their parents when he left 20 years ago.) The 400 men were perceived as a threat, but now they are understood to convey greater respect—a greeting party rather than a posse. Apparently, Esau has had a change in heart, if not character. Is it water under the bridge at this point? Have the passions of youth faded? Is life too short—and too long—to wisely harbor resentment? Has God moved lightly or profoundly in Esau's life?

Esau's material contentment in refusing Jacob's gifts contrasts nicely with Laban's endless striving for wealth. Perhaps Esau was upset at the material loss of the stolen blessing, but he has more than enough now. Jacob expresses gratitude and insists that Esau take the gift. Esau accepts, signaling full restoration of the relationship. (Imagine if he had refused!) Is this just cultural for Jacob? Or is he assuaging his guilt? Is he still worried about Esau's "true" feelings? (We'll see this problem again with Joseph and his brothers.) Or is Jacob merely insisting on justice? The word for "present" (33:11) is the same as the word "blessing" in Genesis 27. In Jacob's words (if not his mind), this is restitution for his earlier crime.

Curiously, Jacob says that he has now seen "the face of God." Perhaps this is more kindness or flattery. But taking it seriously, it must have been powerful to see God move in Esau's heart, to imagine God's mercy through

---

6. Jonathan Sacks calls this "the choreography of self-abasement" (*Covenant and Conversation*, 221).

Esau, to experience grace in Esau's desire to forgive and fully restore the relationship. When we see God move so decisively, have we not seen the face of God too? When we receive forgiveness, from the depths of our sin against God and others, is anything more poignant and powerful?

Esau offers to accompany Jacob's crew and to have fellowship with him. Jacob gives a polite but firm refusal with appropriate rationales, while promising to visit Esau later. What are Jacob's motives here? It would be unreasonable to force Esau to go at Jacob's pace, given all of the livestock and family. Jacob would be really busy and distracted in administering the move. And why risk ruining the moment? It's gone so well; let's leave it here. Or maybe Jacob is still nervous, wanting to be able to breathe again. (What if Esau changes his mind?!)

So, Jacob heads west and there is no record of him visiting Esau later. The always-gracious Matthew Henry speculates that Jacob did—and maybe so. Perhaps he never meant to keep his word or he just never got around to it. At the end of the day, while this seems to be a missed opportunity, Jacob and Esau have separate lives to lead and they're on separate paths going forward. Even though they're brothers, they avoid being "unequally yoked" (II Cor 6:14). Remember too that they were probably never all that close—and that reconciliation does not imply that the two would be best buddies. Sometimes it's more than enough to repair the relationship, such as it is, and just move on.

WRAPPING UP . . .

When I think about placating someone in the Bible, Jacob is notable, but Abigail is the first person who comes to mind. Her husband Nabal is a hothead. Before David becomes king, he and his 600 men are on the run from Saul. Nabal refuses to be at all hospitable, despite his wealth and David at least indirectly providing security for him. Worse yet, he talks all kinds of trash to David's men and picks a fight with a great warrior who has a militia. Without her husband's knowledge, Abigail intervenes by bringing a feast and kind words to David, whose anger is appeased.

In Romans 12:18, Paul writes: "If it is possible, as far as it depends on you, live at peace with everyone." Paul continues by counseling against revenge and says to overcome evil with good rather than more evil. Sure, that's wisdom too. But it starts with trying to live at peace with everyone— and not just the easy people. "If you love those who love you, what reward will you get . . . Do not even pagans do that?" (Matt 5:46–47) In trying to handle the tough people in our lives, I love the two caveats that Paul adds here: "if it is possible" and "as far as it depends on you." It isn't always possible and it's certainly not completely up to us. But as best as we can, we should aim to live in peace.

When I think about wrestling stories in the Bible, Jacob is more memorable, but my favorite is Daniel 1—when young Daniel and his friends have been taken into exile in Babylon. It's a great narrative, especially for young people away from home for the first time, making decisions about how they will live in light of how they were raised. Is this my faith or the faith of my parents? Are these my principles or theirs? Daniel and his friends famously say *no* to the king's wine and meat, tactfully advocating with the king's official for a diet of water and vegetables. Not so famously, Daniel and his friends say *yes* to Babylonian language, literature, and culture—and having their names changed. It's easy to say *yes* to everything or *no* to everything, but they wrestled with what they could accept and what they must reject from the Babylonian training regime.

Really, we see the same principles in play throughout Scripture. Think back to the use of questions in Genesis 3. The first recorded conversation in the Bible starts with a question from the Devil (3:1) to stir doubt rather than to seek truth. In the subsequent conversation, God starts with four questions (3:9–13) to promote introspection rather than to seek information, to substitute repentance and restitution for shame and guilt, to offer grace beyond mere mercy. Either way, as Leon Kass puts it: "Questions stir the soul."[7] For good and for ill, questions invite reflection and wrestling, where statements can inform but often serve to close down thought. Along the same lines, it's noteworthy that the gospel writers record 301 questions from Jesus in His ministry.

Questions can be used for "violence" and some questions are so useless as to be equivalent to "silence." Questions can be used to attack and to tempt. Questions can dominate "small talk" and accomplish little good. But questions can also be wonderful for developing relationships, in teaching and learning, in gently poking and prodding for evangelism and discipleship—in a word, for wrestling.

In I Kings 18:21, Elijah asks a question and calls the people to choose, but they remain on the fence in silence. Joshua and Caleb are faithful in delivering their report about the Promised Land and pose a question through

---

7. Kass, *Beginning of Wisdom*, 82.

the alternatives at hand—but the people respond in violence by threatening to stone them to death (Num 14:10). Some people are unwilling to wrestle and others will try to destroy you if you promote wrestling. Neither response is admirable.

Let me close by discussing three more examples from Paul's writings. In I Corinthians 9:19–22, he concludes: "I have become all things to all people so that by all possible means, I might save some." This obviously didn't mean caving on every principle, but being uncompromising on first principles, willing to submit on secondary matters, and wrestling with discernment through prayer to know the difference.

In Acts 16:3, Paul had Timothy get circumcised to promote the Gospel. But in Galatians 2:3, Paul refused to have Titus circumcised, because the Galatians would have understood this as agreeing with the Judaizers about the (heretical) need to become Jewish before one could become a Christian. When do we submit our rights for the good of others and when do we stand against legalisms? We have to wrestle, since it's not always easy to tell the difference.

Finally, in I Corinthians 10:13, Paul confidently tells us that we will not be tempted beyond what we can bear. But in II Corinthians 1:8, he tells us that he despaired of his own life, because the trials were so difficult. Which is it, Paul? Well, both. The divine reality is in I Corinthians, but the human perception is sometimes in II Corinthians—and Paul had to wrestle with the gap between his circumstances and his faith, his contentedness and his hope, his subjective perception and the sovereign reality.

It's easy to be kind to nice people, but can we handle ornery folks? Can we placate the yahoo at work, handle the challenging teenager, or finesse a struggling spouse—instead of crushing them or writing them off? It's easy to adopt a set of legalisms as rules of living, but can we walk in the Spirit and wrestle with the complexities of the wild and crazy world in which we live? Can we recognize the inherent tradeoffs in public policy instead of devolving into partisan bias, simplistic analysis, and demagoguery? Will we rely on the spirit of the law or the letter of the law, as we administer justice and mercy in our daily lives? May we wrestle well with the difficult people and circumstances in our lives.

12

Vengeance and Jealousy

COMPLETE TEXT: GENESIS 34-37
RECOMMENDED READING: GENESIS 37
POTENTIAL MEMORY VERSES: 37:3, 37:4

THE FEUD BETWEEN THE Hatfields and McCoys started with a battlefield death toward the end of the Civil War. The spat really picked up pace with the disputed ownership of a hog. Perceptions of weaponized law enforcement and a biased judiciary added fuel to the fire. In the vicious cycle of violence which ensued, more than a dozen family members died. Because the families lived in two different states (Kentucky and West Virginia), the federal government got involved. The subsequent court cases resulted in seven life imprisonments and an execution. From a hog to a hanging, the Hatfields and the McCoys became the stuff of (real) rural legend.

Years ago, P.J. O'Rourke wrote about blood feuds in Albania. When a boy came of age, he was responsible for "killing members of the clan who killed members of his clan, who killed members of their clan, and so forth—a sort of pyramid scheme of death, if you will." O'Rourke cited estimates by anthropologists that 2% of the country's population were involved before closing with an example: "A man was beheaded with an ax in a Tirana hotel lobby—revenge for a murder his father had committed in a northern village more than 40 years before."[1]

In Genesis, the threat of sibling rivalry has been a significant piece of the narrative: Cain and Abel, Isaac and Ishmael, Esau and Jacob, Rachel and Leah—all with ripple effects across generations. We can read between the lines and infer some parental responsibility for these outcomes: the passivity of Adam and Isaac extending to their role as fathers; the likely emphasis on Isaac as the promised child of Sarah over Ishmael as the surrogate child of Hagar; Isaac and Esau vs. Rebekah and Jacob; and Jacob's favoritism of Rachel over Leah.

Is sibling rivalry the natural state of affairs? What can be done to foster good relationships between them? Joseph and his brothers will provide another example, with the famous story of Jacob's favoritism and the "technicolor coat" in Genesis 37. At the least, the text gives us solid counsel: Parents should avoid favoring one child over another. In the long run, Joseph will show us a beautiful way of dealing with his brothers. For now, his brothers will show us another.

That's inter-family rivalry, but what about intra-family rivalry? Abraham rescued Lot, but then worried about his opponents seeking revenge. Isaac repeatedly deferred in the feud with Abimelech's shepherds. Although quite different approaches, both seem legitimate, at least in certain contexts. Especially with Jacob's family growing larger (and more powerful)—and looking forward to Jacob the person becoming Israel the nation—we wonder how he (and they) will negotiate the world around them. In Genesis 34, we'll revisit "international" relations with the ugly story about Jacob's family and the Shechemites.

DINAH AND THE SHECHEMITES

What sounds like the name of a rock-and-roll band ends up being one of the most under-rated stories in the Bible. It gets overlooked because it's strange by modern standards and R-rated for sex and violence. In the Church today, we often reduce the Old Testament to a hodgepodge of heroes for pre-teens, despite its power and relevance. As we'll see, the content in Genesis 34 is for "mature audiences," so this memorable story often falls through the cracks. After Jacob's wrestling match in Genesis 32, preachers

---

1. O'Rourke, *Eat the Rich*, 52.

Vengeance and Jealousy

and teachers usually prefer to nervously say "there's nothing to see here" and scoot along to the life of Joseph.

At the end of Genesis 33, after his reunion with Esau, Jacob heads west and puts down some roots. He buys land, establishes a place for his family, and builds shelters for his livestock. We're introduced to the locals—in particular, Hamor and his clan in the town of Shechem. Jacob hadn't wanted to live near Esau, but now, his neighbors are pagans. Is this a desire to be near "the city," trying to avoid Esau, a Lot-like attraction to good land, or something else? In any case, the careful reader wonders if this foreshadows trouble ahead.

Without this ominous angle, everything looks good for Jacob at this point—after a remarkable and providential set of successes: family, wealth, and returning to the Promised Land; wrestling and largely prevailing with Laban, God, and Esau; and spiritually, more wisdom, humility, and dependence on God. Jacob is also following in Abraham's footsteps: He bought land, dug wells (John 4:6), built altars, and engaged with the outside world.

Life seems to be "returning to normal." Jacob has settled down, but is everything settled? For better and for worse, the answer is no. He formally acknowledges God (33:20) and he will talk with God and deal forcefully with idolatry in his household (35:1-4). But in between, God's name and presence will be notably absent. As crazy as the early years were for Jacob and his family, it's about to get a lot rougher in Genesis 34 and 37. Externally, he will wrestle with the Shechemites and eventually Egypt. Internally, his favoritism toward Joseph will prove to be fateful.

At the beginning of Genesis 34, we're introduced to Jacob's only (recorded) daughter, Dinah. She is between 12-16 years old, given the Hebrew term and the chronology—a young woman in that culture. She is the first recorded family member of this generation to engage the world and it doesn't go well: Hamor's son Shechem rapes her. (Notice that she is referenced by pronouns rather than her name; he objectifies her and the narrative's grammar conveys the same.) Then, we get strange references to his heart, love, and speaking tenderly to her. Better than abandonment, I suppose—but post-rape, she has no good options for marriage. Shechem tells his dad to "get me this girl for my wife"—not exactly submission to the authority of his father and not an impressive way to pursue a woman for marriage. Again, we're squarely in a might-makes-right man's world. Not good!

Gen Men

PROPOSALS FOR MARRIAGE AND "MINOR SURGERY"

Hamor travels to Jacob's place to try to make marital arrangements—and Jacob defers until his sons return home from the day's work. Is Jacob overly passive here—in allowing Dinah to get into trouble and in letting his sons take action? When Hamor visits, Jacob is not in a position to act with any strength. Moreover, it's probably wisdom to get a corporate response. The responsibility is perhaps theirs, given his age and their coming of age. In any case, when the boys hear the news, they are furious. But they hide their anger long enough to negotiate with Hamor and Shechem, who are interested in the opportunities of inter-marriage.[2]

To cut the brothers some slack: They're in a tough spot. Dinah is, in essence, being held hostage (34:26) in a walled city. They're dealing with the city's leader, run by pagans with a might-makes-right mentality. Asking nicely would probably not suffice. Attacking them directly would not work out well. Marrying pagans is not advisable. Can they ignore the violence done to their sister? The options seem to be revenge (which requires guile and surprise) or acquiescence. As God did with Sodom, maybe He would intervene again. Or perhaps Israel should be the agents of righteousness and justice in this matter. Unfortunately, there is no record of Jacob's family consulting God on such a big decision!

Jacob's sons follow in Dad's footsteps and deceive the Shechemites. (The writer uses the same word as in 27:35.) They offer circumcision as the rite of entry into the family. This might be fitting as an external manifestation of an internal reality, if faith and obedience are at hand. But there's no mention of God here at all, so this is not about religion. In one sense, this is a big ask; in another sense, it's one and done. (Note that the Shechemites require no explanation, implying that they were familiar with the practice and understood its cultural weight.)

Why did Jacob's sons make this proposal? Maybe they thought the offer would be declined and they could get Dinah back through an unusual negotiating tactic. In any case, it seems to show how little Jacob's sons valued the things of God. They're using something that represents a blessing—and symbolized God's desire for them to bless others—to do harm to others. They're twisting a sacred ceremony into an instrument of vengeance. (In a Christian context, think of drowning people with baptism

---

2. For those interested in the topic of anger, I highly recommend Garret Keizer's fine book, *The Enigma of Anger: Essays on a Sometimes Deadly Sin*.

or poisoning them through the Lord's Supper.) It's a pretense of religion as a mask for malice.

It's been said that "minor surgery" is a procedure that happens to others. But anticipating the short-term marriage opportunity and long-term material benefits, Shechem quickly bears the costs and persuades the others to join him. Leon Kass has a clever line here: "The Shechemites circumcise themselves wholeheartedly for gain, not—as did Abraham—to gain wholeheartedness. What they gain, in fact, is their own death and the ruin of their city."[3]

Among the brothers, Simeon and Levi (the 2nd and 3rd sons of Jacob/Leah) emerge as the leaders of the pack—the two key vigilantes who lead their family into the melee. As Leah's children, they are full siblings of Dinah, signaling "favoritism"—or more charitably, greater empathy and allegiance. The Shechemites are "still in pain" when the brothers attack and kill them. (One might call this a "surgical" strike!) The rape of Dinah was a serious crime, but the punishment is too strong and indiscriminate. We see good intentions with tremendous zeal, but wrong methods and "execution"—in a word, a poor semblance of justice.

On the other hand, maybe collective punishment was appropriate, given the collective sin, their endorsement of Dinah's rape, and their plan to "rob" Israel over time—as manifested in the collective circumcision. In this sense, the execution is an ironic, perfectly just reversal of Shechem's might-makes-right approach to Dinah—as their marital request yields a martial response. Her name means justice—and when Shechem defiled her and the city's men went along, they brought down "justice" on themselves. Circumcision was centered on the organ that got Shechem in trouble—an eye for an eye, if you will. And Shechemite circumcision is a parody of righteousness, just as Shechem's request to be given a bride he had already taken.

Finally, a few thoughts on the politics of the moment. The plunder by Jacob's sons at the end is unfortunate, since it muddies the water on their motives and avoids the comparison with righteous Abraham who refused loot from the King of Sodom. And as a practical matter, merely killing Shechem the rapist probably would have led to a counter-attack and revenge killing by Shechem the town. Ironically, they would have seen Israel's revenge as unjust, instigating a Hatfield-McCoy-style cycle of violence and vengeance.

Even so, the narrative ends with Jacob's reasonable concern that this would lead to more trouble. Sadly, he doesn't worry about harming God's

---

3. Kass, *Beginning of Wisdom*, 492.

name and doesn't seem to trust God's protection. Is this in line with Jacob's earlier passivity or part of the post-wrestling transformation of his character? After these events, God will command Jacob to go to Bethel, paralleling Genesis 15:1 where Abraham has just acted with great courage, but then realizes the full consequences.

The sons rebuke Jacob for this concern—a strong response that asserts the righteousness of their actions, implies his lack of concern for Dinah, and communicates little respect for him. There is no response from Jacob recorded. There is a measure of truth in what they said and what good would it have done to reply? Likewise, we should eat crow when deserved and be quiet when we can't improve on silence.

THREE DEATHS, A BIRTH, AND TWO CONVERSATIONS WITH GOD

There's not much exciting in the narrative until Genesis 37, but there are still some important nuggets. Genesis 35 opens with Jacob's call for the family to destroy its idols. Why does he need to do this at all? It indicates that idolatry is a recurring problem—as it will be until Israel's period of exile. We recall Rachel taking Laban's idols when they left home; we remember her painful idolatry toward children (30:1); and then, we wonder if there's any connection to her ironic death in childbirth later in Genesis 35.

Jacob's call to get rid of the idols is in response to God's command to build an altar at Bethel and perhaps the items taken as plunder at Shechem. Bad news: Jacob failed to do this before. Good news: He takes care of business now—and without a direct command from God. It's also encouraging that God shows up so soon after the fiasco. Notice that God doesn't say anything about the Shechemite episode, underlining the inherent dilemmas (was there a good decision available?) and signaling more interest in what it reveals than the particular choice. If anything, the command to settle in Bethel seems to be removing Jacob from Shechem where the fateful decisions had been made. But most directly, God is commanding Jacob to complete his earlier vow (28:20-22). Had he forgot or was he procrastinating?

We're also told about the death of Rebekah's nurse, even though Leah and Rebekah's deaths are not mentioned in Genesis. The nurse, like the idols, are buried under an oak tree, symbolizing the elimination of cultural influences from the homeland. Or maybe the mention is simply to honor her greatness and faithfulness, even though it was behind the scenes. God cares about the patriarchs, but he cares about Abraham's servant Hagar and Rebekah's nurse too.

Before the stone pillar altar (did this remind Jacob of his stone pillow pillar in 28:18?) and the offering at Bethel, God reiterates the patriarchal promises and reminds Jacob of his name change to Israel. They travel along toward Bethlehem and Rachel dies in childbirth, after Benjamin is born—the only child born in the Promised Land. She gets another stone pillar as a memorial—the death and burial of Jacob's favorite wife giving birth to his last son.

At the end of Genesis 35, Isaac (finally) dies, 43 years after the blessing fiasco and Esau's threat to kill Jacob after Isaac died. As Isaac and Ishmael had buried Abraham together, Jacob and Esau bury Isaac. (Was this an awkward or cordial moment?) In Genesis 36, Esau gets an entire chapter of the Bible devoted to his descendants. Why so much space for this when Genesis leaves out so much we'd like to know? This honors Isaac; it shows the fulfillment of God's promises to Abraham; and it provides the origins of peoples who would later be involved with Israel.

In Genesis 35:22, we get a side remark about first son Reuben bedding his dad's concubine, making a premature claim on something he would have received later and at least implicitly challenging his father's authority. This turns out to be a big deal—or at the least, to foreshadow big problems. From Reuben's actions, we can infer that Jacob's time is limited and his authority is fading. Looking forward to the next generation, Reuben seems to disqualify himself from leadership here. (Jacob doesn't say anything until throwing hammers in 49:3-4.) With the Shechem debacle, Simeon and Levi have also disinherited themselves—at least from being key patriarchs going forward. That's three sons down, with nine candidates remaining. Who will lead the family in the next generation?

JACOB AND HIS SONS

In Genesis 37, we start into "the account of Jacob"—the last and longest of the 12 accounts in Genesis. It's named after Jacob, even though he is now a secondary character compared to Joseph and Judah. The family is dysfunctional—in particular, multiple wives, 12 sons (none of whom look promising so far), and a patriarch who is something of a mess. The rivalry between Leah and Rachel now manifests as sibling rivalry among the sons, exacerbated by Jacob's favoritism toward Joseph.

Can this family be preserved instead of destroyed by internal problems and external threats? If so, can the family be unified—particularly in transmitting the faith and perpetuating the covenant with God? Can they grow from a household into a nation that can be a blessing to the world's people, as God had promised Abraham? Is Jacob up to the task of leadership—and with notable flaws in the oldest three brothers, which son can lead the way forward?

What follows is a gripping narrative, told by a master story-teller, who gives us robust character development, raw emotion, and edge-of-the-seat suspense. As Kass puts it: It is a "riveting story described so economically yet so powerfully . . . an affecting family story, a tale of malice and mastery, of near fratricide and forgiveness, featuring one of the Bible's most talented and charismatic figures, Joseph."[4] This sounds like good theater, but the story has already been done many times on Broadway!

As Genesis unfolds, God continues to become "less visible," playing an increasingly indirect providential role behind the scenes—apparently, moving toward a long-run equilibrium of moving more subtly through events. (Eventually, in the New Covenant, this culminates with the Holy Spirit dwelling in the hearts of believers to inform and to empower us.) We're immediately introduced to the frequent subject of that Providence in this account: Joseph, a 17-year-old man who will soon be subjected to staggering trials in a foreign land. For now, he's a shepherd, leading animals with an allusion to his later leadership of people.

We're told about Jacob's greater love for Joseph—the reality and, as it turns out, its problematic perception. Why? Perhaps because Joseph was born later in Jacob's life, but most likely, because he is the first son of his favored wife Rachel. Favoritism will cause trouble for a third consecutive narrative: Rebekah and Isaac with Jacob and Esau; Jacob with Rachel over Leah; and now, Jacob among his sons.

The favoritism famously manifests as a "richly ornamented" robe. As with many other blessings, this one will become a curse of sorts—for Joseph and the family. Every man had a robe in those days, but Joseph's probably resembled royalty: long sleeves, ankle-length, and colorful. In essence, Jacob seems to be choosing Joseph for future leadership. And as we'll see later, Joseph has impressive gifts, charisma, integrity, and faith in God. Since the first three sons of Leah have disqualified themselves, maybe Joseph can be a fine candidate for the position.

---

4. Kass, *Beginning of Wisdom*, 509.

Joseph brings his father "a bad report" about his brothers. We're not sure whether this is inaccurate and slanderous—or accurate but critical. Hopefully, it's the latter, foreshadowing the integrity and courage Joseph will show later. Even so, it may be gossip—and nobody likes a narc. (This is a warning for us: What are our motives for telling and how will our words actually function?) Not surprisingly, the brothers aren't big fans of Joseph or their dad's favoritism. In a word, Jacob's love resulted in the brothers' hate. All of this is exacerbated by Joseph's bad report, the annoying robe, and probable jealousy about his giftedness and charisma.

Then, Joseph tactlessly tells them his two God-given visions of greatness. There are lessons here for both the telling and the hearing of things. If you're Joseph, know your audience. Relating the visions to his brothers is somewhere between poking the bear and offering pearls to swine (Matt 7:6). Don't do it. As per Matthew Henry: Joseph was "more a prophet than a politician."[5] But that said: If you're the brothers, just laugh off the absurdity of it; be the bigger man and say, "We'll see, little brother!" Dad knew better, rebuking Joseph the second time, but also keeping it in mind.

JOSEPH AND HIS BROTHERS

Later, the brothers are tending flocks and Jacob asks Joseph to check on them—near Shechem (cue the ominous music). But they're not there. The music relaxes for a while until Joseph finds them 13 miles down the road in Dothan. His willingness to go the extra mile signals his perseverance—a crucial trait for him later on. But for the brothers, it's a few short steps from jealousy to hatred to murder. This is pre-meditated and otherwise rough business: brother-on-brother crime (although this is a pattern in Genesis); by a group against an innocent individual; and if his visions are divine, attacking God's anointed.

They throw Joseph in a cistern, trying to figure out what to do with him while they eat lunch. (Imagine the scene!) Reuben aims for a moderate solution (or maybe he intends to come back for Joseph later), but his leadership is ineffective. Is he trying to get back into Jacob's good graces? Is he trying to show that he can lead? As the firstborn, would he be held responsible? Does he act out of a greater moral sense? In any case, the brothers give no response. They're capable of listening and following; they will soon

---

5. Henry, *Commentary*, 170.

agree with Judah in 37:27. But whether from a lack of integrity, *gravitas*, charisma, or moral authority, the brothers blow off Reuben.

Judah's plan is to sell Joseph into slavery to some merchants on the busy trade route. Is this what Judah *wanted* or did he sense this was the best he could for Joseph with the brothers? One hint in the text: Judah will leave the family before the next episode is recorded. More humane—and whether to reduce guilt or to gain some money—they set Joseph on a path that God can and will redeem. Reuben failed; Simeon and Levi are silent; Joseph is promising but now out of the picture; only Judah looks effective and he's about to hit the road too.

When the brothers get back home, they deceive Jacob; like father, like sons. Ironically, just as Jacob had done to Isaac, the brothers use a goat and a brother's garment (27:9,16). In a sense, wild beasts did get him; they're just animals of the human variety in his own family! So, it's not an explicit lie, but they're certainly deceptive, covering one sin with another. Jacob mourns and is inconsolable. He's lost Rachel and now Joseph. Does Jacob suspect anything? Is this naivete on his part—or worse than he could have possibly imagined? Does he feel responsible for sending Joseph on the trip alone?

Spoiler alert: There will be a happy ending. But interestingly, both Jacob and Joseph endured 20 years of separation from their family. And both stories conclude with the reunion and reconciliation of brothers. But for now, what a mess! If they can't get family right, how can they get a nation right? How can this possibly work as part of God's plan?

WRAPPING UP . . .

In our own lives, how do we handle those who seem to have it better than us? It starts with gratitude for what we have. In her immensely helpful book, *1000 Gifts*, Ann Voskamp explores the connections between grace, gift, joy, thanksgiving, and the Eucharist. To combat her own struggles in this area, she practiced the discipline of noticing and writing down things to express thanks. Gratitude and thanksgiving are antidotes to jealousy, resentment, depression, and so much more.

Beyond that, we should simply avoid making comparisons. For one thing, we're not good at it. We tend to pick certain people and contexts to make the comparisons more favorable for us. We take credit for things we don't control and blame outside factors when we do have control. For example: If you're slender, you probably put too much weight on the role of genetics and take too much credit for your diet and exercise; if you're overweight, you probably blame your body and downplay the importance of healthy choices. We tend to give ourselves the benefit of the doubt and jump to harsh conclusions about the motives of others. And really, we don't know enough to judge well anyway—in particular, failing to understand the complexities of others' blessings. For example, when people are beautiful or wealthy, it can be easy to depend on the gift, to be independent of God, and to have people around who want to enjoy the gift instead of loving the person.

And how do we handle those who harm us? In big things, we often leave it to government. After the anarchy, dictatorship, and mixed family governance of Genesis, God gives the Law to the nation of Israel in Exodus. He will prescribe punishment for capital offenses, restitution for property violations, and "cities of refuge" to deal with vengeance. In developed countries today, we generally have recourse to law enforcement and court systems that protect our rights to life and property. But how do we handle the smaller things? Certainly, bitterness and resentment are not advisable. Jesus will preach loving and praying for one's enemies. Gratitude for God's grace and a recognition that "there but for the grace of God go I." As feasible, redemption and reconciliation are Kingdom priorities.

Perhaps more important: What do we do when the rights of *others* have been violated? God intervened with the crime of Cain and the sin of Sodom—when the ground cried out from the injustices they were committing. Abraham battled to rescue Lot and argued with God to save the righteous in Sodom. Jesus got upset when the rights of others were violated. But God let Lamech's murders go unaddressed and He will let the injustices against Joseph play out for years. One can make a case for intervention, especially to prevent more damage. But when should we get involved—and how best to do so?

This could take us on a long tangent about Christian political economy—the relatively few contexts when government is a godly means to godly ends for Christians to pursue. But this requires another book that I've already written, *Turn Neither to the Right nor to the Left*. So, let's give Paul the last word from Romans 12:17–21:

> Do not repay anyone evil for evil. Be careful to do what is right in the eyes of everyone. If it is possible, as far as it depends on you, live at peace with everyone. Do not take revenge, my dear friends, but leave room for God's wrath, for it is written: 'It is mine

to avenge; I will repay,' says the Lord. On the contrary: 'If your enemy is hungry, feed him; if he is thirsty, give him something to drink. In doing this, you will heap burning coals on his head.' Do not be overcome by evil, but overcome evil with good.

13

Purity and Productivity

COMPLETE TEXT: GENESIS 39-41
RECOMMENDED READING: 39:1-41:1
POTENTIAL MEMORY VERSES: 39:9, 39:23

My friend Kristen Sauder used to tell a story about Cliff Barrows, the long-time worship leader at Billy Graham evangelism crusades. She got to meet him backstage and wanted a picture with him, because her grandma would get a big kick out of it. When they posed, she put her arm around him. He politely but firmly put her husband Kurt between them. Even though Cliff was decades older than her, he reflexively practiced purity and integrity through a simple choice.

The idea came out of Graham's amazingly productive ministry. He was famous for what became known as "the Billy Graham rule" (most recently popularized by folks criticizing Mike Pence for doing the same thing): Never be alone with someone of the opposite sex. I'm not sure how far Graham extended the rule—cousins and grandmas, hospital visits and rides in elevators. But the principle is sound. Especially when you struggle with certain temptations, when there is good reason to be worried about perceptions, when people may look to create trouble—and especially when it has little inherent value—then why do it?

My long-time pastor Bob Russell has also practiced the Graham Rule in some form—and for many of the same reasons. Like Graham, Russell has been remarkably fruitful because of his humility and his passion, his preaching and leadership skills, his integrity and faithfulness, his hard work and his dependence on the Spirit. He is best known for his 40 years as lead pastor of Southeast Christian Church in Louisville. But arguably, his decades since "retirement" of pouring into church leaders have been even more influential.

In partnership with Thomas Clarkson, William Wilberforce was the parliamentary leader of the British abolitionist movement from 1787 until the passage of the Slave Trade Act of 1807. Later, he worked to end slavery in the rest of the British Empire, dying three days after the passage of the Slavery Abolition Act in 1833. As an Evangelical Christian, the Lord lit a fire in him to fight slavery in England. His obedient Christian life, his single-minded focus, and his productive perseverance rocked the British Empire and eventually, the world.

So, purity and productivity are related, but there's more to productivity than mere purity. We are blessed by God with gifts and talents. We invest in knowledge and skills. Wisdom is gained through experience and useful counsel. It is helpful to avoid distractions and steward time effectively. We should delegate and empower others to extend our impact. It is crucial to work hard and diligently, depending on the Spirit. We prune the good to pursue the best. We serve and worship, but we also practice solitude, meditation, and introspection. We thank God for what He's given us and we faithfully steward God's grace to us in its various forms.

In this chapter, we'll take our second look at Joseph's roller-coaster life. We'll see his purity and his productivity in Potiphar's household. But his integrity ironically leads to prison, where his patience and God's providence pay huge dividends. He emerges from prison to productivity in Pharaoh's court as the top cabinet member of his administration. Throughout, God's presence and provision will be in partnership with Joseph's participation— as God's plans move forward.

JOSEPH IN POTIPHAR'S HOUSEHOLD

Genesis 39 opens in Egypt—a culture shock for Joseph and the reader. It's not just the foreign country, but moving from rural backwater to urban cosmopolitan, from large family to all alone, from freedom to slavery. The first thing we learn about Egypt here is its systemic slavery. In terms of powerful, competing worldviews, this is in line with the might-makes-right world critiqued throughout Genesis and in marked contrast to what we've seen from the patriarchs—what God wants for Israel and all peoples.

We've already seen several references to the temptation of assimilation in Genesis. Abraham was so worried for Isaac in this regard that he sent a servant to get Isaac a wife from the old country. God told Jacob to return to the Promised Land, apparently given a concern that he would settle near Laban. We've seen passing descriptions of life in other settings—for example, the obvious problems with Babel, Sodom, and Shechem. And we've seen the seemingly innocuous leadership of Pharaoh and Abimelech. But these differences will get a far-fuller exploration here. Joseph and ultimately Israel end up in Egypt. Of immediate concern: How much will Joseph struggle with the potential for compromise? Among the longer-term worries: How can Israel remain holy and effective while immersed in a foreign culture with values opposed to what God wants?

God's providence immediately places Joseph in Potiphar's household. Joseph is prosperous—through his participation and God's provision. Potiphar sees the success, attributes it to God's blessing, and gives Joseph more authority. Joseph effectively deflects credit from himself to God. In our lives, this can be easy; often times, it's challenging. But in this, Joseph is fulfilling Genesis 12—blessed by God in order to bless others.

JOSEPH WITH POTIPHAR'S WIFE

Genesis 39:6 opens with the irony that Potiphar is unconcerned with Joseph in charge. But in fact, Potiphar has good reason to be concerned—about his own wife! Joseph is handsome and her interest in him grows "after a while"—probably enhanced by his personality, his productivity, and likely, the forbidden fruit aspect introduced by his refusals. Whatever the causes, she is attracted to Joseph and continues to make shameless advances toward him.

Notice that Joseph is careful to provide reasons for declining, rather than merely saying "no." His answer in Genesis 39:9 is one of my favorite lines in the Bible: He says he can't do it for himself, his master, and his God. He opens with the fact that it's not in his best interests—in essence, "I'm better than that." We saw Adam and Eve have trouble with short-run benefits and long-run costs, but Joseph does a much better job with the economic analysis here. Then, he describes the respect he has for her husband—in a word, "I can't do that to him." And then, the bottom line: it would be a sin against the Lord.

Joseph's answer is eloquent and comprehensive. If his threefold rationale was off-the-cuff, that'd be impressive in a way. But I suspect that he had been rehearsing the answer for some time, getting ready for a likely confrontation. (Joseph was not allowed to practice the Billy Graham rule!) Surely, with her persistence, Joseph was wise enough to get ready for the big moment. He avoids her as much as possible, but he prepares for the likely crisis. (It's noteworthy that he doesn't take his concern to Potiphar; presumably, this was not a good option.) As we face similar temptations and trials, it's smart to spend some time thinking about and rehearsing our answers.

Just as likely: Joseph had already wrestled with a variety of possible rationalizations for engaging in adultery with her. He's away from home with little accountability. (What happens in Egypt stays in Egypt. Hey, nobody will know—except everyone who reads Genesis later!) She's probably attractive. It wouldn't be smart to make her mad. She's in a high position and could help me fulfill the dreams given to me by God. My family deserted me; I deserve it. And so on. But he doesn't fall for any of these—instead, choosing faithfulness, righteousness, and integrity.

It's worth noting that Joseph is the only biblical example to explicitly conquer the giant of sexual temptation. It sacked plenty of other biblical heroes, including David, Samson, and Solomon. This victory will come with a heavy cost. But at each turn, Joseph chooses well and does his best with every task put in front of him. How was he able to do this? He believed in God's sovereignty, supplemented by his boyhood dreams from the Lord. He believed that God wanted the best for him. And he was strengthened by the Lord's evident hand in his life—then and in the past. As we deal with temptation, the same trio of beliefs is crucial: We should trust that God is sovereign, personal, and benevolent—and we should remember moments in our life that undergird those beliefs.

There are many lessons here for us and the situations in which we find ourselves: how to think about temptation; how to avoid and resist temptation; how to talk and act in difficult circumstances; how to anticipate trouble before it arrives. Do we really believe that God knows what's best for us and wants what's best for us? If so, we're morons when we go our own way. Too often, we rationalize and make excuses; underestimate costs and the persistence of temptations; overestimate benefits and our ability to avoid temptation; fail to stay away and run away as necessary; and so on. I love a

Purity and Productivity

Dallas Willard line about this episode: "If Joseph had filled his mind with thoughts of romance or sexual indulgence with Mrs. Potiphar, she would have got *him* and not just his coat."[1]

Joseph does his best, but it is insufficient to avoid her advances and the consequences when she persists. She tears off his cloak. (Clothing is key to many of Joseph's big moments.) I like Matthew Henry's quip here: It's "better to lose a good coat than a good conscience."[2] She quickly gets the servants involved, invokes prejudice against a foreigner, blames Joseph and her husband, and sets up Joseph as the fall guy. In all of this, Joseph is Christ-like. Henry makes the comparison: They are both "the best of men . . . falsely accused of the worst of crimes by those who themselves are the worst of criminals."[3] She's willing to violate the 7th Commandment (adultery)—and now, she breaks the 9th (false testimony), setting up the possibility of his execution and the 6th (murder).

Potiphar is angry—whether at Joseph or his wife, we don't know. Or maybe he's upset at a situation where he loses his amazingly productive lieutenant. Who would he have trusted more? As with many accusations of sexual harassment, it would have been difficult if not impossible to know. One suspects that his wife had exhibited low character in other contexts. There's good reason to think that Potiphar believed Joseph—or at least, suspected his wife's story. If his wife was trustworthy, Joseph would have been executed. And he is imprisoned in a not-so-bad place—under Potiphar's control and maintaining some connection to Joseph (40:3; 39:1). If so, why not release Joseph or sell him to another master? Those are not options either—if he wants to preserve his marriage and domestic tranquility.

The narrative closes as it opens—with two hopeful references to God's providence: "the Lord was with" Joseph (39:2,3 and 39:21,23). Joseph's trust in the Lord is well-placed, despite the turn of events in the face of his integrity. In good times and in bad times, with injustice despite righteousness, Joseph had the Lord's presence. Again, the result is that Joseph found favor, gained trust, and was given authority—in prison, as he had in Potiphar's household.

---

1. Willard, *Great Omission*, 59.
2. Henry, *Commentary*, 179.
3. Henry, *Commentary*, 180.

THE BUTLER, THE BAKER, THE CANDLESTICK MAKER

In Genesis 40, the scene changes to Joseph in jail. The previous story ended with a supposed offense; this narrative begins with an unspecified offense. The jobs of the baker and the butler (or "cupbearer" in most translations) may seem menial, but they were testing drinks and preparing food for Pharaoh—trying to avoid his assassination. (From a game theory perspective, knowing that the king had a "taster" would make it far less likely to even attempt to kill him.) Beyond this, they're called "officials," since they probably had an advisory role in his administration. In a word, they are trusted and wise—helpful, but ultimately disposable.

The cupbearer and the baker are suspected of serious crimes—probably a conspiracy against Pharaoh and his kingdom, rather than lousy coffee and burnt brownies. They've been in prison for some time and then both receive a dream on the same night. Joseph notices that they are "dejected"—presumably, above and beyond being bummed out from their prison stay! Are they worried about the dreams—or are they encouraged to hear from the divine, but are frustrated that they don't know what to do with it?

In any case, Joseph is not self-absorbed with his own problems. He practices discernment and empathy. And beyond mere observation, he takes action. He ministers in the midst of his own suffering and waiting. He points them to God and His sovereignty—and thus, God's ability to deliver them. What a wonderful example! Joseph is filled with compassion for his fellow prisoners. Beyond purity and productivity, he loved others well.

Joseph offers to interpret their dreams. The cupbearer steps up first. Why him? Was he confident, expecting good news with a clean conscience? Was he more aggressive by temperament or the suspense was killing him? In any case, he gets great news: He will be set free from prison and restored to his old position in three days. Here, "lift up your head" is translated as "release." Joseph makes a reasonable request after delivering the pleasing interpretation, but we'll have to wait and see how that turns out. Then, the baker steps up. Does he find courage from the cupbearer's good news?[4] Instead, Joseph tells the baker that they will "lift *off*" his head. Here, we see that Joseph is able and willing—although presumably not eager—to deliver the bad news.

---

4. Whenever I read this, I think about "brave Sir Robin" from *Monty Python and the Holy Grail*.

Purity and Productivity

The next scene is Pharaoh's birthday party. Apparently, it was customary for him to blow out his candles, release a prisoner, and execute a prisoner. Good times! Then, Joseph's prophecy is fulfilled: a general encouragement to Joseph when he has been used by God in a powerful way—and then specifically, to imagine that he will be released from his unjust prison sentence soon.

Unfortunately, the next word in the narrative is "however." What happened? Was the cupbearer selfish? Did he forget initially and then combine this with procrastination and rationalizations why it was risky? In any case, Joseph now endures another sort of injustice and trial: his brothers, Potiphar's wife, and now, being ignored and forgotten. Which hurt him more? Probably his brothers, but this is terrible—when you expect something to be resolved quickly and it just drags on and on. It must have been excruciating to have his expectations and hopes raised, but then to be forgotten and his hopes fade.

A DREAM COME TRUE

In the opening of Genesis 41, we read that two full years pass until the next (providential) episode, as God intervenes again and finally frees Joseph. What were the purposes of God's timing here? From what follows, it appears that God was just lining things up to fit current events in the kingdom. Beyond that, did Joseph need two more years in prison or did prison need him for two more years? As with the brothers selling Joseph into slavery, God's ability to "work all things for good" does not excuse the cupbearer's guilt. But God is in control—and Joseph seems to endure the trial faithfully and trust God's sovereignty fully. Ironically, Joseph saw the cupbearer's deliverance clearly, yet only had a dim view (and a promise) of his own. So, he walked by faith, continued to persevere through hope, and did the best he could with the opportunities in front of him.

Now, Pharaoh is the one having a pair of dreams! This time, it's cows and grain, alluding to food and famine, ominous but unclear. He is troubled and asks his wise men to interpret. They are unable to understand the dreams or are unwilling to bring bad news. (Remember Joseph's willingness to say tough things in Genesis 40.) The cupbearer suddenly remembers Joseph, assumes responsibility for the oversight, and takes a risk, implying his confidence in Joseph despite his youth, ethnicity, and status. Pharaoh sends for Joseph, who confidently gives credit to God—before he even hears the dreams!

There are two dreams, but only one certain and impending interpretation: seven years of great abundance followed by seven years of ravaging famine. Perhaps better news than they expected—and good news in that they had time to prepare. But the famine would be so bad that it would cause people to forget the abundance.[5] Beyond the dream interpretation, Joseph moves to provide practical advice in addressing the imminent crisis. Beyond the warning, he provides a plan and a way forward. Beyond what was asked by Pharaoh, Joseph boldly provides more, taking the opportunity and the initiative. Sometimes, such counsel is unwelcome, but it's usually smart to have some ideas in your back pocket. One smiles to read that Joseph is careful to recommend someone "discerning and wise," without specifying himself as the obvious choice. And in sum, he is really quick on his feet in a challenging situation.

Pharaoh is smart to take the wise counsel, putting Joseph to work and overlooking his youth (he's 30 years old in 41:46), his ethnicity as a foreigner, and his status as a prisoner. Joseph will report to the king, but is placed in a powerful position as his top lieutenant. The years proceed as prophesied. Joseph's strategy keeps the country from starving. But his plans also enrich and empower Pharaoh, ironically setting the table for the slavery that will eventually burden the Israelites in Egypt.

Joseph goes from the pit to Potiphar's house, prison, and now, the palace. What a roller coaster ride! He is given a new name and an arranged marriage. Like Daniel centuries later, Joseph accepts some parts of the culture. But unlike Daniel, we don't read anything about him rejecting aspects of the culture. As a people called to be holy and separate, we wonder if Joseph—as a potential leader for Abraham's descendants—will succumb to the temptation to Egyptianize. If so, all of his giftedness and integrity will not be able to offset his willingness to compromise.

Joseph also has two sons, Manasseh and Ephraim, both of whom will become prominent tribes in Israel. Manasseh's name means "forget (troubles)" and Ephraim's name means "twice fruitful." The names represent two important traits, especially for someone who has endured such trials—the abilities to forgive (if not forget) troubles and to celebrate new beginnings. On the other hand, will forgetting his trouble imply that Joseph will forget his family, the promises of God, and his faith?

---

5. Drought and famine were rare in Egypt because of the Nile River. This may be part of the reason why Pharaoh's wise men doubted what might have otherwise been an obvious interpretation.

Purity and Productivity

WRAPPING UP . . .

In Hebrews 12:1, the writer exhorts us to "throw off everything that hinders and the sin that so easily entangles. And let us run with perseverance the race marked out for us." I love the combination of the two things to "throw off." Obviously, we should get rid of "sin that so easily entangles." Sin can cause so much trouble and drama in our lives, undermining our effectiveness. But we should also avoid "everything that hinders." This speaks to neutral or even good things that distract us from running as well. Greater productivity stems in large part from focusing on the goals that God has put in front of us, and then not straying to either the left or the right as we run our race.

In his classic book, *The 7 Habits of Highly Effective People*, Stephen Covey talks about "private victories" that are built around the first three habits he describes. First, Covey encourages us to "be proactive." Throughout the book, I've emphasized this principle—in particular, by avoiding subtle sins of omission. Second, "begin with the end in mind." When we do this, we will have a robust vision and workable strategies for making good things happen. Third, "put first things first." As in Hebrews 12:1, it's important to avoid both sin and distractions. In the language of this chapter, "private victories" and productivity come through a combination of mind and action, purity and focus, personal growth and redeeming mistakes. For the believer, this includes growing in Christ-likeness through experience, submission, obedience, and increasing dependence on the Spirit—as He informs and empowers us to be more productive in what God wants for us and from us.

Friends and colleagues often say they're amazed by my productivity in wide-ranging endeavors. I suspect that I'm above-average in this regard, but it's difficult to measure such things. And at the end of the day, it's not how much we produce, but how well we use the time, talent, and treasure that God has given us to steward through daily dependence on the Spirit. One way to be productive is to be a workaholic. But my wife and I spend a lot of time together; I've invested heavily in our four sons; we practice relatively radical hospitality; and we have a handful of close friends who we routinely enjoy. To the extent that I am productive, what are the causes?

First and foremost, the credit and hopefully the glory go to God. He has blessed me with a quick mind and placed me in environments in which learning and thinking are encouraged. I was blessed to be raised in a family that valued education. Through my undergraduate and doctoral studies, I was in a position to sharpen my mind. And as a professor, I've continued to invest in knowledge and the ability to process information—as well as thinking, analyzing, and modeling problems—in the iron-sharpening-iron environments of teaching, research, and service within academia.

Second, I've had a relatively simple and pure life. I was blessed to mostly stay away from common problems when I was younger—pornography, bad relationships, alcohol, and drugs. And as an adult, I've consistently chosen simplicity and options with minimal drama. Our marriage has always been at least good and generally improving. My wife and I are both frugal, so we haven't had to think much about finances. I hold myself to high standards, but I'm not a perfectionist. So, I do many things at an A- level, avoiding the extra chunks of time required to reach an A level.

Third, I've largely avoided activities that others give a ton of time. I was a late adapter on cell phones and spend little time on my pocket computer. I follow sports, but don't spend hours on that every week. We don't watch much TV or see many movies. I try to move beyond small talk as quickly as possible—to be more purposeful in my relationships. I'm able to say no to opportunities and to drop good things to do something better. And probably most important: I have a job and career with tremendous flexibility, allowing me to be productive in other arenas while excelling in the workplace.

Fourth, I have Kingdom work that I really want to do. I thoroughly enjoy the primary aspects of my work—teaching and writing about economics and public policy. I love my vocations—making disciple-makers and developing layleaders for the church, teaching the Bible (in person, on radio, and through podcast), our young-adult ministry, and writing all sorts of things (from op-eds to books). I wake up most every morning with things to do that are enjoyable for me, helpful for others, and productive for the Kingdom.

Can you be more productive? In large part, it stems from a good mind, a pure heart, and active hands. If you have a good conscience, a simple lifestyle, and an eagerness to love and serve others, you will become more productive. Christians should generally be among the best workers, bosses, students, and citizens. The first institution given by God to Adam was his "work"—not just his job and career, but all of the work God put in front of him to do for the Kingdom. Made in God's creative and productive image, we should strive to be more creative and productive.

14

Repentance and Leadership

COMPLETE TEXT: GENESIS 38, 42–44, 46–47
RECOMMENDED READING: 38, 44
POTENTIAL MEMORY VERSES: 38:26, 43:9, 44:33, 49:10

THE BIBLE IS FILLED with memorable confrontations: Abraham bargaining with God about the Sodomites; Moses advocating for the people of Israel in the Wilderness; Joshua and Caleb vs. the 10 spies; Jesus telling Peter "Get behind me, Satan!"; Paul with the Galatians and the Corinthians—and over and over again, the Old Testament prophets with the Israelites in the face of their idolatry, injustice, and iniquity. But my favorite biblical example is Nathan rebuking David after his sins with Bathsheba and Uriah.

In the beginning of II Samuel 11, we're told that David is home instead of battling the Ammonites. He goes to the roof of his palace, where he sees lovely Bathsheba bathing on *her* roof in the cool of the evening. He's not where he should be, looking at things he shouldn't be seeing. He sends for her and sleeps with her. She becomes pregnant, but her husband Uriah is off at war. So, David hatches a plot to blame the pregnancy on him, calling him home. But Uriah has so much integrity that he is unwilling to sleep with his wife, given the deprivations of his fellow soldiers. When Uriah returns to the battlefront, David's Plan B is to have troops pull back from battle, leaving Uriah exposed. This strategy works—and now, David is guilty of adultery, murder, and so much more.

God is displeased and sends the prophet Nathan to confront David. But the rebuke is clever and subtle. Nathan tells a story about a poor man whose only lamb is stolen by a rich man. David responds with indignation at this injustice and demands that the rich man be put to death. Nathan then drops the hammer: "You are that man!" David is immediately broken and eventually writes the amazing Psalm 51 about sin and repentance, the Lord's forgiveness and grace. In part, David is a great man of God and an effective leader because he is able to repent.

As we come into Genesis 38, we're wondering how God's "Abraham project" can succeed. Abraham was amazing, but Isaac was never as impressive and fades at the end. Jacob is a mixed bag and his family is dysfunctional. The most promising son (Joseph) is in Egypt and presumed dead. The three oldest sons (Reuben, Simeon, and Levi) all seem unable to lead the family forward. Judah is the only other son we've met, but we're not sure what to do with him: Does he get credit for rescuing Joseph or is he fully complicit in what happened to him? In any case, we learn at the start of this narrative that he's left the family to live elsewhere.

Who will lead this mess? How can God have a holy and effective nation if the chosen family can't function? How can this motley crew be a blessing to all people? In Genesis 38, we'll read a memorable but overlooked story which explains how Judah gets back to his family and is chastened in a way that allows him to be the leader they need. Then, in Genesis 42–44, we'll see how God's providence and Joseph's ingenuity allow for an authentic test of the brothers. Finally, in Genesis 46–47, we'll see how the family is eventually reunited (if not fully restored) in Egypt.

MY THREE SONS

As with the narrative in Genesis 34 (Simeon/Levi, Dinah, and the Shechemites), we have another amazing but strange and R-rated story which gets overlooked because of its unsettling content. This is an unfortunate omission because it explains how Judah emerges as the foil to Joseph—and ultimately becomes the *primary* leader of Israel going forward. Arguably, this is the most under-rated important chapter in the Bible. But since its details are awkward, we often avoid it. In our desire for safer stories, we can miss the wilder stories that point most vigorously to redemption and the amazing work of God.

Repentance and Leadership

In terms of the overall narrative's structure, Genesis 38 builds literary tension as an interlude between the *descent* of Joseph into slavery in Genesis 37 and the *ascent* of Joseph in Potiphar's household in Genesis 39. We learn at the start that Judah has left his family. The narrative leaves it unstated, but it seems as if Judah refuses to live with his brothers any longer—or at least, wants a fresh start—after they've sold Joseph into slavery and crushed their father. Abraham is meant to bless the nations. So, maybe it's promising that Judah is interacting with the outside world. (How can you bless the world if you have no encounters with it?) But we've also seen trouble in Genesis from friendship with the world (as Lot in Sodom) and other encounters with the world haven't gone so well either (most recently, Dinah in Shechem).

Judah finds a Canaanite wife—not prohibited (yet), but not a great sign either, given what we've seen from the efforts of the patriarchs to avoid marriage with the Canaanites. He and his wife have three sons. The oldest (Er) marries Tamar. But he commits some sort of unspecified wickedness and is subsequently judged by God with death. Then, we encounter the provocative institution of "levirate marriage," where a "kinsman redeemer" marries a widow. He takes responsibility for her and fathers a child with her to carry on the brother's name. (Jewish law not only endorses but actually commands polygamy in this context!) Of course, this arrangement would also provide care for widows and any daughters. But in addition, it also points to the purposes of marriage for procreation and the transmission of name, land, and hopefully, faith in God.

Unfortunately, second son Onan is not interested in doing his part. Many have interpreted his sin as masturbation, but the real problem is *coitus interruptus* as a form of "birth control." He didn't want the burdens of another child or to reduce his estate. (It's ironic that he didn't want to "leave a legacy" with Tamar, but the fancy term for masturbation is named after him: "*onan*ism"!) By having sex with her, he was pretending rather than performing his levirate duty. He was using Tamar for sexual gratification without embracing his responsibility. And he was violating God's will, also judged by God with death. (It makes you wonder what Er did!)

OK, two sons down; one to go. As you might imagine, Judah is gun-shy about arranging a marriage between Tamar and his last son Shelah. In 38:11, Judah says one thing, but he's thinking another. Reasonable delay for Shelah's youthfulness becomes unfortunate procrastination, which eventually leads to clear disobedience by Judah and despair for Tamar. She is unable to marry Shelah or anyone else. She is unable to bear children—for their own sake, for herself, or for the name of her husband. In a word, Judah is not his daughter-in-law's keeper and is preventing Shelah from being his brother's keeper.

THAT'S (NOT) WHAT FRIENDS ARE FOR

After "a long time" (38:12), Judah heads to Timnah, soon after his wife dies. In his grieving, he may be more vulnerable to temptation. And it's ironic that veils are meant to limit lust and sin, but it doesn't work here! His "friend" Hirah isn't much help either. This is the first mention of a friend in the Bible. Naomi/Ruth and David/Jonathan are the most prominent biblical examples—both quite impressive. But the concept gets off to a rocky start here; Hirah's passivity is underwhelming.

We often use the term friend, when it's often more accurate to say buddy, colleague, or acquaintance. (We also describe someone as a man, when they're really a guy, a dude, or a boy.) True friendship implies loyalty and intimacy, a desire to love and an ability to love, the wisdom and courage to ably call someone on the carpet. It's popular in the church to have "accountability partners." And that's fine. But it's better to develop authentic, transparent friendships to get accountability and so much more!

Genesis has been sobering on sibling rivalry, but siblings can be close friends. In fact, they have some inherent advantages for friendship and can be a tremendous blessing to each other. They know each other from the beginning; they share many of the same experiences (albeit from different perspectives); and they are roughly the same age. Can siblings rise beyond the problems depicted in Genesis to be a blessing to each other? Families have challenges and friendships require cultivation, but the payoffs can be immense.

As in Genesis 27, the narrative gives us someone in disguise and a goat as a prop. And as sprinkled throughout Genesis, we're wondering if Tamar is taking things into her own hands—or doing what she can (and should) do, within the constraints she faces. Her invitation is similar to the demand of Potiphar's wife, but Judah is not nearly as virtuous as Joseph. Judah doesn't have cash or a credit card, so Tamar collects an ID and collateral for future payment. She becomes pregnant—a sign of God's providence in opening a womb (not always a given in Genesis). And when Hirah is unable to find her and pay the debt, Judah thinks he's gotten off easy.

Repentance and Leadership

Tamar's illicit pregnancy becomes known. As the father-in-law, Judah is also responsible for her in terms of this sin—and he's willing to put her (and the baby) to death. His over-reaction is reminiscent of David's response to Nathan's story. He probably sees this as an excuse to get rid of her—to avoid the responsibility of marrying her to Shelah. But the hypocrisy is staggering. He had sinned against Tamar as her father-in-law and then sought the services of a "prostitute." Can Judah be redeemed?

Fortunately, the answer is yes. She pulls out his ID and the gig is up. No other defense is required. She had resembled a prostitute, but she was actually pursuing what is owed to her (justice) instead of payment. And Judah has unintentionally fulfilled the responsibilities of the levirate marriage. As such, Jonathan Sacks praises her: "With great ingenuity and boldness, Tamar has broken through the bind in which Judah had placed her."[1]

Even better, Judah is convicted of his sin, noting Tamar's greater "righteousness." In this, he becomes the Bible's first "penitent"—apologizing and repenting for wronging her. For this, he is a hero in Judaism. Of course, acknowledging sin and engaging in repentance are at the heart of a good relationship with God and others—and at the center of the Gospel. So, Judah should be a hero to Christians as well!

Tamar has twins—Perez and Zerah—ironically, replacing Judah's two dead sons at once. In Ruth 4:18–22, we learn that Perez will have a famous future descendant: King David. And ultimately, this story leads to the genealogy of Jesus Christ in Matthew 1:1–3. In fact, the parallels with the story of Ruth are remarkable. Both feature Gentile mothers (as Hagar earlier in Genesis)—another indication that God is quite interested in both Jew and Gentile. In both, two sons die, leaving childless widows who deal with in-laws. Levirate marriage was supposed to address widowhood and childlessness—and the institution works, albeit with daring and creative behavior by Ruth and Tamar, and through men who were not first in line to be a kinsman redeemer.[2] In both cases, the women are praised by the men—and in both cases, these amazing stories are in the lineage of David and Christ. Without both, the line from Abraham and Judah to David and Christ would have been broken.

Judah is not just chastened but changed. He has learned what it takes to be a father, a father-in-law, a brother, and a son in Israel for God. When

---

1. Sacks, *Covenant and Conversation*, 261.

2. The kinsman redeemer is usually a brother, but any surviving relative is eligible. In Ruth 4, Boaz becomes the kinsman-redeemer for Ruth when a closer relative refuses.

we next see him in the narrative, he has returned home, exerts impressive leadership, and leads his family into a surprise encounter with his long-lost brother Joseph. In all of this, the narrative makes the point that repentance and growth are a key part of relationship with God and effective leadership.

QUITE A FAMILY REUNION

In the previous chapter, I described Joseph's adventures in Genesis 40–41, which concluded with a prophesied famine, Joseph's policy proposal, and his promotion from prison to the palace. So, we now skip to Genesis 42–44 where the brothers' lives intersect once more—in a drama directed by Joseph. The catalyst: Jacob tells the ten oldest sons to go to Egypt for food. (Benjamin stays behind because of his age, more favoritism, or Jacob's concerns about a terrible sequel with the second of his favored wife Rachel's two sons.) It's noteworthy that all three patriarchs are tested by famine in the Promised Land. In this, we can see an analogy to the Christian life: In our dry times in Canaan, how will we handle our temptations and encounters with Egypt? But here, the reader sees the foreshadowing: What will happen if the brothers meet again? Or more broadly, what will happen when "Israel" encounters Egypt?

Joseph is in charge and doing the work of the Egyptian kingdom.[3] His brothers bow down to him and call him "Lord," fulfilling the first dream in Genesis 37. Joseph recognizes them immediately, but they don't recognize him. For one thing, they're a group and he's one man. They're all considerably older, but he was a young man when they last saw each other and would likely have changed more. Most important, he is shaven, wearing Egyptian clothing, and speaking Egyptian. (Again, a "disguise" plays a key part of the story!) Joseph "pretends" for now. He's probably stalling for time at first. But then, he comes up with an ingenious way forward—teasing them in part, but certainly testing them.

It's also noteworthy that Joseph had not gone home (or sent spies to ask around) even though he traveled a lot on business (41:45–46). Granted, it would have been a long trip. And he had no assurance that Jacob was alive or that his brothers wouldn't try to kill him again. It would have been a risk to leave behind his new family. He had just started a "new job" and

---

3. It's a little strange to see the "vice president" doling out grain. Is this servant leadership or micro-managing? The most likely and gracious interpretation is that Joseph will have good opportunities for "foreign policy" when meeting so many people.

it may have been perceived poorly by his boss. (Not enough paid vacation yet?) Maybe he had assimilated and wasn't all that interested in going back. In any case, hopefully he was content where God wanted him to be—in line with the dreams he had received and the remarkable providences he had experienced.

Joseph messes with the brothers repeatedly as the larger narrative unfolds. Remember that he knows the length of the famine and that they will need to return for more food. As it turns out, the plan is to learn about Benjamin and Jacob—and to see if the brothers have changed. (The narration repeatedly signals that Joseph gets no joy from the charade.) Joseph doesn't see everything, but the narrator tells the reader about the self-torture of the brothers—still harboring a ton of guilt and believing in a sense of karma for what they had done to Joseph years ago.

As an aside, we see Reuben in action again, blaming them with an "I told you so" (42:22)—not particularly helpful, other than aggravating their consciences. No surprise: His attempt at "leadership" again falls on deaf ears and elicits no response. Joseph detains Simeon, perhaps indicating Reuben's relative innocence or allowing the oldest son to return home to persuade his father. Or maybe, Joseph expects that if the brothers leave Reuben in Egypt, they're less likely to return to get him!

Joseph messes with them by secretly returning their money. Their terrified response is somewhere between amusing and pathetic. They can't turn back without risking everything—if they don't return without Benjamin. With the silver as a prop, note the parallels to Joseph being sold into slavery: The sons return home to Jacob with silver but without a brother; it looks like they have successfully "sold" *another* son for silver! They tell Jacob what happened and what has been offered, but he's not interested in the deal at this point. (Again, notice Reuben as a "try-hard" in 42:37—as if killing two grandsons would offset losing another son!)

THE RE-EMERGENCE OF JUDAH

As Genesis 43 opens, Jacob finally assents to a return trip to Egypt when they run out of food. Who steps up? Judah. Reading between the lines (and comparing him to Reuben): Judah delivers the message with a firm but dignified style—neither too little nor too much emotion; just the facts with little rhetoric. He offers personal accountability. He doesn't tell Jacob what to do or dismiss his concerns, but points him to the best solution. Leon

Kass sums it up and connects this episode to what Judah had experienced in Genesis 38: "Judah brings Jacob back to his senses ... he gently instructs his father in the lesson he learned from Tamar: one must not sacrifice the future of the clan out of selfish regard for oneself and one's youngest and dearest son."[4]

And it works. Jacob is stirred to faith-filled action and turns to God for His mercy. From here, Judah will be the leader of the family. He supersedes Reuben and ultimately "competes" with Joseph. It's easy to get excited about Joseph—a great and faithful man in his own right, but the line of David and Jesus will go through Judah. Joseph will receive the double blessing, but the birthright and spiritual blessings will proceed through Judah. (Why not Joseph? That's an angle we will explore in the next chapter.)

Once back in Egypt, the drama has some twists, but unfolds about as we would expect—until Joseph plants evidence on Benjamin and has the brothers brought back to Egypt again. This sets up the final exam. As God with Abraham in his ultimate test, the brothers are challenged to sacrifice a prized son. Earlier, they had sold Joseph into slavery for silver; what would they do with Benjamin? Judah steps up again, starting in Genesis 44:16. He owns the situation; he doesn't defend anything or make excuses. He doesn't beg or bargain. He doesn't desert Benjamin and he attributes their capture to the providence of God rather than Joseph. Judah opens by suggesting slavery for all except Benjamin, but Joseph refuses. And then in one of the most beautiful and poignant passages in Scripture, Judah makes a passionate and persuasive speech (the longest in the book of Genesis).

The speech is bold diplomacy in substance, but quiet and modest in style. Judah approaches Joseph to talk man-to-man. There is no groveling; he does not challenge the facts; he simply argues and pleads for mercy. His words are carefully chosen, angling toward persuading Joseph to extend mercy. Note his deference in using "lord" and "servant" (44:18), referring to Benjamin as a boy (44:22), and mentioning his grieving father eight times. Judah closes by taking responsibility and offering the more reasonable but still-staggering solution of sacrificially substituting himself for Benjamin. As a type of Christ, Judah offers to pay the price for Benjamin's "sin." Like Paul with his fellow Jews, Judah was willing to condemn himself if it meant saving others (Rom 9:3).

What an offer; what a speech; and what a change in Judah! We see why he is fit to lead the family. Judah had sold Joseph into slavery, but here,

4. Kass, *Beginning of Wisdom*, 585.

he offers to take Benjamin's place *in* slavery. The Bible's first penitent in Genesis 38, Judah leads his family by his willingness to give up his freedom for his father and youngest brother. Kass sums it up nicely: "Judah in effect tells Joseph: I may be your slave . . . but I belong first and most to my father, to whom I am pledged for my brother."[5]

Judah is his brother's keeper and his father's keeper. He keeps his word to his father with remarkable courage, creativity, loyalty, and determination. Fittingly, the tribe of Judah (the bulk of the Southern Kingdom) will stay with God longer than any other tribe. Joseph was second to the king of Egypt, but Judah would be the father of kings in Israel. And "the lion of Judah" (Gen 49:9; Rev 5:5)—first David and then Jesus—will come through his descendants.

As soon as Genesis 45 opens, we'll learn that Joseph is blown away and the drama resolves beautifully. For now, the big picture is that neither fraternal envy nor filial trouble with a favoring father are enough to sack God's project with Israel. It's funny that we've seen schemes throughout Genesis, but only Joseph's plans work so marvelously. He had put his brothers in a situation where they would have an overwhelming temptation to repeat their earlier crime by abandoning Benjamin to slavery. Joseph recreates the past so they can move forward in the future. And Judah passes the test with flying colors.

ISRAEL GOES TO EGYPT

We're skipping Genesis 45 for now. But I do want to cover Jacob/Israel and the rest of the family settling in Egypt in Genesis 46–47. Here, we see the resolution of the recent drama, the reconciliation of the brothers, and the reunion of the family—albeit in Egypt instead of the Promised Land.

Jacob/Israel "sets out"—as if on a journey from which he will return. The patriarchs were mostly wanderers, but Jacob's descendants will end up settling in Egypt—for centuries of slavery, before the Lord delivers them from another Pharaoh and brings them into the Promised Land under Moses and Joshua. Jacob brings all of his stuff, not wanting to be dependent on Pharaoh, not wanting to abuse hospitality, and trying to avoid cultural pressures. His sacrifice at Beersheba (on the way out of Canaan) is met by God's gracious and reassuring appearance.[6]

---

5. Kass, *Beginning of Wisdom*, 603.
6. For Jacob, this is the first time that God has appeared to him in 22 years—back to

When they arrive in Egypt, it's provocative that Jacob sends Judah to interact with Joseph, requiring Joseph to make the trip to see him. Is this too much travel for an elderly man or looking to maintain some distance? Is this requiring Joseph to meet him halfway or making sure to bolster his authority as the father? Joseph counsels his brothers and seeks to separate them from the Egyptians, establishing them in a fertile area. In addition to Israel's call to holiness, the Egyptians aren't big fans of shepherds anyway.

Jacob's encounter with Pharaoh is interesting to imagine. The blessing parallels (and reverses) Melchizedek's blessing of Abraham and explicitly accomplishes God's promise in Genesis 12:3. Joseph has called himself "father to Pharaoh" (45:8), but it's Jacob who plays the role of Pharaoh's superior. He twice blesses Pharaoh, does not bow down, and doesn't call himself a "servant." Pharaoh accepts all of this without a fuss. Is he graciously accommodating an old man? Is he exceedingly thankful for Joseph and the father who raised him? Finally, a small but interesting detail: Jacob thinks he's close to death (47:9), but he has 17 years to go. He lives with Joseph for his first 17 years and then another 17 years when they reunite.

The rest of Genesis 47 recounts Joseph's policy maneuvers in response to the famine. The 20% was double what the Lord will require with the tithe in Israel. Seems a bit presumptuous for the State! On the other hand, a 20% flat tax looks good by today's standards. Walter Williams used to tell a story about messing with a British friend on July 4th. Finally, the Brit asked him why America had fought the war—and Williams replied "taxation without representation." The Brit quipped: "How do you like it *with* representation?"

Perhaps the people didn't handle their money well. (To cut them some slack, living in a blessed agricultural setting, they may never have had to practice much thrift.) Some combination of public policy and the public's behavior results in poverty for the people. They give up their money, their livestock, their land, and eventually themselves. Part of the complicated legacy of Joseph is that his policies led to slavery for Egypt and eventually Israel. In our day, it's always strange to hear people profess suspicion about the competence or motives of politicians and bureaucrats, while cheering when the State grows in size and reach under their preferred political leaders.

As the chapter ends, it's clear that Jacob (if not Joseph) is intent on getting back to Canaan. He makes Joseph take a vow to return his bones to

---

35:9–15 after the Dinah/Shechem fiasco. And this is the last recorded speech from God until Moses in Exodus 3.

the Promised Land—a powerful signal of Jacob's preferences for himself, connecting to his ancestors and influencing his descendants. (Practically, it would help Joseph persuade Pharaoh to let him return to Canaan for the funeral when the time came in 50:5–6.) And it would be a useful step to promote their eventual journey home. In a word, Jacob will continue to lead his sons toward Canaan even when he is dead. What a legacy!

WRAPPING UP . . .

I'm eager to meet Peter when I get to Heaven; I think we would have been good friends. I love his willingness to risk—to do and say things that others would not, for better and for worse. He had the faith to get out of the boat. He had the insight and the courage to declare that Jesus was the Messiah. But he also denied Jesus three times and found it difficult to embrace the Gentiles. I'm firmly convinced that the Lord is more bothered by sins of omission than we are. (Remember that Adam's passivity is a significant part of "the original sin" in the Garden.) Then again, maybe that's because I (like Peter) apparently prefer to commit sins of commission and avoid sins of omission!

As with Judah, Peter was an effective leader who made tremendous mistakes, but was able to repent and be restored. (In this, Judas is a sad foil to Peter in his inability to turn back and seek forgiveness.) In John 21, Jesus messes with Peter three times around a charcoal fire, completely reversing Peter's three denials around a charcoal fire in John 18:18 (the only two times the word is used in the Bible).[7] When I think about profligate sin, the story of Hosea comes quickly to mind—where the prophet is called to marry a prostitute as a picture of Israel's unfaithfulness to God. Another R-rated story that is too often overlooked, it underlines the staggering and amazing grace of God offered to bozos like us. Will we embrace it?

What does all of this mean for us? First, leadership often includes saying you're sorry for specific things. We should be quick to apologize to family at home and colleagues at work. We should be aggressive to repent,

---

7. In Acts 10, the Lord sends Peter a vision, compelling him to visit Cornelius and to see the Gentiles as full citizens in God's Kingdom. The book of Acts is structured around the three accounts of Peter's "conversion" in Acts 10–11 and the three versions of Paul's conversion in Acts 9, 22, and 26. As the most prominent leaders of the Early Church, both experience tremendous forgiveness, restoration, and redemption after their repentance and accepting God's grace.

taking steps to turn away from sins of omission and commission. And we should model this behavior to those around us, especially our children.

Second, reconsider the importance of sins of omission and the limited value in God's Kingdom of "staying out of trouble." Jesus could have come to Earth for a week and gotten on the Cross to pay for our sins. Instead, He led our kind of life, was tempted in every way, and modeled a disciple-making ministry. In God's economy, salvation could have been followed by commands to avoid mistakes and sit on a shelf until the Lord brings us home. Instead, we're called masterpieces who have works prepared in advance for us to do (Eph 2:10). We're called ambassadors of reconciliation (II Cor 5:17-20). And we're empowered by the Spirit to do great things in His Kingdom (Gal 2:20).

If you tend toward passivity and fear, look for small ways in which you can risk and be obedient. In your words, commit to honesty and more candor. After your mistakes, commit to apologize and repent. Don't be a weirdo about it or go off the deep end, but err on the side of saying and doing too much—as you follow heroes of the faith who did likewise.

15

Guilt vs. Grace

COMPLETE TEXT: GENESIS 45, 48–50
RECOMMENDED READING: 45:1–10, 50:15–21
POTENTIAL MEMORY VERSES: 45:5, 45:7, 50:20

THE SPITFIRE GRILL is one of my favorite little-known films from decades ago. It's the story of Percy Talbot—a woman released from prison, looking for a fresh start in the small town of Gilead, Maine. It can be challenging to welcome a stranger into life and community. But it's one thing when the newcomer is "normal" and another to learn that she is a felon. What does it look like to repent and restart—and then, to be restored and redeemed by others? When someone has damaged us, how can we forgive—if not forget or fully trust? In practice, our limited information about people and circumstances can make it difficult to interpret actions, words, and motives.[1] Reality is one thing; perceptions can be another.

In Galatians 6:1, Paul says that those who are spiritual (or Spirit-filled) should "restore a sinner gently." I love the verse, because it gets to God's robust goals for redemption in His Kingdom. The ideal (when possible) is not merely toleration, but restoration—a far more difficult and beautiful

---

1. This leads to the universal practice of "stereotyping"—what economists call "statistical discrimination." Given imperfect and costly-to-obtain information, we judge individuals and specific situations by their group affiliations, based on our sense of the data and through our experiences.

opportunity. The verse also alludes to the difficulties in doing this well. This is a "spiritual" matter, to be done with wisdom and courage, informed and empowered by the Spirit.

After Peter and Judas betray Jesus, Peter repents and is fully restored, but Judas is overcome by guilt and commits suicide. James goes from being a skeptic, thinking his brother Jesus is crazy (Mark 3:31–35) to the head of the Church in Jerusalem. Paul is "the chief of sinners" (I Tim 1:15)—in part, because he persecuted the Early Church—and yet, he's used by God as the chief apostle to the Gentiles. The grace of God is the exemplar here—both in terms of establishing a relationship with God and continuing a relationship with God, especially in the face of serious and continuing sin.

One of the twists in *Spitfire Grill* is that the townspeople slowly learn that *they* need redemption—in particular, with respect to how they've perceived Percy and how they've treated her. We see some of the same elements in the drama with Joseph and his brothers. The family is reunited. But what does it look like for Joseph to forgive when the brothers are an abstract reality in a different country—and now, when they are standing before him? And if Joseph can extend forgiveness well to the brothers, will it be perceived properly, received graciously, and accepted fully?

THE GHOST OF CANAAN'S PAST

Genesis 45 opens with Judah's words breaking Joseph's composure, overwhelming his heart, flooding his eyes, and bringing an end to both the test and the charade. Judah has passed the test with flying colors, willing to trade his life for Benjamin's, to sacrifice his freedom for another favored son, reliving and reversing the earlier decision to sell Joseph into slavery. Joseph is fully convinced that his brothers have changed (at least Judah) and that Jacob was not implicated at all. Joseph is relieved that his decision to test the brothers is over—and excited that it has ended so well.

Not surprisingly, the brothers respond as if they've seen a ghost. It probably seemed supernatural; in a sense, this is a resurrection of sorts—and perhaps even more difficult to believe. Adding to their confusion, Joseph easily switches languages—no longer relying on interpreters. Aside from guilt, shock, and fear, they're probably trying to remember what they had said earlier, now knowing that he could understand them the entire time! He had toyed with them. Would they now get what they deserved?

GUILT VS. GRACE

Did they remember his teenage dreams and now imagine that his lording over them would involve slavery, torture, or death?

Instead, Joseph asks about his father again, pushing for reunion and aiming for reconciliation. He directly addresses what they had done to him. (Sometimes it's better to overlook an offense; sometimes it's better to get it out in the open!) But he doesn't dwell on it or explore the details. (That's rarely useful.) Most important, he calls them close, forgives them, and provides a wonderfully providential perspective for their dastardly decisions. Joseph connects his history to God's plans to save lives—and ironically, *their* lives. Through a divine lens, he had found purpose in his sufferings and redemption of their choices. He does not excuse their actions, but turns his focus toward blessing and God's will.

Joseph's monologue is surely rehearsed and certainly powerful. It's noteworthy that he encourages them not to be angry with themselves or each other. He proactively addresses their fears and their guilt; he has seen both from them! He doesn't ignore their sins, but forgives them and hopes they will forgive themselves as well. C.S. Lewis said that he used to think it was silly to say "hate the sin and love the sinner," until he realized that he did all the time ... with himself![2] Joseph walks this line quite nicely.

How was Joseph able to do this? In the story, we see the principle that forgiveness is easier and more meaningful when it is rooted in beneficial events—when we can see God's hand and sovereignty at work. Things worked out really well here. That's not always "enough," but it always helps. Related to our discussion in chapter 8: Joseph is practicing both reason and faith—a reasonable faith, if you will. He trusts God, but Joseph can also see and understand how God has been working. As possible, we should do the same. And Joseph chose to forgive. Sometimes, we want to wait until we feel like it, but the command to forgive (as we've been forgiven by God) is for our benefit and the benefit of others. Joseph released his worldly "right" to retaliate; he chooses not to harbor resentment.

We don't see the details in the narrative, but surely, Joseph worked through a process of forgiveness. Jesus said to forgive "70 times seven" times. I usually think about this as 490 separate offenses (if it was mathematical instead of figurative). But it can also be 490 times that we need to forgive the *same* offense. Some moments can scar us so much that they continue to revisit us. In this, we continue to take those terrible thoughts captive instead of coddling them (II Cor 10:5).

---

2. Lewis, *Mere Christianity*, Book 3, Chapter 7.

Another principle not relayed in the story: When forgiving others, it is important to clear one's part of the table, pointing to and repenting from whatever sins we've committed in the relationship. For Joseph, maybe he would acknowledge being a jerk as a teenager. Without this, we fail to allocate blame properly; we needlessly heap up guilt on others; we lessen our own effort to forgive; and we miss the opportunity to be explicitly forgiven.

One can quibble about the particulars of Joseph's approach. For example, he seems to show favoritism to Benjamin (45:14–15). But overall, Joseph is a great example of how to deal well with really bad events. He doesn't hold a grudge or act as if it didn't happen. He shows mercy when he had the power to crush them; a might-makes-right approach would have resulted in their deaths. From the brothers' perspective, they did not expect to see Joseph—or then, his forgiveness, mercy, and grace. How well do we receive grace when offered? Are we frustrated when others don't accept grace? In every case, our responsibility is faithfully administering grace in its various forms (I Pet 4:10). What others do with the offered grace is between them and God. Forgiveness requires one person; reconciliation requires two people.

In the big picture, this is a huge moment for the brothers individually, the family, the emerging nation, and God's plans for Israel. Forgiveness and repentance are central to what God wants to accomplish in each person: from Judah's compassionate and courageous response to Joseph's forgiveness and grace toward his brothers. And again, Judah's penitence with Tamar in Genesis 38 sets up this moment.

As Jonathan Sacks notes: "The book of Genesis is, among other things, a set of variations on the theme of sibling rivalry: Cain and Abel, Isaac and Ishmael, Jacob and Esau, Joseph and his brothers. The book begins with fratricide and ends with reconciliation."[3] In the four key stories about brothers in Genesis, there's been considerable progress. We've seen Cain murder Abel and walk away; Isaac and Ishmael standing together at dad's funeral; Jacob and Esau making up but going separate ways; and now, reconciliation with ongoing relationship between Joseph and his brothers.

GETTING ISRAEL TO EGYPT

Joseph tells the brothers to go home and bring Jacob to Egypt. At least in the short-term, this is smart since Egypt has the food. And with Joseph's

---

3. Sacks, *Covenant and Conversation*, 326.

Guilt vs. Grace

position in Pharaoh's administration, it may make sense in the medium-term. But how does the move fit into God's plans for Abraham's descendants to be in Canaan, which is decidedly not the environs of Egypt? More broadly, when should we anticipate that reasonable short-term decisions may well have unfortunate long-run implications?

What is Joseph thinking? Is this purely practical? Is this who Joseph is now—Egyptianized in a way that is troubling to the future of God's project for Israel as a holy people? Is Joseph merely worried about losing his position—that he has too much to lose professionally? He's been boasting to his brothers about being "father to Pharaoh" and "ruler of all Egypt." If that's how you see yourself, how do you forsake that to become a shepherd again in the backwaters of a famine-stricken "Promised Land"? Or maybe he's just rationalizing that it would be poor stewardship to relinquish what God had clearly given him.

Joseph is also excited because he can set up his family in Goshen—in the fertile eastern part of the Nile River delta. It was an area where they could live largely separate from Egyptians, allowing them to more easily preserve their distinctiveness. And it was in the area of Egypt closest to Canaan. Joseph probably sees this as merely extending the provision to his family that he's been granted; he and God are "taking care of" the family.

But there are also reasons for concern. The narrative continues somewhat ominously in 45:16-23 by reminding us that Pharaoh and Egypt are (really) in charge. Pharaoh is happy with Joseph's arrangements for his family—and that's fine, at least short-term. But it also foreshadows the difficulties that will come when a new ruler is not so inclined. When you give power to the State, it is wisdom to worry about how it will be wielded in the future.

From there, Joseph sends the brothers home, exhorting them not to quarrel. It sounds like a motherly quip, but it's practical too. This speaks to Joseph's discernment and his ability to analyze a difficult situation despite the emotions at hand. You can picture them debating and blaming each other on the way home. Instead, Joseph wants them to leave it in the past—as he has done. And it's not like they can completely ignore the conversation. They must get a story together to tell Jacob. How do we deal with the revelation of past sin, especially in our immaturity? How do we explain ourselves in a way that doesn't misrepresent the past or cause more damage?

Genesis 45 concludes with a stunned Jacob hearing the amazing news when the brothers return home. The narrative is tight, but it masks an exceedingly dramatic scene. And there are some noteworthy details. The brothers don't share Joseph's version of the story with Jacob—either overcome by the power of the moment or not caring for Joseph's angle. They mention his position, but unfortunately, they do not attribute it to God. They also leave out the grandiose titles conveyed by Joseph—either trying to diminish him or thinking the details were not helpful. Not surprisingly, Jacob is in disbelief. Beyond the extraordinary outcome, it's always difficult to believe someone who has lied to you before!

BLESS YOU!

In the previous chapter, we covered Jacob's family settling in Egypt (Genesis 46–47). And in Genesis 50, we'll see similar themes to what we've been describing so far in this chapter. But in Genesis 48–49, we see a series of blessings from patriarch Jacob to his sons and Joseph's two sons—as the end of Jacob's life draws near.

At the end of Genesis 47, Jacob had come to Joseph, commanding Joseph to bury him in Canaan. Now, Joseph visits Jacob while he's ill, perhaps anticipating his imminent death and probably looking for a blessing for his two sons, Manasseh and Ephraim. Jacob reiterates the covenant and the promises of population and land (in Canaan, not Egypt). Then, we're surprised to hear Jacob say that he is *adopting* Joseph's sons! At least symbolically, this communicates an expectation that Joseph's Egyptian-born sons will be absorbed into Israel.

Joseph does not protest at all. Maybe he was excited by the decision. Maybe you just follow your dad's direction when you live in a patriarchal society. Maybe God had already communicated this to him. Or maybe he doesn't care all that much—more interested in his profession than his parenting. Here's one thing we do know: Jacob was also honoring Joseph by blessing his two sons instead of him. Recall the birthright and the blessing with Esau and Jacob in the previous generation: Esau sold the birthright for a bowl of soup; Jacob and Rebekah connived to defraud the blessing from Esau and Jacob. Joseph's two sons will get the double material blessing, but Judah will get the spiritual birthright. Judah was the oldest of Leah's children (who had not disinherited himself) and Joseph was the oldest son of Rachel.[4]

---

4. If you're doing the math at home, Joseph's two sons will make up two of the 12 tribes receiving land. How do 12 sons plus two grandsons equal 12 tribes? There is no tribe of

Guilt vs. Grace

In another sense, if Jacob is worried about Joseph becoming Egyptianized, Jacob "sacrifices" Joseph, but recovers his two sons to take Joseph's place. The mention of Rachel is a bit odd and probably telling as well. Leon Kass runs with this angle and concludes: "Jacob may now understand the symbolic meaning of his decision not to bury Rachel with the other patriarchs and matriarchs. Rachel's burial . . . had left her on the outside of the new way. Now her preeminent son has chosen to assimilate himself to outside ways. Rachel had clung to her father's idols; Joseph now clings to the land of the idolaters. Jacob . . . sees that—like mother, like son—the beautiful Rachel and her beautiful Joseph are both detours on the way to the promise that God Almighty has made to them."[5]

Things get even weirder when Jacob switches hands during the blessing, giving the greater blessing to the younger son. Both tribes will be prominent, but Ephraim will be more important—and later, the nexus of political power in the unfaithful Northern Kingdom of Israel. Careful readers are not surprised by the flip, since we've seen the birth pattern reversed throughout Genesis. God continues to upset the worldly norm of prioritizing the older over the younger. Like his father Isaac, Jacob is nearly blind, but his trouble with sight is merely physical—and he blesses the sons properly in accordance with God's values. More specifically here, choosing the older son would also imply that things are fine as they are. But this cannot be the case as long as Israel remains in Egypt instead of the Promised Land.

After the blessing in Genesis 48, Jacob blesses all of his sons in Genesis 49. This implies both diversity and unity within the family—that the blessings differ, but they're all given together. Not surprisingly, Judah and Joseph dominate here, receiving almost as much space as the other sons combined. The blessings seem strange to us moderns, but they should be read as a combination of prophetic speech and an analysis of the strengths and weaknesses of his sons. The blessings are not a matter of determinism as much as they are a recognition that our past shapes our future.

Some of the blessing details are especially noteworthy. Oldest son Reuben is first and his blessing includes a reference to his earlier indiscretion with Jacob's maidservant more than 40 years earlier (35:22). Without any apparent apology or repentance from Reuben, the consequences multiply and full reconciliation is impossible. Simeon and Levi are "blessed" together with a reference to their anger, as they had acted together violently in Genesis 34

"Joseph"—and Levi, the priestly tribe, will only inherit cities rather than larger territory.

5. Kass, *Beginning of Wisdom*, 641.

against the Shechemites. Judah will become the leader, with prophetic references to David and messianic references to Jesus Christ. Joseph's blessing is focused on fruitfulness. Wealth often connects to power—and many of Israel's most famous leaders (Joshua, Deborah, Samuel, Jeroboam, Gideon, and Jephthah) will be descended from Ephraim and Manasseh.

BURYING THE PREVIOUS GENERATION

Genesis 49 ends with the death of Jacob. He had given instructions to all of his sons about his burial—perhaps worried about whether Joseph would follow through or treating his sons with equal dignity and respect. The command to bury him in Canaan is a weighty symbolic expression: Egypt is not my home; Egypt is not *our* home. It also forces Joseph to return "home"—with all of the emotions, memories, and vision this would entail.

Genesis 50 opens with Joseph weeping in contrast to the stoicism of the other brothers. Is this the long-term result of favoritism? Has Joseph experienced more loss and is therefore more sensitive? Was he less accepting of death, given his immersion in Egyptian culture? The long embalming process (including the removal of organs) was Egyptian custom, but here it's quite useful given the long trip ahead! And then, they take 70 days to (officially) mourn and as a sign of official respect.

It's noteworthy that Jacob's death and funeral get so much space, compared to every other passing in Genesis. This underlines Jacob's desire to be buried in Canaan rather than Egypt. It emphasizes Joseph's obedience to his dad's command. And it shows the level of respect that Pharaoh had for Joseph and Jacob—which unfortunately will fade badly as we transition to the book of Exodus.

It also illustrates the supreme tension between an Israelite and an Egyptian worldview: here, the grand parade and embalming from Egyptian culture, followed by the simplistic burial of sons carrying a coffin to a cave in Canaan. The competition in worldviews will continue silently over the next 400 years—and then noisily, as God sets his people free from Egyptian bondage in a might-makes-right world. But really, the history of Israel and the Church is to wrestle with the tensions of being a holy people who are in the world. How can we be in Egypt without becoming Egyptians? How can we be ambassadors to another world without being unduly influenced by that world's systems and its citizens? As for the soul-searching that was surely occurring for Joseph, Kass asks the question this way: "Am

Guilt vs. Grace

I the Egyptian viceroy in the chariot or am I the dutiful son of the Israelite ancestors?"[6]

For us, funerals are an opportunity to mourn—to give and receive comfort. Hopefully, they are also an opportunity to celebrate—to remember positively but honestly, while giving thanks. In a word, we look to grieve the loss and celebrate the life. For the Christian, they are an opportunity to testify to our hope in Jesus—for the next phase of our eternal life in Christ Jesus with our resurrected and glorified bodies. When you can, be present for others as they grieve. When appropriate, contribute meaningful words to eulogize the person and to help personalize the ceremony.

Sadly, with Jacob gone, the brothers are worried that Joseph will *now* take his revenge. The narration finally reveals that they never fully trusted his forgiveness! They continued to torture themselves with grief for their actions and disbelief about Joseph's heart and motives. Many times, we know about grace, but we haven't experienced it. It seems too good to be true. For Joseph's brothers, the grace of God and Joseph was not yet real to them. This saddens Joseph, but what can you do? Only your best. And Joseph tries to reassure them again. Will it stick this time? We can only hope.

The book ends with Joseph's death at 110—the ideal age for death in *Egyptian* culture (is this another ominous sign, biblically?) and 50 years after Jacob's death. The mention of grandchildren and Joseph pointing them to God are both encouraging references. Finally, Joseph is embalmed and buried, but his bones will not be delivered for a really long time—when the Israelites would be freed from Egyptian slavery and finally get to the Promised Land. Cue the dark and foreboding music: Joseph does not receive the State funeral that his father Jacob had received. In what can be the long slow grind of history and God's providence, His promises of population, land, and covenant would be fulfilled, but it would take centuries.

Genesis has a gloomy ending, but God is clearly present and active all the way through. Matthew Henry describes the dark conclusion this way: "Thus, the book of Genesis, which began with the origin of light and life, ends with nothing but death and darkness; so sad a change has sin made."[7] The reference to Joseph's bones is a hopeful ending, foreshadowing trouble but also eventual success. Things look uncertain as the book closes, but the narrative points forward to the faithfulness of God and His promises.

---

6. Kass, *Beginning of Wisdom*, 655.
7. Henry, *Commentary*, 210.

WRAPPING UP...

The story of Zacchaeus in Luke 19 is a childhood Sunday School favorite. On what seems like an average day in the ministry of Christ, a wee little man climbs a tree and gets to have lunch with Jesus—and everybody lives happily ever after. Good stuff for kids to be sure. But the narrative should have a lot more pop for adults.

Zacchaeus could have been fully seduced by wealth and power, jaded by those who responded poorly to his abuse, or blanketed by guilt for how he had oppressed the Jewish people for the Roman state in a might-makes-right world. Instead, he is somewhere between desperate and inquisitive about the man from Galilee. Zacchaeus drops the pretense of power—a grown man climbing a tree in his robes to see Jesus. The tax collector ignores the nasty looks of the taxpayers to get a look at the Messiah. Zacchaeus doesn't let his terrible past get in the way of his curious present or his hopeful future.

When Jesus invites himself to Zacchaeus' home, it starts a chain of events that quickly leads to his salvation. Was it a response to the grace of being chosen? Was it an Ecclesiastes-like despondence from realizing that his way of life was financially profitable but spiritually bankrupt? Was it seeing Jesus persist through the complaints of the people about his lunch decision? Was it awe at the knowledge that Jesus had said *no* to so many other people that day so he could say *yes* to Zacchaeus?

I'm struck that Jesus declares Zacchaeus' salvation and that Zacchaeus provides such strong evidence of his own salvation. He provides four-fold restitution for those he has cheated (Exod 22:1). He gives half of his possessions to the poor. He goes well beyond the Law to exhibit extravagant grace as a reflection of the amazing grace he has received. And you can tell from his eagerness and the title he gives Jesus ("Look, Lord!") that these actions emanate from the heart of a new man, born again into God's good and great Kingdom.

How do we know when others have changed? When they take costly steps, aiming for restitution, repentance, and redemption. How do we know when *we* have changed. It's the same. In James 2, the brother of Jesus asks, "Can such faith save?" When our actions line up with the beliefs we profess and the heart we claim, then we can be confident that we're "watching our life and doctrine closely" (I Tim 4:15–16). Accept and extend grace. Forgive and restore. As with Abraham, may we be blessed in order to bless God and others.

Epilogue

I HOPE YOU'VE ENJOYED this walk through the masterpiece of Genesis. It has so much to offer in terms of understanding God's character, His work in history, and what He wants for each of us and from each of us. From the staggering work of Creation to His relationships with Abraham and his descendants, we see a powerful God who loves us and wants to partner with us through His provision and our participation.

In chapter 1, we discussed the silence of Adam and the violence of Cain. On the one hand, some of us have a greater tendency to be passive, lazy, and cowardly, committing sins of omission. Aside from their frequent subtlety, these can be counterfeits for virtues—for example, complacency that looks like patience. On the other hand, some of us are generally too active in word or deed, committing sins of commission. Whether being a knucklehead or acting out of malice, we often do and say things we should not. *Which category is more of a struggle for you—and what are your strategies for growing in this?*

In chapter 2, we compared the obedience of Noah with the greatness of Abraham. While Noah was good at following directions in building the ark, he was unable to impact his neighbors and he struggled after the Flood. In contrast, Abraham makes more mistakes, but grows in his walk, has remarkable faith, and goes beyond mere obedience. He invites nephew Lot to join him when he had been told to leave family behind; he practices radical hospitality and goes to battle for strangers; he negotiates with the Lord about the righteous in Sodom; and so on. *What would it look like for you to strive for the greatness of Abraham in your daily life?*

In chapter 3, Abraham obeys the Lord's call to "leave and go," forfeiting the comforts and stability of Babylon to embrace the unknowns and adventure of following a good and great God. In theory, it may be feasible to "stay" and become what God wants you to be. But in practice, following God usually implies leaving things behind. We may not be called to move to another country, but we are called to crucify the Flesh and the World. We may not be called to change jobs, but we are called to redeem our work. We may not be called to leave family and friends behind, but we are called to new relationships with Gospel purposes. *Is there anything you need to leave—and is there anywhere you need to go?*

In chapter 4, we talked about Abraham's lies to Abimelech and Pharaoh—and then more broadly, the power of the tongue for good and for ill. Telling the truth is important, but not always easy to define. False testimony, slander, gaslighting, and gossip are clearly problems. But our standard here should be Ephesians 4:29. Avoid whatever is "unwholesome"—words that do not help people become "whole." And more important, aim to "build others up, according to their needs," so they may benefit from what you say. *What is one thing for you to remove and one thing for you to add with respect to your tongue?*

In chapter 5, we praised Abraham for his magnanimous generosity with Lot and then his tactical use of strength to rescue his errant nephew and a bunch of strangers. Abraham was wealthy, but did not worship wealth—and thus, was comfortable in allowing Lot the first choice of land. Abraham also used some of his resources to train his household and prepare for trouble. He was ready for war if needed, but reluctant to use his power, even in a might-makes-right world. *How do use your resources for the good of others?*

In chapter 6, we critiqued Lot for drifting toward Sodom. After his unfortunate choice of land, he moved near Sodom and was eventually a leader in Sodom. In this, Lot provides a terrific and terrible picture of compromise—and the tension between being in the world and of the world. The ideal is to be strong in the Lord so that you can stand against temptation, but there are also times when it is wise to flee. *What is one area in life where you have fled, but you should stand—and one area where you have stuck around but should flee?*

In chapter 7, we revered Abraham's radical hospitality, but we mostly discussed the question of timing. We can say or do the right thing with the right motives, but still mess up *when* it's done. We might walk with the Lord

EPILOGUE

or be obedient for a time, but we struggle when a trial lengthens. When we get impatient, we often take things into our own hands, rather than patiently waiting on the Lord. *What is an example where you got the timing wrong—and where do you need to be more patient?*

In chapter 8, we described the testing of Abraham with the binding of Isaac. (Remember that a test hopes for our success, while a temptation hopes for our failure.) How well do we respond to trials, tests, and temptations? We also wrestled with the relationship between faith and reason. Faith is a universal phenomenon, as the way we necessarily bridge the gap between logic, evidence, and the inferences we draw. This begs questions about the extent and the objects of our various faiths. *Where should you be using more reason—and where should you question your "faith" in something or someone, given the available evidence?*

In chapter 9, we saw the apathy of Esau and the passion of Jacob. Even though Jacob is a mess, he at least cares for the things of God. Esau is a better guy by the world's standards, but he is uninterested in the divine, rendering him ineligible for transmitting the faith (or perhaps, even being in the family of God). While it might be easier to measure behavior and tempting to imagine that behavior is ultimate, the crucial factor biblically is relationship with the Lord. *What is something where you are relatively apathetic but should be passionate?*

In chapter 10, we detailed the battles between Jacob and Laban over wives and wealth. Laban tricked Jacob with Leah, but he persevered to get Rachel. Laban rigged Jacob's wages and wealth, but he found a creative way to get around Laban's plans and was blessed by the Lord. We tend to undervalue perseverance and creativity in following God. Short-term obedience is fine, but we often quit when the going gets tough; we're not a persevering people. Other times, people keep plugging and we praise them for it, but they should be mixing in some creativity. *What small disciplines can you embrace to develop your ability to persevere? Where have you been banging the same drum, but might benefit from some creativity?*

In chapter 11, we described Jacob's wrestling match with the preincarnate Christ and explored wrestling as a metaphor for Jacob's relationships with Esau, Laban, and God. Sometimes, we avoid wrestling with God because it seems presumptuous or wrestling with others because it doesn't seem nice. But wrestling with God and others is applauded in the Scriptures—just as God changes Jacob's name to Israel, to commemorate his wrestling with God and man. *What is an example where you need to get on the mat and wrestle with God or others?*

In chapter 12, we covered the first of two overlooked R-rated stories in Genesis (the rape of Dinah) and then, arguably the most famous story in Genesis (Joseph and the "technicolor coat"). We described the tradeoffs of pursuing justice in a broken world and handling tough situations well. After Dinah has been raped, what is the best response in a might-makes-right world? Then, Jacob favors Joseph over his other sons; Joseph foolishly shares his dreams with the brothers; they are jealous and willing to murder their little brother; and oldest brother Reuben is unable to lead well. *What is a context where you are tempted to jealousy or envy—and how can you focus on gratitude instead?*

In chapter 13, we saw Joseph's remarkable purity and amazing productivity. He was impressively righteous in the face of Potiphar's wife and her sexual advances toward him. He was exceedingly effective as the manager of Potiphar's household. Purity and productivity are both important to pursue—and we discussed the relationship between the two: If we live a life with more purity and integrity, we will tend to be more productive. *Where is a lack of purity or focus keeping you from being more effective?*

In chapter 14, we discussed the other overlooked R-rated story in Genesis—the wild story of Judah, his three sons, and Tamar. She creatively pursues justice, leading to Judah's repentance, her restoration, and eventually, King David and Jesus Christ. Then, we saw how Judah returned to his family, effectively leading them and eventually passing Joseph's test—expressed as Judah's willingness to sell himself into slavery for one of his brothers, reversing what they had done to Joseph years earlier. *Echoing Judah as the Bible's first penitent, what is a specific situation or relationship where you should be much quicker to apologize and repent?*

In chapter 15, we saw Joseph extend amazing grace to his brothers—and then years later, after Jacob died, their apparent inability to receive that grace. Joseph was able to offer grace because of his relationship with God; his gratitude for God's presence and promises; and his ability to see God working in history and his own story. But grace given is not the same as grace accepted—in terms of salvation and everyday life. *What is an area in life where you need to be better about extending or receiving grace?*

All of these stories are instructive about God's character and His work in time and place. As examples for us, some of them are inspirational; others are illustrations of what to avoid. All of them are memorable, even though

Epilogue

we tend to overlook certain stories because they're awkward or too colorful for a child's eyes. But let's go back to "the beginning" to close this out.

In Genesis 1:26–28, we have the opening commission to Adam and Eve—and thus, to all mankind: Be fruitful, multiply, and extend godly dominion over the Earth. In other words, increase the population through marriage and family; take care of the world as good stewards of God's good creation; and live a fruitful life, working hard to produce things of value while depending on God's provision. We are made in God's image—God's likeness—to act like God: creating, building, loving, serving, sacrificing.

The commission is reiterated as biblical history moves forward. Noah is a post-Flood fresh start. Abraham is called out of Ur and blessed to be a blessing to all peoples. After Genesis, Moses is given the staggering task to deliver God's people from Pharaoh. Judges are chosen to lead as proxies for God. Prophets are commanded to speak the truth forcefully. Saul, David, and Solomon are anointed as the first kings of Israel. But all of this points to the second Adam, the Ark door which saves completely, the greater fulfillment of Abraham's blessing, the full-blown forgiveness of the penitent, the second Passover Lamb, and the ultimate Judge, Prophet, and King: Christ Jesus.

The first commission in Genesis 1 is matched and extended by the five commissions of Jesus—one at the end of the four Gospels and one just prior to His Ascension in Acts 1. The most famous of the set is Matthew 28:18–20—to make disciple-makers as we go through our daily life. We baptize them and then we get to the rest of the calling—to teach them to obey all that Jesus has commanded; to grow in the grace and knowledge of Christ (II Pet 3:18); to be remembered for our work produced by faith, our labor prompted by love, and our endurance inspired by our hope in Jesus (I Thess 1:3).

This parallels Paul's command to church leaders in Ephesians 4:11–13: "So Christ himself gave the apostles, the prophets, the evangelists, the pastors and teachers, to equip his people for works of service, so that the body of Christ may be built up until we all reach unity in the faith and in the knowledge of the Son of God and become mature, attaining to the whole measure of the fullness of Christ." Paul continues by describing the move from infants to adults; from blown by the wind to steady in the face of the wind; from vulnerable to strong against deceit; from spectator and consumer to each part doing its work.

May the stories in Genesis inspire us to pursue the path that Jesus and Paul have laid out for us and our churches. In Genesis, we see God's hand at work—from the creation of the universe and mankind to his providential "behind the scenes" presence with Joseph and his brothers. And we see a range of choices by the people in those stories—as they participate within God's provision. May they serve as examples to us as we walk with Jesus.

Select Bibliography

Ariely, Dan. *The (Honest) Truth About Dishonesty: How We Lie to Everyone—Especially Ourselves.* New York: Harper Perennial, 2013.
Babylon Bee. "Church Unsure Why Men Are Struggling Spiritually in Spite of Quarterly Pancake Breakfast." Apr. 4, 2025. babylonbee.com/news/church-unsure-why-men-are-struggling-spiritually-in-spite-of-quarterly-pancake-breakfast.
Bonhoeffer, Dietrich. *The Cost of Discipleship.* New York: Scribner, 1963.
Corbett, Steve and Brian Fikkert. *When Helping Hurts: How to Alleviate Poverty Without Hurting the Poor. . .and Yourself.* Chicago: Moody, 2014.
Crabb, Larry. *The Silence of Adam: Becoming Men of Courage in a World of Chaos.* Grand Rapids, MI: Zondervan, 1995.
Devlin, Elise, and Jayson Jenks. "Gregg Popovich Is a Coaching Legend. He's Also a Master of Tough Conversations." *New York Times,* June 22, 2025. nytimes.com/athletic/6432607/2025/06/18/gregg-popovich-is-a-coaching-legend-but-hes-also-a-master-of-tough-conversations/?source=athletic_pulsenewsletter&campaign=13874700&userId=20507302.
Evans, Hannah. "No Sex, No Booze, We're Off to Church: Gen Z Have Found God." *The Times (London),* Apr. 22, 2025.
Graham, Ruth. "With Gen Z, Men Are Now More Religious Than Women." *New York Times,* Sept. 25, 2024. nytimes.com/2024/09/23/us/young-men-religion-gen-z.html
Henry, Matthew. *Matthew Henry's Commentary on the Whole Bible, Volume 1: Genesis to Deuteronomy.* Peabody, MA: Hendrickson, 1991.
Johnston, Andrew, et al. "Divorce, Family Arrangements, and Children's Adult Outcomes." NBER Working Paper #33776, May 2025.
Kass, Leon. *The Beginning of Wisdom: Reading Genesis.* Chicago: University of Chicago Press, 2006.
Kearney, Melissa. *The Two-Parent Privilege: How Americans Stopped Getting Married and Started Falling Behind.* Chicago: University of Chicago Press, 2025.
Keizer, Garret. *The Enigma of Anger: Essays on a Sometimes Deadly Sin.* San Francisco: Jossey-Bass, 2002.
King, Florence. *The Florence King Reader.* New York: St. Martin's, 1995.
Lewis, C.S. *Mere Christianity.* San Francisco: Harper, 2001.
Lewis, Robert. *Men's Fraternity: The Quest for Authentic Manhood.* Nashville: Lifeway Church Resources, 2005.
O'Rourke, P.J. *Eat the Rich: A Treatise on Economics.* New York: Atlantic Monthly, 1999.

Select Bibliography

Ortberg, John. *The Life You've Always Wanted: Spiritual Disciplines for Ordinary People.* Grand Rapids, MI: Zondervan, 2015.

Pearcey, Nancy. *The Toxic War on Masculinity: How Christianity Reconciles the Sexes.* Grand Rapids, MI: Baker Books, 2023.

Peck, M. Scott. *People of the Lie: The Hope for Healing Human Evil.* New York: Touchstone, 1998.

Peterson, Eugene. *A Long Obedience in the Same Direction: Discipleship in an Instant Society.* Downers Grove, IL: InterVarsity, 2000.

Peterson, Jordan. *12 Rules for Life: An Antidote to Chaos.* Toronto: Random House Canada, 2018.

Reeves, Richard. *Of Boys and Men: Why the Modern Male Is Struggling, Why It Matters, and What to Do about It.* Washington, DC: Brookings Institution. 2022.

Renn, Aaron. *Living in the Negative World: Confronting Challenges in an Anti-Christian Culture.* Grand Rapids, MI: Zondervan, 2024.

Rodrigue, Jourdan. "How a Phone Call from a College Football Legend Reset Sean McVay's Coaching Career." *New York Times*, June 2, 2025. nytimes.com/athletic/6398004/2025/06/03/sean-mcvay-coaching-career-rams-nfl/.

Ross, Allen. "Genesis." In *The Bible Knowledge Commentary: Old Testament*, edited by John Walvoord and Roy Zuck. Wheaton, IL: Victor, 1985.

Sacks, Jonathan. *Covenant and Conversation: A Weekly Reading of the Jewish Bible.* Jerusalem: Maggid, 2009.

Sarna, Nahum. *Understanding Genesis: The Heritage of Biblical Israel.* New York: The Jewish Theological Seminary Press, 2015.

Sayers, Dorothy. *Letters to a Diminished Church: Passionate Arguments for the Relevance of Christian Doctrine.* Nashville: Thomas Nelson, 2004.

Schansberg, D. Eric. *College 101: What Students and Parents Should Know About Universities.* Louisville, KY: Further Still Ministries, 2025.

———. "Joshua 22's Failure to Communicate." *The Word Diet* podcast, episode 189, January 18, 2024.

———. *Inheriting Our Promised Land: Lessons in Victorious Living in the Book of Joshua.* Greenville, SC: Alertness, 2003.

———. "The Great Omission." *Touchstone* 31.3 (May/June) 2018.

———. *Turn Neither to the Right nor to the Left: A Thinking Christian's Guide to Politics and Public Policy.* Greenville, SC: Alertness, 2003.

Solid Steps Radio. "#16 Parts 1 and 2 Marriage—Being a Good Guy Is Not Enough." Episode 16, February 6, 2016.

Thomas, Ian. *The Saving Life of Christ: You Can Have a Dynamic Faith and Victorious Spiritual Life.* Grand Rapids, MI: Zondervan, 1989.

Voskamp, Ann. *One Thousand Gifts: A Dare to Live Fully Right Where You Are.* Nashville: Thomas Nelson, 2011.

Wilkin, Jen. *In His Image: 10 Ways God Calls Us to Reflect His Character.* Wheaton, IL: Crossway, 2018.

Willard, Dallas. *The Great Omission: Reclaiming Jesus's Essential Teachings on Discipleship.* New York: HarperOne, 2014.

www.ingramcontent.com/pod-product-compliance
Lightning Source LLC
Chambersburg PA
CBHW051056160426
43193CB00010B/1209